CONSPIRACY FOR GREATNESS

MASTERY OF LOVE WITHIN

Step-By-Step Caching and Guidance for a Peaceful, Effective and Fulfilling Lifestyle

HOW TO ACCESS AN EXTRAORDINARY LIFE

By: Behnam Bakhshandeh

PRIMECO
EDUCATION
Your vision is our business

Conspiracy for Greatness... Mastery of Love Within

Step-By-Step Coaching and Guidance for a Peaceful,
Effective and Fulfilling Lifestyle

How to access an extraordinary life

Written by: Behnam Bakhshandeh
Published by: Primeco Education, Inc.
Edit by: Sandra Rea-McGinty
Graphic Design by: Lynch Graphics, Inc.

Cataloging-in-Publication Data is on file with the Library of Congress
ISBN: 978-0-615-30400-7
ISBN: 0615304001
All Rights Reserved

Printed in the United State of America
First Edition: September 2009

To purchase additional copies, please visit our website at
www.PrimecoEducation.com

1. Success
2. Life Coaching
3. Education
4. Transformation
5. Enlightenment
6. Happiness
7. Self-Help
8. Accountability
I. Title

Primeco Education, Inc.
204 N. El Camino Real – Suite 444
Encinitas, CA 92024
1-877-942-6076

To Erin;

Behnam.

Aug. 2010

Great minds discuss ideas;

Average minds discuss events;

Small minds discuss people.

--Eleanor Roosevelt

I am dedicating this book to:

My fallen hero, my brother Behzad Bakhshandeh on behalf of

all fallen heroes who fought for freedom and against ignorance;

Your life made a difference. You will live forever in our hearts.

My mentor of all times, my father, Hussein Bakhshandeh;

I learned from you how to live with distinction.

You are my king forever.

هرگز نمیرد آنکه دلش زنده شد به عشق

ثبت است در جریدهٔ عالم دوام ما

--خواجه حافظ شیرازی

One whose heart has been enlivened by Love would never die.

And that is how our permanence has been guaranteed in the Book of Life.

--Hafes-e Shirazi

Table of Contents

Testimonials

"I was nervous, scared and completely stopped with the thought of starting my own practice. Within a month of coaching with Behnam, I have done it! I am absolutely fulfilled and happy in my life."

Lydia Banuelos, M.D.

Pediatric Ophthalmologist-Tucson, AZ

***

"Behnam's commitment to my success is unwavering. I don't always like the coaching he gave me, but I always love the result."

Bert Carder, CEO

Your Beauty Network, Inc.-Oceanside, CA

***

"My team and I are producing even better results than I'd hoped. We are making more money, having more fun and using less time than before. Thank you again for results that I can take to the bank."

Chris Heller, President

Keller Williams Realty-Encinitas, CA

***

"As a person who has always been interested in having a high quality of life, the coaching program with Behnam has been a driving force in helping me to achieve that quality."

Susan Kolesar, President

Artemis Media Group-Plain, PA

"Coaching with Behnam has opened up a new world of possibilities in my life personally and professionally. It has made a difference in my relationship to others and to myself."

Brian Dallmann

Sr. Controls Engineer–St. Louis, MO

***

"I highly recommend Behnam's coaching for any area you are interested in working on. You will get so much more than you pay for."

Nazanin "Naz" Meftah, CEO

Pacific Crane Enterprises, Inc.- Tucson, AZ

***

"It has been truly an honor to meet and work with Behnam. With his unique way of coaching, I have realized phenomenal results in my personal, professional and business life."

Kenneth G. Patton

Business owner and Mayor-Laceyville, PA

***

"I have learned through my coaching to live for what I believe in and be content and happy. Thank you Behnam for helping me see myself for who I am and loving it."

Myra English

Myra J A Salon-Defiance, OH

***

"My ability to lead and accomplish has been taken beyond the next level."

Captain Mark Bringhurst

United Airlines-Temecula, CA

Acknowledgments and My Eternal Gratitude

During the years of my personal growth and development as a human being, I have come across many great people, life altering disciplines and principles and open minded organizations that are making a difference. In some way, shape and form all those interactions contributed to me and my life. All those experiences made me be who I am today, personally and professionally.

Gratitude unlocks the fullness of life. It turns what we have into enough, and more. It turns denial into acceptance, chaos to order, confusion to clarity. It can turn a meal into a feast, a house into a home, a stranger into a friend. Gratitude makes sense of our past, brings peace for today and creates a vision for tomorrow.

--Melody Beattie

From the time I was born until the time I attended high school and through my sports phase, to college, to the time of Iranian revolution, to the time of the Iran and Iraq war, at the time of work and career, in all travels, during the time of marriages and divorces, to the time of my immigration to the United States, to the time of awareness, enlightenment and transformation, to the time of reinvention of who I am now… a whole new era of my life and my existence… I am grateful. I have read, observed, learned, felt, cried, laughed, missed, succeeded, failed, experienced pain and joy, and I have grown. Overall, I have lived!

I am grateful to my parents, Hussein and Paridokht Bakhshandeh, forever. Thank you for my life. I watched you and learned how to live life based on love, honor and integrity. I learned what it means to be a decent human being. I have not completely done what you had directed me to do or to be, but I did what I did and I caused what I caused. Maybe that was my journey to take me to being who I am today. I am sorry for any hardship I have caused you during my upbringing. I was a just a kid who was not sure of who he was!

I am also grateful to my three brothers, Behzad, Behyar and Bardia. You are my knights. Behzad, you are not here with us today, but I know that you know you are my hero and my inspiration! You stood for what you know is right for our people and for freedom in all aspects of being human. You gave your life to people like me, so I can be free and express myself freely. For this I am forever grateful. Behyar, you have always been there when I need you! You have been there for all of us. You are the spirit of our father, and your generosity and kindness is amazing, I am in debt to you. Bardia, I love your free spirit and who you are for your family, you are true friend, and I am proud of you.

I am grateful to all of my uncles and aunts, who taught me many great things about life. Especially I am grateful to my uncles who taught me how to work hard and work honestly. I learned a lot from you!

I am grateful to all of my teachers during my school days. I am grateful to all of my friends, cousins, and all the people who went through different parts of my life with me, good, bad and ugly, everywhere and in all times

11

before I came to the USA. Especially my buddies, boys and girls during high school, in Abadan-Iran. Those times were an adventure of lifetime!

I am grateful to the three wonderful ladies I was married to during different periods of my life over the last 30 years. Thank you each for so many great years of love and happiness, years I choose to remember. And thank you for my children, Poneh (Renee), Shima and Behzad, to whom I am grateful. You kids are my hope, my love, my life and my future! Thank you for your patience with your old man. You are all I have. I love you.

I am grateful for my new country, the United State of America. I made my life here. I failed a lot and I succeeded a lot! But I always had my chance to succeed, just as long as I was working hard, being honest and not being a burden to my government. I have pride and I am grateful for the opportunity to make something of myself … speaking and writing English for a living! Are you kidding me? It is nothing but a miracle! But everything is possible here in the land of opportunity. At the same time, I am grateful for my old land, my mother country, Iran. I am as much American as Iranian, and being Persian is in my heart and soul. I love my culture, our art, our food, our music, our people, our heritage and our dignity. We are Persians. Being hospitable, welcoming and open hearted are some of our most precious values. We are a contribution to humanity. I am proud to be and Iranian American.

I am grateful to my family members and friends who took care of me when I immigrated to the U.S. while I found my way around, especially my friends in Northern California and both of my uncle's families in Southern California. I am also grateful to the people who hired me to work for them

12

and make my life work here, especially my dear first boss in Los Angeles, who hired me for my first real job in the U.S. as a welder and a workshop supervisor. Thank you for your generosity and support!

I am grateful to friends who took me in when I moved to U.S. During my time in Los Angeles and San Diego I have been fortunate to meet many more wonderful, generous people. You all are my family. I am also grateful for my friends who took care of me during my time in Philadelphia. Lovely and friendly people. Thank you for your generous love. I hope I deserved it.

I am grateful to my best friend, Ata Hassani, for his courage to look within himself way before I looked into my own soul, and having courage to share it with me and others!

I am grateful to the Landmark Education as an organization, its Forum Leaders Body and staff, current and former, for the outstanding work they do and the difference they make in others' lives, and for their mentorship of me during the time I had the privilege of being with them. Thank you for touching my heart. I will never forget the difference we made together! I am grateful for the program leaders I had the privilege of working with in the San Diego and Philadelphia centers. I will never forget the awesome work we did together! I am sorry if ever I have disappointed you.

I am grateful for my teammates in Primeco Education, current as well as former, for their work, their passion and their partnership with me in making a difference in this world. Especially, I thank Angel Haag. You are my partner. Thank you for believing in me, and thank you for your loyalty,

13

for standing by me to cause our vision "Inspired by others success, having fun and creating abundance," every day for so many years for so many people! I am also grateful for all of our clients, individuals, organizations, communities and or anyone who was so generous to us and so trusting that chose us as their mentors, coaches and/or consultants.

I am grateful for my friend, Debbie Ford. Thank you for inspiring me to write a book and express myself. Thank you for leading the way and thank you for the great work you do.

I am grateful for my life partner, Cindy Gillen, for never giving up on me and always pushing me forward. Thank you for loving me! I know it is a big job, and I know I am not easy to live with at times, but you are the woman for the job! Thank you for believing in me, for your trust, for your partnership and for sharing your kids with me.

To everyone I mentioned or I forgot to mention – family, friends, co-workers, teammates, known or unknown, near or far – you made me who I am today. Our relationships, the outcome of our relationships and everything that we went through together made me who I am today. Thank you! I am grateful.

All experiences, good or bad, fun or sad, exciting or terrifying, they all made me who I am today and think what I think today.

I am grateful to be alive.

Security is mostly a superstition.
It does not exist in nature, nor do the
children of men as a whole experience it.

Avoiding danger is no safer in the long run
than outright exposure.

Life is either a daring adventure,
or nothing.

--Helen Keller

Recognition

During my research and writing of this book I have come cross and mentioned wisdom and knowledge of so many great thinkers, writers, historians, poets, scientists, religious figures, industrialists, public servants, public figures, cultures and heroes.

I would like to mention their names in order of their appearance in this book and bow down to their wisdom, their enlightenment, their love and contributions to humanity and their bright knowledge.

Molana Jullaledin "Rumi"
Eleanor Roosevelt
Hafez-e Shirazi
Melody Beattie
Helen Keller
Mark Twain
Sufism
Zoroastrianism
Debbie Ford
Dr. Martin Luther King Jr.
Ebn-i-Yamin
Cherokee Native American Indians
Alfred D'Souza
Anthony D'Angelo
Henry Ford
Lester Levenson
Tom Landry
John Scharr
Chinese Proverb
Kwan-Tzu
Archbishop Desmond Tutu
Eleanor Roosevelt
Persian Proverb
President John F. Kennedy
William Shakespeare
Norman Cousins

Benjamin Franklin
Zen Proverb & Stories
Albert Einstein
Plato
Galileo Galilei
George Bernard Shaw
Michael Jordan
Jawaharlal Nehru
Ron Edward Disney
Marianne Williamson
Nelson Mandela
Publilius Syrus
Shearson/Lehman Brothers
William A Foster
Mother Teresa
William Hutchison Murray
Johann Wolfgang Von Goethe
Sir Winston Churchill
Judy Armijo
Jack London
Buddha
Buddhism
Mahatma Gandhi
Edward Estlin Cummings
Carl Gustav Jung
Omar Khayyam

I would like to acknowledge the Iranian artist and scholar Mr. Koorosh Angali, for his generous insights on translating the Persian poems cited in this book.

Special thanks to my friend and former Primeco Education Coach Miss. Aprille Trupiano for her notes and assistance on the Chapter Seven "Vision & Values".

My gratitude to one of my great participants of the Bravehearts Program 2007 in Saint Louis, MO, Miss. Hillary Gokenbach, who out of her powerful and beautiful sharing we took the name "Conspiracy for Greatness".

I also do not want to forget to say thank you to the following people who supported me during development of this book:

- Miss. Angel Haag my operation manger for reading and correcting my English!
- Miss. Sandra Rea-McGinty with "Book Candy Studios" from Lake Forest, California for her book editing work.
- Mr. David Lynch with "Lynch Graphics, Inc." from Asheville, North Carolina for the beautiful and classy book cover design.
- Mr. Ken Patton with "LB Printery" from Laceyville, Pennsylvania for helping me with the page set up.

About The Author

Behnam Bakhshandeh, an accomplished business manager and business development professional known widely as a dynamic personal and business coach, implements his skills as a passionate, visionary leader. Using these skills and drawing from his own life experience, he produces extraordinary results in record time.

Behnam brings his broad expertise and successful track record to each project, whether it involves personal development, implementing customer-focused programs, integrating technologies, marketing, redesigning operational core processes, or delivering strategic initiatives.

Born in 1957 in one of Iran's southern states, in a small town called Abadan, Behnam is the second brother of four sons from a family who was raised by loving and caring parents. Behnam's father had much influence in Behnam's upbringing, raising him as man of honor and integrity.

Behnam arrived in the United States in April of 1986 and has been a proud US citizen since 1999, though he remains a proud Persian in his heart and soul. Behnam has an absolute commitment to transforming the view of Iranians in the eyes of the western world, wanting them to understand his people are not what is painted by media and negative political propaganda.

In his teens, Behnam became interested in human development and began studying with advocates of personal transformation. He became interested in the study of the ancient Persian religion, "Zoroastrianism" *1 and the ancient Persian philosophy of transformation "Sufism" *2 eagerly consuming the books of Sufi masters and poets like Rumi *3, Shams *4, Hafez *5, Saadi *6 and Omar Khayyam *7 and so many other ancient and modern Iranian poets, writers and great thinkers of his era. He was fascinated by the simplicity of the main rules and aspects of Zoroastrianism which focus on *"Think kind, Talk kind and Do kind."* At the same time, he totally finds himself related and connected to the message of Sufism, which is *"Love within."* These simple yet powerful philosophies became some of the most influential elements of Behnam's writing and designing programs.

Between his high school graduation and his arrival in the U.S., Behnam went through many changes, personally, professionally, socially and sociologically. During that period he put in time doing mandatory military service. This was also a time of tremendous personal development as a man during which he developed leadership skills.

During his college years he went through one of the biggest political alterations in the 20th century in his country, the Iranian Revolution in 1979. This was a great deal for any Iranian, regardless of age, religion, race or sexual orientation. It was and still is one of the biggest political and social mysteries of our modern time.

Soon after the Revolution, Behnam married his high school sweetheart. Out of that marriage came his first-born daughter, Poneh (Renee). Within less than a week of his wedding Iraq attacked Iran's borders. His hometown of Abadan was on the border of Iraq. Like any other courageous Iranian, Behnam volunteered to serve and did what he had to do to defend his hometown during that chaotic time.

Eventually, Behnam was able to return to his education, during a time when the Iranian regime was being really hard on any anti-suppression movement in the universities, colleges or on anybody with any idea of

19

reform. During that time Behnam lost many close friends and family members, including his older brother and his first cousin. These losses have an emotional impact on Behnam's life to this day and is one of the main reasons for his overwhelming passion for life and living it full out. It is not easy to forget! However, he has forgiven, which is why he is free of the attachment to his writings and free to express his love to his three children (daughters Poneh and Shima, and his only son Behzad named after his murdered uncle).

Between the ages of 19 and 39, aside from learning and reading about Zoroastrianism and Sufism, Behnam studied the philosophies of Buddhism *8, followed by studies of many major world religions, and later the most notable Greek and Western philosophers, including Aristotle *9, Socrates *10, Plato *11, and the more modern philosophers, such as Nietzsche *12, Goethe *13 and Freud *14. This was the beginning of his understanding of Ontology *15 and since then he is fascinated by this since. To this day you can hear him say:

What is the big deal? All these organized religions have the very same message of love, respect and integrity!

Behnam has a tremendous amount of respect for all of the Major Prophets, such as Abraham, Moses, Jesus and Mohammad, but believes that people's interest of personal gain, political agendas and social dominations turned organized religions into something that it was never meant to be. On this issue, Behnam remains very passionate.

Behnam was always known as a "hardcore and take no crap from anyone" kind of guy. He is very well aware that this posturing was only a defense mechanism he designed to keep his emotions and feelings protected. While he continues to be straightforward, he no longer takes the hardcore stance he once did. Behnam expresses his artistic abilities and passion in many different ways. He draws, paints, dances, and plays the Saxophone.

He also has a strong passion for ancient Iranian and new age poetry. He even writes old fashioned poetry from time to time. Today, his friends know him as a passionate, sensitive, generous and romantic man who finds a lot of satisfaction and good from alone time, when he rides his Harley-Davidson V-Rod motorcycle along the beautiful San Diego North County coastline.

Behnam arrived in America after many hardships and problems with less than $100 in his pocket and little knowledge of the English language. Instead of touting his educations in industrial design engineering and business, he accepted several menial jobs, such as working for a dry cleaning shop and for a small boat-building shop during his first few months in California. All the while, he concentrated on improving his English while keeping his eyes and ears open for better opportunities.

That better opportunity arrived when a Los Angeles fire protection company hired Behnam as a welder. Thanks to his commitment to honor and hard work, Behnam built a strong relationship with the owner of the company, and quickly advanced from welder to production supervisor. After Behnam redesigned the company's production line, their productivity increased 25 percent during the first year and continued upward for each of the following four years, increasing production four-fold between 1986 and 1990.

In 1990, Behnam founded his own residential construction business in partnership with one of his relatives. By 1994, he had grown his company into one of the most respected and reliable businesses of its type in the Los Angeles area. Behnam also served as project manager for several federal and state construction projects in the San Diego area and consistently completed his work ahead of deadline. He always says, "You are either producing results or you have no results, plus a pretty good justification or reason!"

Since moving to the United States in 1986, Behnam's continuing commitment to informal education profoundly influenced his personal development. Behnam used whatever means he could find to make his wide-ranging knowledge of philosophy and personal growth available to the public.

Using his mastery of the teachings of history's great thinkers, Behnam began to focus on the elements and practices essential to become a complete, self-realized human being! He participated in different courses, seminars and developmental events to learn more about himself and his effectiveness in communication and relatedness. One of his favorite quotes that he always uses is from an American master writer, Mark Twain, is,

I never let schooling interfere with my education!

Before 2001, Behnam led educational and transformational seminars and programs for a global educational organization for more than eight years. During that time he also successfully managed business operations for that company in two major U.S. cities on two coasts, San Diego and Philadelphia.

By the end of year 2000, Behnam personally worked with more than 23,000 participants. He was accountable for expanding customer participation, training program leaders, increasing sales, improving the finance department's efficiency and management of the overall operations for the staff and their team of over 400 volunteers, who together served an annual client base of over 10,000 people.

If you ask him about the number of people he has led, he will say,

It doesn't matter anymore! I don't know, but it must be a lot of people.

For awhile I thought it meant something. I was counting my participants to prove something to myself and to others. I made it mean something about my experience. I stopped counting in the year 2000!

But now after so many years and so many people, there came a time when I started learning from people, too. Now, I am just enjoying being with different people, from different locations, from different cultures and who each have different experiences.

It is a lot to learn! People are very generous and so amazing that I want to know them all. They listen to me like I have something great to give them.

How generous! It is very humbling.

Behnam started his own education and coaching company in 2001. Since then, he and his team members have helped countless businesses and tens of thousands of individuals achieve their goals and transform their thinking to a much more effective way that allows them to have access to fulfillment, success and peace of mind. His proven methodology is based on his extensive experience in business and human relations, fueled by his burning passion for life.

Behnam consistently delivers and works with others to produce results beyond what was predicted or expected. This exceptional rate of business and personal growth is the result of integrity, unprecedented teamwork, open communication and a contagious, unflinching commitment to excellence in all business operations, personal relationships and professional interactions.

Behnam and his team are a shining example of how combining vision and goals with hard work consistently pays off beyond even the highest expectations.

Behnam is known among his friends, family and clients to be a patient, compassionate and a no-nonsense individual who loves to make a difference in all aspects of his life as well as the lives of others.

His work with individuals in personal and life coaching has created rewarding intimate relationships, loving and supportive families, flourishing careers and thriving health. His work with businesses has resulted in successful teams building companies through a shared vision, efficient process redevelopment that causes increased revenues, and work environments that support employee satisfaction and retention.

Behnam is widely known for his commitment to making a difference in every life he touches. He is distinguished in his field for delivering outcomes that leave each and every client fulfilled and living their dreams.

His rigor ensures that results are produced, while his compassion and sense of humor brings play to every working relationship.

Behnam dedicates his life to his three children and to serving others.

CHAPTER ONE

WE ARE ON OUR OWN WAY

SETTING UP THE JOURNEY

If you can find happiness
without someone else in the picture,
then you can welcome anyone
into your happiness.

Thank you for selecting my first book, *Conspiracy for Greatness …
Mastery of Love Within!*

For many years, I was fascinated by our ability as a human race to shift our
thinking. One of the main elements that define us from other species is this
ability to "think," and to decide and redirect our minds to what we always
knew we could do! Look at our collective recorded human history, and
you will find all those wonderful, brilliant and fascinating human beings
who directed their thinking to an area or topic, producing unprecedented
results, incredible inventions and so many amazing creations that we can
barely keep count. Now, you and I are taking advantage of the outcome of
those brilliant thinkers!

All inventions, all new methods and all new ways to do something new or
improve something that someone else came up with a long time ago has
come from our thoughts. What makes a human being think the way these
geniuses have thought? You can see them everywhere, in science, in
technology, in politics, medicine, sports, aerospace, architecture,
engineering and many different areas. This list can go on and on.

Why do you think Thomas Edison did not give up after trying over 900 different materials that would make the light bulb work? Why did Louis Pasteur not give up on finding a cure for so many human illnesses and diseases? Why did Dr. Luther King, Jr., not give up on his dream for social equality? Why did Mahatmas Gandhi not give up on dream of a free and independent India? Why did Leonardo Da Vinci not give up on coming up with a new invention year after year, after year? As you know, I can give you thousands of examples from thousands of amazing human beings that made the world a better place for you and me. An amazing point to note here is that all of them had the same 24 hours you and I have! Why is it that most of us cannot achieve as much as they did?

We Are NOT Different From The Great Thinkers!

Maybe we think they are different from we are, like they have more brain cells than we do, that they have different genes, or that there is something dramatically different about them! I know as well as you know that there are no differences between those people and us! Contrary to what you might think, or want it to be, there is no difference. Not in biology, not in abilities and not in circumstances! We all, as they were also, have and still deal with life's circumstances. As a matter of fact, they had so much more hardship in life compared with what we deal with today. Did they have the Internet, cell phones, computers, a college counselor, a high school prom, a personal trainer, a coffee latte or parents who were committed to their development? No. We have that! We are spoiled and we are lazy! *VERY* lazy!

What made these great minds different was their mentality, their view of life and their vision of their world. In their view of life there were no limits, and if there were, they knew they could work around them, and they knew they could get over that hump. If there was a limit, it was not a limit they imposed on themselves, but rather it is what others insisted on!

There are no limits, there is no hardness, and there is no "I can't" until we say "it is," or we listen to others saying "it is!" What is this amazing phenomenon that some people have created mastery around and for so many others it is still a mystery?

They had vision! They saw a future, and they started planning and designing their actions to correlate to that future they saw. But they did not act like it was a fantasy or some pie in the sky, but like "it is true and I am getting there!" They did not know how, but they knew they could reach their goals. So can you if you change your thinking.

We all are experts in *DOING*. By the way, just *DOING* is not enough for us; we have to *DO* IT GOOD, or *DO* IT RIGHT! Take a look around, you are either good at what you *DO* or you go to school to become good at what you are going to *DO*, or know someone who is very good at what they *DO,* or what you need them to be good at! Or you hire someone who is good at what you want them to *DO*! It is all about *DOING,* and we have to *DO* it right!

That is what makes things work around our lives, and what we need! We have made our environment so complicated and so out of control with *doing* rules, *doing* laws, *doing* governments, *doing* parenting, *doing* this and *doing* that, which forces us to go through many years of education and *do* a lot of other *DOINGS* just so we can afford *doing* the education. We teach our children to *do* the same thing to become someone that does something that will make us proud of what they *do,* and then we are all getting busy doing what we all *do*! How is that for a great picture of our lives and our world that we have created around us?

As I said, just doing it is not enough. We must to do it right! If we don't do it right, we suffer for years and are stuck in a battle with ourselves. We make ourselves wrong for not doing it right the first time, and the first try! Can you see yourself there? I am sure you can, as can I. We have started so many things and have not finished them, because it was not *RIGHT ENOUGH*, it was not *GOOD ENOUGH*. The result? We just dropped it.

When Did YOU Give Up?

We have put aside, stuck on shelves and stored in garages so many dreams and ideas that make us sad to think about them! Look for yourself and see how many dreams, or interests in life, you put aside because you failed after a couple of tries, or maybe you haven't even started because you were not sure if you could succeed or accomplish it. Or you were not sure if you could do it *RIGHT*! How many times and for how many years have you judged yourself or others for not doing "it" right? How many times were you sad? How many times did you cry or get depressed because you did not do something right? In business, work, education, sports, friendships and relationships? If you notice, everyone around you is the same way! Even people who look confident and have succeeded in life have dealt with this issue of not "doing it right," and most important, not being good enough *to do it right*. Or not being good enough to be loved, not being enough for someone or something. Not being enough to be selected on a school sports team. Not being good enough to pass the test in school, high school, college or work. Not being enough to be trusted. You know as well as I do that this list can go on. It was in your life from the beginning, it is there right now, and it will be with you until you leave this earth! Maybe it started when you fell from your tricycle the first time, or when you did not get asked out to your first prom night, and all the stuff in between. Either way, you started developing this mindset a long time ago, and you still carry that big baggage with you wherever you go.

Come back, stay with me, right here and now. There is a good ending in this very sad dramatic story, a very good one, with a great protagonist, and it is called "YOU!" Yes, you are the hero in this drama because you can and you will win! So stay with me here and you will see how you can turn this sucker around.

What is common in all these incidents, and/or events in our lives that cause all that mischief is the *BEING* part of human being that makes us all be in the same boat.

Human Beings vs. Human Doing

Very interesting. We are human beings, but all we do is "human-doing." It sounds funny, doesn't it? That is because it *is* funny! If you pay attention, you will notice that regardless of nationality, race, age, sex, sexual

31

orientations, and even social-upbringing, when a person is upset, angry, sad or happy, we can recognize it without them even talking. Why is that? We can recognize resentment, we can see regret, we can smell unhappiness, and we can recognize so many different ways of *being* in others. We can also see being committed, being interested, being communicative, being excellence driven and having leadership qualities. Even without them doing anything special, we can see those characteristics on others regardless of how hard they try to hide them or express them. "State of being" is what makes us all do what we do, or even feel what we feel. It makes us interested in what we do, it allows us to get related to others, or take ourselves away from them! It makes us succeed or fail, and it makes us love or hate ourselves and others!

I can talk about myself here. I have done this many times in my own life, which has impacted other's lives. If you read my biography at the beginning of the book you know that I was born and raised in Iran, and I am Persian, which brings with it more than 2,500 years of monarchy, over 7,000 years of civilization and more than 10,000 years of history. For a long time, this history separated me from so many people. What kind of people? Anybody who was not Persian! I know this seems pretty arrogant! So, how I was doing that? I did not have any American friends. I was working with them, but not socializing with them. I was taught that I was better than them. I was from a very rich and deep culture, and they didn't match up. I was BEING better than them. I was not saying that I was better to them nor to anybody else, but who I was BEING with them was arrogant and snooty! Can you understand that? I am sure that you have done that toward other people, maybe some of your friends or even some of your family members.

When I realized what I was doing, I saw how shallow it was and how empty my life was. I was isolated and kept myself away from a lot of great people, but I was not seeing it that way. As I said, BEING is like air to a bird or water to a fish. We do not recognize our own way of *being*. Sometimes it takes a shocking incident or event to wake us up. Sometimes a shocking experience of how we have hurt others might wake us up, or sometimes when someone you love leaves you because that your way of *being* is too much and is too destructive. Unfortunately, sometimes we wake up too late. I am guilty of this.

Listen, I am writing this because I have experienced it! I am not writing this to impress you, but to share with you about my experiences, so maybe that will make a difference for you. I have failed, I have three divorces behind me, I have failed in business, I filed bankruptcy in 1991, and I have broken up with people for no solid reasons beyond I wanted to. I have lied, cheated and fabricated. I have taken advantage of others, and for a long time I was thinking about just one person … *ME*! I paid big prices for these ways of being I am sharing it with you so you might learn from my mistakes without the pain. It will not be easy, but it is doable. Through this book, I will share more about my life and what I have done, so you will have a better understanding of where I come from and that I have gone through some of the same issues that you might be dealing with now.

Breaking The Conspiracy Of Thought

For a long time, I was arrogant, cocky, unapproachable and self-centered. I was doing anything to survive and to make it. I was about "get what I

33

want" at any cost! What I did not see is the self-sabotage. I did not see how I was compromising my integrity, my greatness and my future. I was not aware of my BEING. Being aware of who you are *being* is the hardest thing you can achieve as a human being. To know and be aware of the source of your being, it takes a mastery to understand this mystery. The mystery of loving yourself enough so you do something about the future you are about to live. Maybe not from the past you are dragging behind you, but from a great vision that you can create, invent and live for.

This mystery is the topic of this book. ***Conspiracy for Greatness … Mastery of Love Within!*** Because what we are not aware of, but always runs us and controls us is the absolute opposite of this, which is a conspiracy for smallness, for weakness and a conspiracy to oppose limits on our own and others limitations and abilities. A conspiracy for keeping mediocrity in place, a conspiracy for killing possibility as soon as someone tries to bring it up, a conspiracy to be part of the "being norm," meaning to be just like others or what others and society is expecting from you.

Being ordinary is norm! Being small, thinking small, and doing small is norm! Everybody does that. What is opposite of norm or normal? Abnormal, right?

What is opposite of ordinary? Extraordinary, right? So, consider this; for being extraordinary you have to become abnormal. You might laugh because it is funny as much as it is ridiculous. But, you have seen it every day; you deal with it each time you get excited about something in life. Each time you want to go out there and achieve your desires and your dreams, you deal with this phenomenon. Because it is not the norm to be great; it is not the norm to be out there and be extraordinary. People will laugh at you. Others will say "look at him (or her)… they think it's that easy!" This is one of the reasons I call this phenomenon a conspiracy … a conspiracy for smallness!

Have you ever seen a crab basket? Yes, crab basket. Go to a crab fishing boat or place, and watch how crabs are treating each other. Usually one crab will start climbing out of the basket, trying to get away, maybe go for freedom and, suddenly, the rest of the crabs will grab him and pull him down. It is a sad thing to watch. Where else can you see this phenomenon outside the crab-fishing boat? In everyday life with ourselves, when someone pulls you down … every day, someone will say to you, "You can't do that!" or "You will not succeed," or "Are you crazy?" or "Don't be so childish!" And/or, any other disempowering and belittling comments that people will tell you. Sometimes even they don't know they are doing it. I am sure that some of them really love us and do care about us, but they are not aware of their way of being that makes them say what they are saying to us. The reality is sometimes we do the same thing to others! We do! You do! To ourselves and to others! But mostly to ourselves … every day

I have heard myself share my doubts with friends and people I care about regarding their hopes and dreams. I remember my best friend from high school, Ata, who is now living in Los Angeles with his beautiful wife Mahnoosh. When he was sharing with me about the transformational workshop or seminars he had done, I was putting him down, joking and making belittling comments that I am sure now looking back were hurtful, but Ata with his very generous way of being and his manners laughed with me. He did not want me to feel bad. With him I was being a macho man. I am sure you can identify with this. We all have those people around us; we have even done this to people ourselves.

We are the worst conspirators of all time! We kill ourselves off and we kill off others every day. We do not make a stand for others and we do not make stand for ourselves. We make ourselves wrong and make others wrong, too. We judge ourselves, and that is why we judge others. We can't stand our own failures, so we refuse to see others' successes. We see our worst in others. That is the conspiracy I am talking about. Making a stand for oneself and others is not an easy thing; it's scary and it's hard! You have to give something precious away – your ego, your desire and your wants. That makes it hard. Maybe that is why you don't see leadership around you too often. Some people provide that leadership for themselves, and some do it for others.

Look at our history. Anyone who stood for our greatness, anyone who stood for better lives for others, anyone who stood for being or doing extraordinary things and tried to come up with a new way of living was shot, assassinated or suppressed and shut down! Jesus, Caesar, Abraham Lincoln, John F. Kennedy, Robert Kennedy, Dr. Martin Luther King, Jr., and Malcolm X in United States. Mahatmas Gandhi in India, Ernesto Che Guevara in Bolivia, Emiliano Zapata in Mexico, Dr. Mohammad Mosadegh, Khosro Golesorkhy and Samd Behrangi in Iran, Nelson Mandela in South Africa, and so many other great leaders, revolutionaries, thinkers and any person who said:

This is not all of it! There is more in being human and being free!

You can find these great thinkers and leaders in any nation, any religion, any race, any political movement and any freedom-fighting group. You can find them behind the work of any free-spirited writer, poet, musician, artist and speaker. This list can go on and on; the world is full of people who stood for others and were murdered, suppressed or jailed.

We are not going to get to their stories here. However, I hope to make you see that there is no difference between them and you. The feelings are the same. We are assassinating others and ourselves by buying into our *smallness,* and the "I can't do" and "You can't do it" talk. What is the difference? We might not be shooting people with guns, but for sure we are using our tongues to kill their dreams! We talk, we gossip, we lie, we manipulate, we hide, we put them down and we do not acknowledge them. Why do we do that? There is no difference between us and the crabs in a pot. Maybe because we don't want to see how easy it is to succeed in life. Maybe we don't want to face that we can be and are responsible for the quality of our lives.

You Can If You Think You Can!

If you look around carefully, you will see either now or maybe in your past you have given in to so many ideas that were not powerful, and quite frankly pretty small. Some generated from yourself, and some you adopted from others around you, and some you just made up during your upbringing or that you get when you become part of the "work force."

We have surrounded ourselves with people who buy our *small talk*, our excuses, our justifications, our explanations, our complaints and our opinions. Why? Because we do it for them, too! That is why I call it a conspiracy! Everyone is in it; you and your family, your friends, your co-workers, even society as whole. Look, when was the last time you talked to a family member or a friend and asked them to tell you what they think about you, and they told you the truth about what they really think about you? When was the last time you told them about what you want to do in life and your future, and they kicked your behind so you do what you need to do to become that?

How many times when you nagged and complained about life not being fair they told you to shut up and do something about it? How many times have you gossiped about someone, and they stopped you and said I don't want to listen to gossip? How many times have they bought your complaints, your smallness and given in to your justifications? How many times have you done that for them? You and I both know you have done that a lot! Actually, almost all the time as much as they did for you! That is the way a conspiracy for smallness works.

It is all designed for keeping you small and in your comfort zone. You don't have to do anything! You don't have to become someone who can fulfill one's dream. You can say "I can't," and everyone will say you are right, you can't. You can say, "It could not get done," and everyone around you would agree with you. You can say, "The world is not taking care of me," and everyone will give you their same experience to tell you how accurate you are. All of it is a conspiracy. A conspiracy for smallness, and for mediocrity! Because you and I know if you stop doing that, if you stop listening to that nonsense, if you get yourself out of that "rat hole," if you stand firm and declare that you are the master of your life, then you can do anything you put your heart and soul in, then you will fulfill your dreams. In that case you have to alter who you have been being in your past so you can do something different in your future. Not in terms of your shape or form or race or nationality or religion, none of those, but in terms of thinking and developing your new view of life and your world around you. And that, my friend, will be the beginning of a new world, the start of something way bigger than what you have done before. It is a conspiracy for greatness. For whose greatness? For you first, and then for anybody and everybody around you! Thinking is the biggest challenge of all. Why? Because you have been trained to think in a certain way and we will try to show you that there is a whole new way of thinking that allows you to get to your greatness, and actually maintain it!

As Dr. Martin Luther King Jr. said:

Rarely do we find men who willingly engage in hard, solid thinking. There is an almost universal quest for easy answers and half-baked solutions. Nothing pains some people more than having to think.

Start Thinking Differently NOW!

We have to develop our new trend of thinking, and the only way I know is to become responsible for where we are; you know you can't go anywhere new without knowing where you currently *are*. For you to start your journey, you must become absolutely responsible for all aspects of your life.

That is the hardest thing you will ever do. It is not easy, but it is doable! As you are going through this book, be responsible for what you are learning; be responsible for writing that experience down in the designated area that is in the end of each chapter. Be responsible to follow the coaching, and dig into the questions and inquiries I throw at you, because those inquiries are the things that will make a difference! As I have said before, I have no answers for you. I have very good questions that allow you to find your own answers. When you get that answer from yourself, then you will never forget what you discover, and you will know what to do to alter that way of being that caused that way of doing! And that, my friend, is the best way to learn! Be responsible to follow the instructions and directions throughout this book. I promise you will get value and you will get more than you asked for. We will work more on responsibility in the future chapters.

Who Are You; Who Are You NOT?

For you to become more responsible for "who you are" you have to get who you are not!

Who you are is not your home, your checkbook, your car, nor the people with whom you associate. Who you are is your passion, your vision and your dreams. Who you are boils down to your values and your principles. That is what media, marketing companies for the fashion, the beauty, the cigarette cartels, and the movie industries and any other big money-making organizations know already! They know people in general are not relating to themselves to the rest of the human race as whole. There is a big void within these people that no certain look, body size or association with others or even money can fill. Because of this mindset, they fall target to the marketing campaigns of products galore that promise to give them fulfillment, which never comes.

We can never get to that space and that point that we are whole until we understand fully who we are and how we grow to become who we are. So many great thinkers and writers have written and dig into this great phenomenon. One of the best books on this topic is *The Dark Side of Light Chasers* by Debbie Ford. I have the privilege and honor to call Miss Ford a friend. She definitely had, and continues to have, a great influence in my development as a responsible and accountable person.

In her first book, *The Dark Side of The Light Chasers*, Debbie Ford talks about all areas of our lives, and the fact that we do not own our entire humanity – where we like to just be our light, but not our dark, where we like to be known as our generosity, but not our stinginess, we would do anything so others know us as our love, but not our hate. We fail because they all come together, and that makes us whole and complete as a human being. Meanwhile, we suffer because we don't want others to see both sides; we want them to see only one side … the good side! That is the beginning of in-authenticity and fakery! That is dressing up your past and wanting to *sell it* as your future. That is painting your lies with colorful colors and trying to pass them off as the truth. That is where you will be found out and will be called on your lies.

41

Without owning "who you are" and how you become "who you are" on a *good day,* you are just practicing and repeating your past, and nothing will ever change. Yes, you will make more money and you will have a bigger house, but you will not be happy and nor fulfilled. In this book, I attempt to bring you to a point that you will be responsible for your past, all of your past practices, behaviors and choices, and then assist you in creating and inventing a whole new vision for yourself and your life worth living and one worth sharing with others.

After so many years of suffering and failing I have created a vision for my life. My vision for my life is:

Life fulfilled. Passion, love and laughter expressed.
Inspired by people's success, having fun and creating abundance.

I know who I am now. I am my possibility, I am my passion, and I am the cause of my own life. Who I am is the possibility of other's greatness and excellence. This is what I do every day in fulfilling my vision. My commitment is to remove the obstacles people face in building sustained growth and success, personally and professionally. What I do to fulfill that commitment and vision is coaching, consulting and mentoring.

The liar and the cheater could not create this amazing, powerful and enrolling vision, nor could I live it or make it real! I had to transform that guy to be able to see his own greatness and his own power. I cleaned house! Where? I started from my heart and soul. I started telling the truth about all aspects of my life, the good, the bad and the ugly! I started cleaning up my messes. With people, with the ones I hurt, lied to or stole

42

from. I started to pay off my debts to others. Some debts were money, some were in time, some were in friendships, and some were in love I needed to return, but it was debts I owed. That is the responsibility I'm talking about. You have to take life by the horns. As I have said before, it will not be easy, but it is doable! It will get harder before it gets easier. Start by loving yourself. You have to clean the years of dust from your heart caused by anger, resentment and upset! Forgive yourself for *not* forgiving others! Let go of the stinginess and open the door for generosity, and let go of the hate to make room for love!

I could not become who I am today if I did not let go of the years of hate, anger and resentment after my older brother was murdered in Iran during the government crackdown against freedom fighters. We lost two cousins and one brother, as well as many friends. I experienced some hardship around them, too. You can just imagine the amount of hate, anger and upset one can carry in their heart after these kinds of dramatic events in life. Those 25 years have passed, but the experience will never leave me!

Making The Change

I was not aware of the impact that those years would have on my experiences in life and my relationships. I was short with my wife, angry for no reason, demanding without any justification, and I looked for ways to express my heavy load of anger, my resentments and my regrets! Years of hardship were piling up. The simplest way I can express it is that I was drinking the poison and wishing for *them* to die! But, I was the one who was dying, and I didn't know it. Until I forgave and forgot, I could not

43

open my heart to love and peace. I had to give up the fight within me if I was to stand for peace. It was not easy, but I opened my heart for love and forgiveness, which opened so many doors for peace and harmony in my life that I am grateful. This is one of the messages in this book. You've had events and incidents that clouded *your* heart for years. I hope by reading this book and our assistance, you can clean your heart and soul and see the light in your heart – light that will illuminate who you are within and the light of your own greatness.

For me to practice who I am and make a difference, I established my own coaching and consulting programs and practices. It is part of my joy and happiness, and it is my playground. It is my place to go and work with the amazing people on my team to spread the message of having a life vision, accountability, responsibility and effectiveness every day.

In our coaching system, we lead individuals to achieve greater freedom, commitment and accountability in their lives. Personal and professional values, vision and goals become clear. Ability to relate to others grows dramatically and individuals become empowered to follow their dreams to achieve unprecedented results in their career, finance, health and vitality. After so many years of education during which everyone taught me what to do, I find that no one taught me how to BE ... how to be present, patient, have compassion, how to deal with upset and anger and be calm, and how to be someone who can handle regrets and resentments. No one taught me how to be a man, to be a father, to be a husband and to be a son. I have always been interested in this way of human development.

I have studied so many ancient and modern philosophies, and have come to a point of gathering all of my thoughts together, drawing from my education and experiences to create these dialogues. During my career, so many people asked me, "What do you mean by coaching? What is coaching? What is the benefit of coaching? How do you do that?"

Coaching Helps In Transition

Coaching is a highly effective tool for individuals and organizations. It is for people who choose to have their future be here and now, instead of maybe someday, if it's not too hard and if everything is okay. It is for authentic, healthy, ambitious, brave and open-minded people who strive for excellence.

There are strong benefits in our system and our coaching. One is increasing your velocity and your success. Another is recapturing your interests and passions in life, and yet another is accomplishing more in less time, then stretching your imagination and self-expression to allow you to invent a vision and put it into practice. You will communicate directly and clearly, you will increase overall efficiency and effectiveness, and most important, you will fall in love with life and live it fully.

How do we do that?

We use dialogues, processes and action plans that are designed to empower participants. You will look closely at the core beliefs and personal realities that determine your direction in life and how well you

45

achieve personal and professional results. As you become more aware of these beliefs and realities, you will learn to take responsibility for your behavior and choices in life. You will dissolve your barriers to self-expression, success and fulfillment.

Our coaching gives you the goals you need to look at your personal and professional life and its challenges from a new perspective. You will develop practices and actions that support a new and empowering way of living. Is coaching a wise investment? Think of it this way, you are either producing outstanding results in life, or you have great excuses for why not. The choice is yours.

In this book, we look at different areas of your life in which you allow yourself to buy into the *conspiracy for smallness*. We coach you, inviting you to look at those areas and become responsible for the results you have created in those areas, such as the way you relate to yourself, others, your work, and the work you have created for yourself. Then we look at how you can have balance in life, your intimate relationships, your communications, and other topics in your life where you have caused some upset.

The best way, I know, to get the most benefit from this book is for you to bring your life to it versus just reading a book to get information. You hear people say, "Knowledge is power." No it is not! Implementation of knowledge is power; application of knowledge is power." That is true. What you know makes no difference, what you do with what you know makes a difference, sometimes good, and sometimes bad. It all depends on your agenda and your goals in doing what you are doing in regard to yourself and others when you use your knowledge. You know how to lose weight, right? You may even be reading a book about it, or have purchased exercise equipment to lose weight, but are you losing weight? No. Unless you get committed to the goal and implement what you know, weight will not be lost. You have to put your thoughts into action.

Changing Your Patterns

You know someone close to you, your husband, wife, life partner, parents, siblings or close friends who have certain "buttons," which if you *push* you will upset them! However, knowing this does not prevent you from pushing it from time to time, right? Funny thing is that as soon as they get upset you say, "Are you upset? I didn't know that would upset you. I am so sorry!" Yeah, right! You absolutely knew, and that knowledge made no difference. You know lying is not good, but you lie a little every day! It all depends on how you justify your actions.

Consider this; if I take away your justifications, explanations and reasons, you have nothing to say about why you don't have what you want in life! Now, if I take away your opinion, you have nothing to say about others' lives either! If you are authentic and honest, you agree with me! Right now you have some explanations, reasons and justifications for why what I said being not accurate, in your opinion. You even have some opinion about me and what I have said! But notice that your explanation, justification, reasoning and opinion made no difference what so ever, and you are still in the same place that you have been before you read this paragraph. If you have any interest, you will start to bring yourself and your life to what I have said, and start looking at your life very closely to become open to learning.

In this book, I try to bring our feelings, thoughts, hopes, notions and desires out on paper, and to organize them in one systematic approach that will make it easy to understand and to help you understand how we operate the "machinery" that we are! How we have become the people we are today. Why things happened the way they have happened in our lives. I can't help the influence of my engineering and business background in this book. How does it influence this book? By organizing the chapters to link together and create practices that will make your thoughts and realizations also link together so you can have the most benefit out of what is laid out before you here. We will have practice assignments and writing exercises, so we can better engage others and think deeper! Your journey is not about knowing … it is about NOT knowing! It is not about how much we can learn but rather about how much we DON'T know, and the impact that understanding can have on our lives.

As I mentioned before I have such passion for ancient philosophy and wisdom, especially Sufism and Persian philosophies that I want to share that passion with you.

The following is one of a short but very famous poem from Ebn-i-Yamin *16 a fourteenth century Persian mystic and poet. Most of his work is a representative of moral aphorism. I make sure to add the Farsi (Persian Language) version of the actual poem to keep the integrity of it.

آنکس که بداند و بداند که بداند

اسب شرف از گنبد گردون بجهاند

آنکس که بداند و نداند که بداند

بیدار کنیدش که بسی خفته نماند

آنکس که نداند و بداند که نداند

لنگان خرک خویش به منزل برساند

آنکس که نداند و نداند که نداند

در جهل مرکب ابدالدهر بماند

- ابن یمین

This is the English translation in a very simple language:

He who knows, and knows that he knows,

    Would lead an honorable and dignified life

He who knows, and doesn't know that he knows,

    Wake him up, lest he remain oblivious

He who doesn't know, and knows that he doesn't know,

    Would gradually, but surely, achieve his goals

He who doesn't know, and doesn't know that he doesn't know

    Is doomed to eternally live in absolute ignorance

                    --Ebn-i-Yamin

An Invitation To Begin Your Journey

I invite you while reading this book to be someone who doesn't know and who is interested in learning to become more effective in his or her life. If you are someone who already knows everything and doesn't need to look at his or her life to be more effective, please take this book back to the place from whence you purchased it and get your money back, because I can't teach you anything new!

In the ***Conspiracy for Greatness … Mastery of Love Within!*** we will examine different areas of our lives, areas that we have impacted with our conspiracies for smallness, and our gatherings of evidence and arguments of our limitations.

We look at some of the most important aspects of our lives, and attempt to get you *present* to the impact of our decisions and choices in our lives. We also take responsibility of how we can turn this life around and design our own future by inventing a vision for our life that is worth living and worth working. Look at the following questions under each of the topics of this book, and see if it is worth finding answers for all of them. See if it is worth having an inquiry into how we have caused our lives to be the way they are;

- **We are on our own way – Setting up the journey**
    - How much of your life has been based on knowing what to do?
    - How do you get in your own way to become who you are?

- **How do you play in life? Opinion versus Possibility**
  - Are you living your life based on your opinions, or are you creating possibilities around your life and your relationships with others?
  - Do you understand how you play in life? Are you on the field or watching from the stands?

- **Internal Conversation – The chatter that ties you down!**
  - How much of your lifetime have you listened to that destructive chatter in your head?
  - How many times have you acted after you listened to your inner chatter and things did not turn out the way you thought they would?

- **Conspiracy for Suffering - Barriers to personal effectiveness**
  - Have you ever judged yourself and others?
  - How much of your time is wasted complaining about yourself, others, what you do and life itself?

- **Own your life results - Inspiration versus Desperation**
  - Are you happy, satisfied and fulfilled in what you do for a living or are you just doing it?
  - Are you moving through life because you "have to," or because you "love to?"

- **Vision and Values – The forces that make things work**
  - What are you valuing in life and why are you valuing them?

o   Do you have a vision for your life or are you just dragging your past with you?

- **Integrity, Responsibility and Accountability – Your source of power, magic and miracles**
  o   Would you like to know how to use integrity as the source of power, magic and miracles?
  o   Are you responsible for the quality of your life, and are you accountable for making sure that those qualities are apparent?

- **Conspiracy for Greatness - Mastery of love within!**
  o   Are you getting "present" to your magnificence and power, and the greatness of life itself?
  o   Do you know how to manage your power and keep your new vision and view of life in existence?

- **Acknowledgment and Empowerment – Access to others greatness**
  o   Are you accessing others greatness by acknowledging, appreciating and empowering them?
  o   Are you aware of the impact you have on others and how you leave them after your interaction with them?

- **What would the rest of your life look like? – What is next?**
  o   Will you live your life based on the past you have experienced?
  o   Or, will you live your life based on your values and a powerful vision that you have created for your life?

As one of the best writers in the world, and a pride and joy of American literature, Mark Twain once said:

I never let my schooling interfere with my education.

There is a relationship here between you and me. Our relationship is like a tripod, a tripod has three legs, and if any of those three legs collapses, the relationship will not work. These legs together will establish the integrity and stability of this coaching process. If you remove any of the legs, what happens? The tripod falls, no matter how strong it looks or how well it is built. For us to get the full benefits from this relationship, we have to get related to these three legs.

1st leg is the leg of "Respect"

I will respect you as a student and a coachee, so I will "swing out," not hold back, and I will be intrusive. I will ask you to dig deep. You bought this book, spent your money and are spending your time to read it. You trusted me to deliver the goods, and because I respect you, I will deliver!

Sometimes you might not like it. It might hurt your feelings. You might not want to hear the truth. Because I respect you, I don't care, and I will deliver. Because you respect me, you won't take it personally. I will smack the back of your head and turn up the heat, because I respect you.

You have already trained so many people in your life to be afraid when you get mad, or when you throw a tantrum, or when you sound this or that way, and it means *back off*! But that is not going to happen with me, because I am not going to get upset with you, I am here and you are there. You cannot play games with me. You cannot be cute or mad or funny to get me to back off. I have nothing to lose; you have a lot to lose! If you don't follow the coaching in the best scenario, you will leave with the same lack of knowledge and understanding of yourself that you started with when you bought this book!

Because I respect you, I will not give up on you. I will not be rude to you, but I *will* be rigorous.

2nd leg is the leg of "Trust"

It is silly for me to ask you to trust me because you don't know me. But, you will benefit if you trust me anyway. I will not ask you to break the law, do something against your religion or do something immoral or wrong. However, I will ask you to do things that will shake up your world. Something that may be so uncomfortable for you to do! Such as cleaning up your messes in life, taking responsibility for what you have done in your life, regardless if you have done it to yourself or to others!

You trust that there is something there for you if you do the process completely. As ridiculous as it may sound, I need to trust that you will do it. I need to trust that you will tell the truth all the time, and not hide anything in this process. If you hide, I cannot deliver this valuable coaching to you. And, you have to trust me that I am on your side. There is big neon letters lit above my head here that say, "I am on your side," even if it looks like I am against you. Because promise you this … I will tell it like it is.

This could be one of the most intimate relationships you have in your life! Because we are not attached to each other, we can just trust the process and get to the bottom of what is in your way to utilize in the maximumizing of *your* power!

3rd leg is the leg of "Concept of Our Relationship"

Coach and Coachee relationship: This is the concept of our relationship. It is not mother and son, father and daughter, therapist and patient, lovers, husband and wife. We are none of those things.

I am the coach, and you are the coachee! We will get into coaching. A therapist will do a psychological profile and address your psychological issues. I believe in what they do, but I care more about your actions. I am more interested in you managing the actions that will come out of your understanding and recognition. I will look at what you do, so I am not so interested in your stories, nor am I interested in your complaints and excuses. I am more interested in what you are going to do about them.

All great athletes and artists have a coach behind them. So when I say jump, you ask how high? You can scream and kick and cry as long as you

55

do it. You agree to bring forth everything in this process and not hide anything. If you want to hold back, it is probably best not to start, because it will not be effective. If you hide, cheat and lie, that will be ordinary. If you want extraordinary, you must rise above that and play *full out*!

I know you are a diamond. I can see it! I can feel it and I am assured of it. But that doesn't matter if you don't see, feel and are sure of it. I can see the diamond within you that has been hidden under so many years of pressure, of lies, gossips, back stabbings, misrepresentations and darkness. As you work through this process, there will be a time that you don't want to look at these layers that are over your diamond within and holding back the light to shine over your life. It will be hard to look at one's darkness, un-forgiveness, and shortcomings as a human being. I know ... I was there. I still deal with my journey every day.

My job is to keep looking at that diamond and to focus on that. Your job is to help me dig into those past layers. As I dig with you and clean our the corners, you may grow tired, resigned and want to stop digging, I will encourage you, hold your hand, and keep reminding you about the amazing shining light of that diamond within. Together, we will get into that process of being *who* you are.

I love the following little story. I don't know who wrote this, but I always share it with others. This little story is a very good example of what we do, and how we are doing it to ourselves. See if you can see yourself in this story:

A Life Lesson

An elder Cherokee Native American was teaching his grandchildren about life.

He said to them, "A fight is going on inside me. It is a terrible fight, and it is between two wolves. One wolf represents fear, anger, envy, sorrow, regret, greed, arrogance, self-pity, guilt, resentment, inferiority, lies, false pride, superiority, ego, and unfaithfulness.

The other wolf stands for joy, peace, love, hope, sharing, serenity, humility, kindness, forgiveness, benevolence, friendship, empathy, generosity, truth, compassion, and faithfulness."

This same fight is going on inside you, and inside every other person, too. They thought about it for a minute then one child asked his grandfather, "Which wolf will win?"

The old Cherokee simply replied, "The one you feed."

Thank you for listening, and I definitely hope this book serves you, and that you learn something great about yourself and start your journey in your **Conspiracy for Greatness ... Mastery of Love Within.**

CHAPTER TWO

HOW DO YOU PLAY IN LIFE?

OPINION VERSUS POSSIBILITY – PART A: OPINION

Make your life a game!
But be out there playing,
not just watching from the sidelines.

We participate in our lives in a certain way. Or we can say there is a way that we "play" in life. The way you have played, or are playing in life, is the same way you are participating in your life or in your job and business.

In this chapter, you will see the ways you are deciding to play or not. The way you decide if it is *safe* to play or not. Just imagine when you and your life partner are talking about different things, especially when the topic of conversation is sensitive. Like when you know you are right, because you know you are right! How do you know you are right? By your knowledge, your evidence, your experiences and your education? It is the exact same way in your home as it is at your work! Same boat, different ocean!

Getting Present With the Here and Now

For you to get the picture of what I am trying to convey to you, I give a relationship as an example. We can use our relationship here and now. Imagine I am the Coach and you are the Coachee. (This happens in our business. Every day, almost each time we have a training or coaching session this phenomenon shows its ugly head!) There is training and

59

coaching going on here, between you and I. By virtue of your reading this book and my writing it we are in a short-term relationship between Coach and Coachee.

For you to get the full benefit of this book, or if I may say *coaching*, you need to notice how you listen to this information. Notice how you apply the distinctions, and whether you are welcoming it or not. How? By getting "present" to your inner chatter. Some call it "internal dialogue" or "internal conversations." They are all the same. It is the chatter and the noise in your head. I will talk about this in length in Chapter Three, but for now just get present to that inner chatter that you have with yourself all the time. You know what I am talking about! The voice that is saying right now, "I don't have inner chatter!" *That* is your inner chatter! Can you hear it? That is the voice that decides for you and makes judgments against everyone, including yourself! (As I said, I will dig inside that voice deeply in the next chapter. It is hard to separate these two chapters from each other, so for now just get present to the fact that you have a "voice" in your head that is making decisions for you.)

While reading this, the same voice will decide if you are getting value out of reading this or not. And, by the way, that voice is doing the exact same thing to your relationship with your life partner, your parents, your friends and/or your boss or business partners, even with your own customers or clients, no exceptions! How? You are reading a section about the way I am digging, describing or distinguishing issues, topics or incidents and you will hear in your head:

I agree with it ... I disagree with it...

Or you will hear the voice saying:

I know all these ... I did not know this...

Or you may hear yourself:

This is right .... This is not right; it is wrong....

Or maybe you hear:

This is bad, it is not good ... This is good...

Or any of the following options or scenarios can occur:

(I am sure by now you can recognize some of these voices, and maybe even all of them. You have to be honest and look for yourself. You might have heard so many different variations of that voice such as the following.)

This is so true ... This is false....
I want this ... I don't want this...
I need this, I can use it ... I don't need this and it is no use to me...
Why he is saying this ... Why he is not saying that?
It should be this way ... It should not be that way...
This makes sense .... This doesn't make any sense...

Or any other way you are relating to this material. You may hear different things in your head. The point is you can't help hearing one, two, or all of these things at the same time in your head. If you notice without judgments, you can see that you have done this in almost all of your conversations with others on a personal level, as well as a professional level. You have done it today; you have done it yesterday, the day before and years before! You know it and I know it. As matter of fact, you are doing it right now as you are reading about how you are doing it.

If you notice and pay attention to what you are saying in your head, the voices have one thing in common. They are all your **OPINION.** Opinion is not bad, it is just not effective. It is not something you can get rid of ever! It will come to you without your control. However, if you can recognize it you can be in control of expressing it.

You can imagine that the *domain of opinion* would look something like figure "A." You can imagine this square box is the world you have created for yourself, full of your opinions, full of your interpretations. Just imagine if you could not use your opinions and interpretations. What would you say? Nothing. Just think about it.

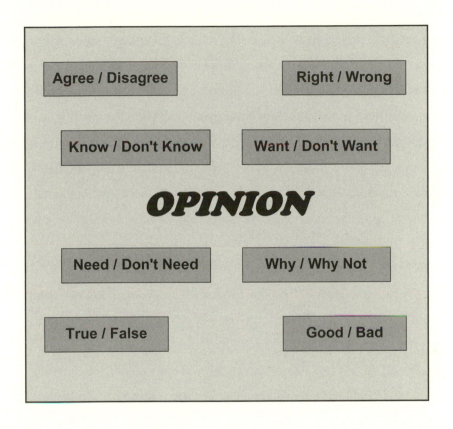

Figure "A"

Run Your Opinion; Don't Let It Run You!

When you are run by your opinion and give into the expressions of your opinion, you are not involved in that relationship about which you have your opinion. For example, here in our relationship your opinion will take you to the "sideline" of our relationship. How? You are not involved with me to learn, but rather you are running your opinion. Even if you look at other relationships you have, each time you have gotten yourself in trouble was a time that you allowed your opinion to take over your wisdom and your love for others. I call this state of involvement "On the Sideline," because it is safe. It is *safe* to be on the sideline without involvement. It is *safe* to not get engaged and just watch life from the sidelines of our own life!

I am not an American football fan, but sometimes I watch it with friends for fun – stay with me, I am trying to make a point. Once, I watched an important game between the San Diego Chargers and the New York Jets with friends. The game was in San Diego and we were all watching the game, but I could not help noticing the reporter. I do not remember who it was, but for sure I remember his opinion about the game and how the San Diego Chargers quarterback should play the game. I could not believe what I was hearing on the sideline at that exact moment that I was watching what was happening on the field. I was watching the Chargers quarterback with the football, and he was scanning the field to pass the ball to his teammates with accuracy, and at the same time four New York Jets players on the defense team were running at him to knock him down and to kill him! Can you imagine? To stay calm, focused and scan the field, and at the same time design your game and make sure you throw a very

64

accurate pass would be difficult. All this is happening in less than three or four seconds! Not to mention those four *running bears* have only one thing on their mind – to kill the quarterback. Can you imagine? It's a really dangerous situation. However "Mr. Reporter," who sat in a very safe box in an air-conditioned room in front of very high-tech TV screen, perhaps with a cold beer in his hand, had an opinion about how that quarterback should play that game! I don't know about you, but I call that arrogance.

Some of us are that way in our lives. We are not on the field of life, but on the sidelines running our opinions. So, how could we be aware of our behavior, and know how we are on the sidelines and running our opinion?

Opinions show their face in so many different expressions. I call them "Red Flags."

Watch For Red Flags

Red Flags are a state of being that we have to be aware of, and that way we can be responsible for what is running the show at that moment. We are not aware of our *own* state of being! "Being" for a human being is like water for fish, or air for birds. Fish are not aware of their existence in water, nor do birds have any idea that they are flying in something called air! Being is the exact same way for us! I will talk more about this in Chapter Four, "Conspiracy for Suffering."

Now, let's get back to the Red Flags. If we have a system to alert us about our state of being that makes us run our opinion and push us onto the sidelines, only then can we turn the game around!

How do you know you are on the sideline? What do the Red Flags look like? Here are a few guidelines that will help you recognize them.

1. Just talking about ideas and goals

You are talking about things versus doing something about them! Do you want some examples? Complaining about your finances, your health or your relationships, yet you won't do anything but complain about them, gossip about them with your friends and just build resentments. You see this in your friends each time you are talking to them, or when you are at parties with them. You hear it in the background when you are talking to your family members ... just talking, talking, talking and doing nothing!

2. Making fast decisions

This is one of the most frequently used Red Flags! We make fast decisions based on what our feelings and opinions are telling us! We decide who is this way or that way, who is with us and who is not. We even make lightning-speed decisions about our relationships with others. We decide in a split second if we are staying in this relationship or not.

How many times have you said something to someone and wished you could take it back within two seconds after it left your mouth? Your opinion runs the show in that moment.

3. Drawing immediate conclusions

This Red Flag usually goes hand in hand with the last one, or sometimes comes just right after making fast decisions. We make up our minds based on our opinions about countries, races, religions, nationalities and/or any other social or political opinion we have about others, and right after that we KNOW who they are! How many times have you made a jerk of yourself by drawing immediate conclusions about something, someone or a situation, and a little later you found out that things were not the way you thought they were? Sometimes we get to that realization a little too late!

4. Not getting involved

This is another Red Flag. We complain about things, people, work situations, society conditions and so many other things, but we do not get involved with *doing* something about them. Even some issues about people who are so close to us bother us, and we even observe their suffering but we don't get involved. Why? Because what would happen if they reject our contribution or say they are not welcoming our input? So what? If you care about them and you see they are going down the wrong path, you show your love and care by getting involved with them.

That is one of the biggest issues in today's modern society, and you see its very negative impact on our society – teenage drug use, teen pregnancy, school violence, and on and on. So what, if they don't like what you say? Are you going to save their lives or not? Or will you show up at their funeral and cry for that wasted life?

5. Listening to your "Inner Chatter"

"You are not the boss of me!" or "Don't tell me what to do!" These statements (or something similar to them) are always showing up as an inner chatter, and it is loud in our head. It usually shows up when someone tells us what to do and/or asks us to be accountable for something. I have seen this in work places, companies, corporations and any organization I have worked with. It doesn't mean that it is not showing up in family relationships, too. Put two people to work together and you can hear it in their heads! You have said this yourself so many times. *Are you married? Are you working for someone? Do you have parents?* See! If you are married, you have a boss or you have parents, for sure you have heard yourself saying it! You have said it, and you will say it again! This is a good Red Flag, if you are present enough to hear it.

6. Always in a hurry

Have you ever being in such a hurry that you could not even think straight? What do you think was happening at that time? At that time when we are running our opinion about how things should be or should not be,

68

we are so entangled with our scarcity for TIME that we become prisoner of our own schedule, or more accurately, we are becoming a prisoner of our own opinion about the amount of time that is available to us!

You notice people who are always in a hurry, are always late or very disorganized. Their first sentence when they see you always starts with "I am sorry…….." (then fill in the blank). In the end, they make a promise to not be late again. However, they can't keep that promise.

I call this behavior "Rocking Chair Syndrome." What do I mean? Lots of actions and movements, but no distance and not going anywhere. Do you know anyone like that? I'm sure you do.

7. Not playing, but telling others how to play

When you are not playing, but you keep judging how others play, this is called resignation, and it's a big Red Flag.

This is your "fast decision" about others and your "immediate conclusion" about what they do. Deep inside we all want to play, but what stops us is what we decide about what others will think of us. So, we stop playing. However, in the back of our minds, we wish others would keep asking us to come and play with them. I know … not you!

I wish I could print a clear picture for you about how your opinions are showing up and kicking you to the sidelines of your own life game, and what the early alarms are, and the Red Flags that could wake you up to what you are about to do. The common concern and question is this: Why are we doing it, and how could we direct our opinion to some other direction?

You know you have done this so many times. You are even doing it right now in so many relationships that you have. I have done it, anybody you know has done it, and anybody who is saying, "Not me," is doing it right now! You have to look back and see how many times you have done it this way, with whom you have done it, and get present to it. It takes a high level of honesty and authenticity to get present.

8. Knowing everything about everything and everyone

I can share some examples of this particularly large Red Flag from my life.

I assure you that like any other human being; I also let my opinion run my life from time to time. Maybe you have never noticed this before, but when you were born a male you were born a "know it all!" I know, shocking. Let me be fair, maybe not every man is a know it all, however, in most cases as a man you were born a "know it all," just like me. How does that sound now? If you were born a Persian male, that's a huge bonus! Tens of thousands of years of history and thousands of years of civilization behind them, and there is nothing you can add to them before they mention to you that "They Know!" I am joking about my own people, but you can see this trait in a majority of men. Why is that? Maybe because we have been taught that we have to be tough and strong to be a man, and strong guys always know everything and if we admit we don't know something we are weak and not worthy. I am not sure, but I can tell you this phenomenon is strong in the male culture. Anyway, being a man, plus being a Persian man, then add engineering to the mix means God help you in a conversation with me when I get into the know-it-all mode. This combination is deadly when you want to convince males like me to see other "possibilities."

For a strong man who has an engineering background, possibility is just what's on the blueprints. It means FACTS. If you are chasing facts, you will not see possibilities. Getting to see someone's greatness and excellence is not just looking at the facts; it is mostly getting present to the possibilities that you invent at any given moment to be able to see *through* someone without getting engaged and entangled with the facts.

This "knowing" thing has held me back to truly know and to learn many things about myself and about others for so many years. I got into fights with people, especially those close to me, just to be "right" about my point of view, and about how I see the situation, which was always the right way to see it, of course. Sound familiar? I have drawn so many immediate conclusions about others, or a situation, that later I realized something happened to be totally the opposite of what I thought it was. How humbling. I have judged, evaluated and run my opinion so many times during over the years that when I think about them it makes me sick to my stomach! It cost me my relationships, it cost me partnerships, it cost me my relationship with my kids, it cost me almost everything I care about. However, what I want you to understand is this: You have a say in the matter and in the final act, and you can become aware of this way of being and be aware of yourself – your opinion is at play!

71

The only difference at this time is I know now. I am aware of all I do, think and of how I am being. I have a choice in each and every moment whether to act on my opinion or not!

Okay, now let's get back to work.

At first, we have to see why we are doing something. Let me ask you a simple question, are you doing anything without compensation? In general cases, we will not do anything if there is not a payoff, payback or compensation available. Would you? Yes, I know, sometimes we do things for personal satisfaction or from the good of our hearts. Yes, we do. That is a payoff and compensation. So, there is something in it for us to keep running our opinion and playing on the sidelines.

There is some juice, some satisfaction, something that will drive us to do what we do by running our opinion about everyone and everything. Something pulls us to this domain of OPINION all the time. What is it? How does this pull and gravitation work?

In this section we look to see what is available to us when we are playing on the sidelines in our lives and running our opinion about others and ourselves all the time.

What would we accomplish by playing this way on the sidelines?

What are some things we are getting by playing this way?

Where is the attraction in playing on the sidelines of our own life?

What is in it for us running our opinion about ourselves as well as others all the time?

Let's get into it and deeply and with honesty look at it!

1. Being right

We would do anything to be right about anything!

We will be right about our limitations. We even argue about our limitations! Such as, "I can't do it" or "It can't be done" or our view of others, such as, "I know she is that way" or "I know he would do that." If you look closely, you can see and hear that this "Being Right" is in every corner of our lives. Notice each time you walk away from an opportunity or a chance to do something that you really want. If you stop, it was because you were right about the justification or reasoning behind your decisions.

73

In my coaching practice, I see this phenomenon a lot. People are a
buttheads to us to prove they cannot do something or be some particular
way. It is so heartbreaking to watch people who are doing that to
themselves. At the end of the day, they are right again about how they
can't and that it can't get done! However, they forgot that so many people
before them were thinking the same way, and they broke through that way
of thinking, and they achieved so many things in their lives and they
accomplished their dreams. They are doing it every day, each and every
moment, while you and I are arguing about our limitations and obstacles!
As Alfred D'Souza said:

*For a long time it had seemed to me that life was about to begin – real life.
But there was always some obstacle in the way, something to be got
through first, some unfinished business, time still to be served, and a debt
to be paid. At last it dawned on me that these obstacles were my life.*

If you are right you are right. Your call. I think that it was Henry Ford who
said:

Whether you think that you can, or that you can't, you are usually right.

2. Judging and evaluating someone or something

When we are right, someone or something has to be wrong. It is a balance!
It is natural, you can't help it, and it comes hand in hand with being right.
You are right; they are wrong! By you judging the situation as wrong or
judging others as wrong, you can justify your lack of relatedness with

74

them, or you can justify lack of effectiveness in what you do. We do this one hand in hand with the first one all the time, every day and every moment when we are not present to the massive cost of it in our lives and relationships.

Right now, if you are running your opinion about what I am saying, you are right about me or the material, and you are judging me and making me wrong, and the next thing you will do is get in a certain position about your decision and opinion. You can see this one all over the place, also. At the work place, in the staff meetings, in any arguments that get started, and that person gets to be right!

3. Taking a position

You have positioned yourself like a battlefield! You are set, you have your foxhole dug out, you check your gun and double check your ammunition, and you are good to go. Let's get to the fight so I can win in my position of being right about that very insignificant issue I am fighting for, over so many years, with each and every person I care about. How crazy and how very dumb!

4. Justifying yourself and your behaviors

Now that you have your position and get to fight, it is time to justify your actions, your behaviors and your attitude. After all, you are right and they are wrong. You are standing in your position and you won the fight. You killed them off and you showed them who is right! You! Perfect! Well done!

Now what? You go home happy and satisfied for a short time as you justify the reasons for your fight and all the explanations about why you had to get to battle, but suddenly it hits you hard. You are going home alone! Nobody to talk to, nobody to cuddle with, nobody to celebrate the win with, nobody to love, nobody to touch. Lonely as a rock in the middle of the desert. How sad. How lonely.

5. Sticking to your guns

So far, you have been right, you have judged and evaluated others, and made them wrong. You justified your actions and your behaviors. Now, you have no other choice but to keep going, digging your heels in. I can see you are calculating how to get yourself out of this hard and lonely situation. By now you are pretty stuck! On one hand you want to be right and keep being right, and on the other hand you miss the intimacy and closeness that is coming from being with others. To have that you have to give up being right, and for some people that is one of the hardest things to do.

You are stuck and you will not admit to any wrongdoing, or you will not apologize for any behaviors that might have caused the fight to continue and the disagreement to last longer. Now you are more stuck because your ego and "looking good" are on the line. Your protection shield is up and is in full functioning mode. If you say you are sorry they might give you grief, and it would not look good. Your apology might also make you look like a weak person. Then what are you going to do? Oh, my God ... no way ... I will stay right ... forget about cleaning that up and having relatedness. I would rather be alone!

You have managed to put yourself right in middle of a very vicious cycle. However you approach it, you will be lonely and it is not fun. You hear the phrase, "sticking to your guns." Do you know why they say that? Because when you are *sticking to your guns,* you are either killing others or they are scared to get close to you! You are always right, and they are always wrong.

6. Being closed and nothing new happening

When you *stick to your guns* or *stick to your ways,* then you will be closed off. You don't have to be a rocket scientist to get this one. When you are sticking to your ways you are automatically closed off to anything new, and the only thing you have left will be the same old way you have operated for a long time! What would come out of that? Again, nothing new; same old lonely ways and lonely days.

Learn A New Way of Playing

There is a whole other way you can participate in life and play that keeps you active and involved in your own life in a very empowering way. There is so much more peace and relatedness in this way of playing.

Think back to the way you related to this relationship, you and me, here in this coaching relationship. One way was to let your opinions run the show and determine our relationship (or any other relationships you have out there) from the point of view of good/bad, right/wrong, true/false, agree/disagree or should/shouldn't, which in the end makes no difference, and eventually will leave you on the sidelines of our relationship and your life, or start relating to our relationship in some other way.

By the way, there is nothing wrong with relating to others and any relationship from the point of view of good/bad, right/wrong, true/false, agree/disagree or should/shouldn't. It is just not effective. It is harder work. It is a more lonely living, and in the end it will leave you resentful and regretful. It will be a matter of choice. Am I living my life on the sideline, or am I getting engaged and getting related to others?

I hope you've enjoyed your journey toward change so far. We are going to continue this discussion of how you play in life in the next chapter, where we look at the other side of the coin and see what else is there. Is this our only option, or do we have other choices?

You will be pleased to see how easy the other choice is. The problem is your ability to see the other side and our other option. That is the reason I am writing this, to share with you about how you can develop yourself into someone who is *able* to get to the other side!

CHAPTER THREE
HOW DO YOU PLAY IN LIFE?

OPINION VERSUS POSSIBILITY – PART B: POSSIBILITY

For us to go anywhere,
we should know where we are first.

Picking up this subject of discussion from the last chapter, we will now see what other options we have to playing life from the sidelines.

There are so many other ways that you can manage to turn that inner chatter around and point your views to different directions Here are a few:

1. Knowledge: Learn from Those in Your Life

You *can* learn something from this book. You *can* learn something from every person in your life. If you are looking for knowledge, you can get it from any relationship you have, even from that jerk boss of yours, if you are truly looking to learn something. You know your boss or manager did not get to where he is "just because." Your parents weren't born yesterday. There are experiences they carry with them that you can use if you choose to be open to learning.

You can relate to our coaching relationship in the same way. I have not written this just because I was bored and had nothing else to do. I wanted to share what I have learned with you, so maybe there is a little knowledge for you to draw on. Is it possible that you might learn something about yourself that you did not know before?

2. Contribution: Contribute without Fear

As you are looking for knowledge, you will have a sense of contribution. That is what any coach or teacher wants to do. Is it possible that you can be contributed to from me or any other teachers in your lifetime? Is it possible that your parents, your spouse, or any of your close friends want to contribute to you when they are talking to you, or telling you to watch out for something?

Maybe that last fight between you and your life partner was not necessary. Maybe last week's argument with your boss or manager could have been resolved faster if you were present to contribution and not domination. Just maybe!

3. Consideration: Learn to be open

When you are looking for knowledge and relating to the conversation as a *contribution,* then the next natural step is considering it and being open to it. Once I saw a funny, but very wise, bumper sticker that read, *"The mind is like a parachute; it only functions when it is open!"* Then I found out it was from Anthony D'Angelo, who became addicted to constant and never ending self-improvement. You get the point! Be open to new knowledge, relate to it as a contribution and consider it, you have nothing to lose by being open.

4. Apply What Your Learn: Try It On

When you are open you are *trying it on* by applying what you learn. Like a new jacket you are going to buy, or a new pair of shoes you are interested in, you will try the items on. If something fits, keep it. If not, gave it back. Simple. If what you are learning here or from anybody else "fits" or it is true for you, you can see yourself in it, keep it. If not, thank you, I'll take it back. Thank you for trying it!

You know very well, from the point of being right and the "I will show you how this will not work," it will not work. Why? Because you said so! Have you heard, *"What you resist persists"*? It is a very powerful statement or phrase, perhaps, from American sage and thinker Lester Levenson. It is so true. All that you tell yourself will happen, will happen *to* you because you said so.

5. Values: Seek and Ye Shall Find

We can look for values vs. looking for being right and making our points. When we look for something we will most likely find it. If we are looking for flaws in others and/or something that will not work, we will find it. At the same time, when we look for some *Value* in what we are listening to, or something we are reading or some conversations with others, then for sure we will find that value.

If you are valuing *communication* or *peace* or *education* then you are going to listen differently and respond differently to any conversation or

83

even any heated dialog. In the case of our relationship, if you put value on learning and expanding your thinking, you will get lots of possibilities.

You see, we have a choice in every given moment to look for and welcome some value from others or not.

6. Being Coachable: You Can Be Great

How and when you apply and try things on is when your coach says it is time to do so. In this particular relationship between you and me, consider me as your coach; consider this book as the game plan, and your life as the game field. Let's play and let's play hard! As you play harder, you will enjoy it more and the price will be greater.

Remember this quote from Tom Landry, the famous Dallas Cowboys football coach:

A coach is someone who tells you what you don't want to hear, and has you see what you don't want to see so you can be who you have always known you could be.

I am doing my best to wake you up to your greatness, the greatness you already possess, and the one that is within you like a diamond in the rough. The diamond is your greatness and the rough is all of your life experiences that you have carried with you up until now. The real ones and the ones you have made up, whatever the reasons, none are important. In the end, the most important thing is for you to get how great you are! We will get to that, I promise you. But there is a catch. Guess what? You have to be coachable! Yes, you have to let go of everything you know about yourself, and start finding the things you don't know about yourself. You have to give up your stubbornness, arrogance and be coachable. This means "do" what the coach asks … the good, the bad and the ugly! You now get to do the things that you don't want to do because they are hard. They are so close to your heart that it will hurt your feelings. Be prepared.

It is appropriate here that I tell you a story from the time that I was practicing platform diving. Yes, I did! If you have met me you will immediately notice that I don't have a diver's body and shape. I was 20 or 21 when I was platform driving, and now I am passing 52. I used to have a six pack. Now I have a keg for a stomach.

Anyway, I was selected for a diving team to play for an Armed Forces competition, so I had to practice on a 10-meter platform. I was good enough on the 5-meter platform, and as you can imagine, a 10-meter platform is a whole different animal. We traveled to another city to practice and to get coaching from a famous and accomplished diver. When it was my turn to dive, right before I started using the stairs to get up to the top of the platform, the coach asked me if I wanted to use a wetsuit for protection. What do you think my answer was? Like any other cocky and over-confident young man, I said, "No, thank you. I can handle this!"

As I was stepping up and going to the top, I had an overwhelming experience of fear that turned to a terrifying anxiety when I got to the top of the 10-meter platform for the first time. That voice in my head kept reminding me of how bad of an idea this was. What an idiot I was for not accepting that wetsuit! I am sure you can identify with this idiocy in some other areas of your life, when someone suggests something to protect you or to take care of you, but you immediately reject the idea because you are the "man." Or you are the woman who can handle it! Yeah, right! So, I was up there and holding on to the handrails for my life. I was scared and shaking. I can laugh about it now, but at that time it was not funny! I was there for almost 20 minutes, and the only thing my coach kept saying was "Jump!" What? Jump? Are you crazy? I will die! Was the only thing I could hear in my head! I was thinking it loud and crazy that someone would jump from this height, I was sure I would die if I would jump.

That's when I started judging the coach. How about that? I am sure none of you readers have done that, but you might know someone else who has done that, right? So, I start saying to myself, "How do you know?" and "You don't know what I am dealing with!" and "I want to see you here jumping!" It was not like I could think about this coach's experiences and expertise or accomplishments. I was just listening to my own opinion about the situation, and about how insensitive and non-compassionate my coach was.

After almost 20 minutes of the coach saying, while using his megaphone, "Jump," he said something else, "Would you like that wetsuit?" Immediately it seemed like a good idea to me. Actually, a life-saving idea! Remember I was the one who rejected the same idea from an expert 20 minutes earlier. Does this ring any bells? I wore the suit and made a very brave act after my coach's support. I let go of the bars and I stood on the tip of the platform. My heart was in my throat! Actually, I am afraid of heights. Yes, I am! You can just imagine how scary it was. You wouldn't know that when you look down from the top, the height seems almost double of what it really is. From 5 to 10 meters was not just 5 meters, it seemed like 100 meters!

Now I have my wetsuit on and standing on the tip. Holy moly! My coach started his famous line again; "Jump," and I was thinking, "My life is over." I was thinking about my girlfriend, my friend, and how sad they would be after they took my body out of the pool. After almost another five minutes of hearing "Jump!" in my head I told myself to just do it. "Just jump straight down without any turn or twist, just straight down!" I can do that! I heard myself saying.

I let go of the platform and jumped straight down. It felt like eternity! But, I hit the water and I survived. I practiced for another two months, and I was able to adjust a timing that was good for the 5-meter platform to the timing for the 10-meter platform. I was fine. I did not get too far in my platform diving career, but I learned a very good and valuable lesson from it.

Why did I share this story with you? I want you to understand the importance of being coachable and following your coach's directions. If you do you will get what you want. Like me with my coach, you will learn a very valuable lesson from listening to your coach. You are not the first person to be in the place you now stand. Others have been there and done that. They know how to help you. Maybe, just maybe, he or she cares about you. Maybe he or she has seen some potential in you, like some possibilities for your life that you are not seeing yet, because you are either too cocky or too afraid.

In that moment that I trusted my coach's wisdom, when I left the platform and was in the air, the possibility of a being a diver emerged. The possibility of being courageous and overcoming fear was right there and that would never, ever leave me, just because I trusted my coach and my dream for my excellence in that area of my life was big enough at that time in my life.

You have to look at your life, look deep inside you and see what your dream is, and decide if it is worth jumping out there in the air to attain it. Is it worth letting go of your comfort zone and what you know to be coachable, and letting go of "what you know" to get "what you want?" I promise you I will not ask you to do anything that I have not done myself, or I am not willing to do. Just be coachable and you will get the freedom to be with yourself and with others, freedom to forgive yourself for all the mistakes you have made, all the bad things you have done, and then you will sleep better! You will fall in love with you again, and you will fall in love with life itself.

In order for you to get there, you have to work hard! I will point you in the direction that you don't *want* to see, and I will say things to you that you don't *want* to hear! You may get mad at me and you may even hate me. But, we will do this for one reason only, for you to get access to your greatness, to your power, and for you to see your love within. I will be straight and not attempt to please you, and/or give up because you are mad. Nor, should you do that. I will not play politically correct because that will not serve anybody. That is not me, and that will not happen on my watch. You and I will push through your barriers to your love within, and we will break through anything that is holding you back from seeing your own greatness, because you are worth it! I am the coach, you are the Olympian, and your life is the Olympics, so let's get our gold medal.

7. Inquiring into the issues at hand

I know you would like answers. Anybody would! We love anyone who has the answers to our problems and gives us the easy way out. That lets us ask "How do I ...?" instead of asking "How to ... ?" We love "How To's," but we will still not do it, because they are a lot more work. Who wants to work? "How To's" make no difference if they are not linked to a greater cause, a future, a vision. What is the point of *doing* if it is not fulfilling something greater than the past we have made or failed to make? We can create some greater events in our lives if we create them first, and then do whatever it takes to fulfill that event or cause. I was reading something from John Scharr, futurist, and this part about future caught my eye:

The future is not a result of choices among alternative paths offered by the present, but a place that is created. Created first in mind and will, created next in activity. The future is not some place we are going to, but one we are creating. The paths are not to be found, but made, and the activity of making them changes both the maker and the destination.

Isn't it true? What I would like you to do is inquire. Yes, I have lots of questions, and not that many answers. You will get your *own* answers, and they are absolutely different from other people who are reading this. Whatever answer you get belongs to you! If the answer you get does not fit in for some reason, then you dig more and be more authentic and honest and you will find the truth for you, but remember the key to it is your honesty and willingness to tell the truth.

See the Possibility

Now, let's look at all of these things together that you have read the things that I mentioned as "the ways you can turn your inner chatter about coaching and relationships around" what do they have in common? **POSSIBILITY!** Yes, if you notice, all of them are possibilities, and will open some doors to possibilities. Knowledge, contribution, applying and trying on, being open, being coachable and having inquiries, are all opening so many doors to possibilities.

When you look at this domain (Figure "B") and compare it with the last domain (Figure "A"), in terms of look and shape or dimensions, they are exactly the same! But, they have two totally different contents. Like talking and thinking. You have options to what to say or even what to think. The language and dialog are all up to you and they all sound the same, but the contents are different.

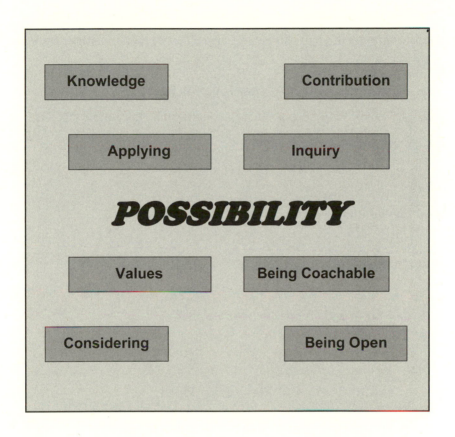

Figure "B"

Choose Your Game Plan: Opinions or Possibilities

As you see by now, you have two options in the way you are playing here, Opinions or Possibilities. As a reminder again, this is the exact way you are participating in your life! Neither one is better than the other. None are good or bad; they are just different. They have different outcomes; they have different end results, ones that have you be on the SIDELINES of your life, as you have seen so far, and another that has you be ON THE FIELD of the game of life ... your life.

How do you know you are on the "field" of your life?

What do the signs look like?

How do I know I am on the field of *my life*?

1- Taking It On and Playing Full Out

You don't just talk about the things you like to do in life, or the goals you have had for the last year without any actions to achieve them! You are in action and you are BEING committed to DOING what you want to do in life, and then you will HAVE what you want to have. Don't be afraid to be completely NOT like so many people who think they have to have something to do in order to become someone they want to be.

You are in the field, you have taken the issue ON and you are moving forward! If you are on the couch and watching sports while you are overweight and complaining about your health, you are eating anything you want and then you are crying about your clothes not fitting you anymore, then you are talking about your health. When you are exercising and being careful about what you eat, you are IN the game of life in regard to your health and vitality. The same thing goes for any area of your life that you are complaining about, your finances for example. You spend more than you make. For example, you're charging purchases on your credit cards when your income cannot afford to pay your bills. During that time you are not ON the field of your finance game, you are on the sidelines running your opinion about how hard it is to save money, or to get ahead. Look at any area of your life and it is clear if you are ON the field. You are in action and you are progressing

The problem is that we want everything to be easy and fast, without any hard times and with the least possible effort. Unfortunately, this mentality has caused so many problems for us as a society. We become a society of "entitlement" and "taking the fast track," which in the long run is not serving anybody. You can see the result of this illusion all across our society.

In this relationship between you and me, right here and right now, are you taking this coaching and direction ON, or are you still running your opinion? If you are taking this coaching ON, it means you are implementing the coaching and you are on the field of this game. Good for you! If not, then you will be where you started before you began reading this book. There is a Chinese proverb that says:

If you don't change your directions in life, you mostly ended where you have headed!

2- Having Compassion and Patience

By establishing compassion and understanding of others and being patient with them we are actually playing on the field of life and not around the field showing impatience and selfishness toward others.

Before we can show compassion and patience for others, we first have to learn to have it for ourselves. It means we must stop judging and evaluating ourselves for what we have not achieved or any goals we have not achieved yet or the goals that we know we will not be able to accomplish anymore. The bottom line is that we cannot have compassion and patience for others if we are not practicing it for ourselves. That being said, I am not talking about how we can now just be lazy and unproductive just to say, "Well, Behnam said in his book that I have to have compassion for myself, so it is okay to not do this work or project at this time." No. I am saying have compassion for how hard you have to try and have patience for how long it will take! Remember, as you might have heard:

Rome was not built overnight!

3- Being Coachable

Being coachable is really simple. Being coachable means doing what your coach has asked you to do, so you can become who you have always wanted yourself to be!

It means giving up your arrogance and your "know it all" attitude and surrendering yourself to your coach. All of it, without holding back. Yes, it is scary; it means you have to trust, even when you don't have that much evidence to trust a coach or you have so much evidence from the past that someone abused your trust. I can totally understand. But that was then and this is now! You have no evidence to not trust this process I am walking you through. Actually, you have access to hundreds of pieces of evidence that this coaching will work. How? By reading other people's experiences and testimonials that they have provided to us about their experience, their results and their breakthroughs using our programs and services.

Trusting your coach is the gift you give to your coach. It is your generosity and your grace. Your coach can succeed with your virtue of your level of being open to his or her coaching and the level of trust you give them. However, your coach does not owe you anything just because you trust them now. It means they will not be careful, and/or walk over eggshells because you trust them. You trust them because you asked for the coaching and you wanted it … and that is that!

That is one of the reasons that *politically correct* speaking is not my favorite thing to do.

I do not speak politically correct, and I will call it exactly the way it is, because I am committed to serving you, not making you feel good. Lots of people are in your life that will make you feel good and have you just feel positive. That is not enough, and that is not going to get you to your "gold medal" in your life. I will not cry for you, and I will not buy into your limited thinking, and I will not be a part of your conspiracy to stay small and unproductive in life. I will stand by you, shoulder to shoulder, and I will fight with you back to back against your limitations, your smallness and your fears. I will be there with you every step of this process. As I mentioned previously, I will never ask you to do something that I have not done or I am not willing to do. But, I will ask you to be unreasonable, fearless and communicative. I will ask you to clean up your past messes, your upsets with others, and to take responsibility for your past and present actions so you can get to that future you have been wanting for so many years. That way you will get to the gold medal in your life.

For you to *get* in this world with your coach, you have to let go of your opinion and be open to possibility. It means taking ON that you might not be as nice as you might think you are! You might not be as great as you think others think you are! Your relationships with others might not be as great as you think they are! They are all out there for examination … by you and by them!

4- Having Inquiries for Resolutions and Solutions vs. Looking for Answers

To get to the world of possibilities, we have to let go of our attachments to KNOWING and to having ANSWERS all the time. We shall look for resolutions to our issues with ourselves or with others. We should try to find solutions to our problems, not from the point of view of looking outside ourselves but rather by looking within ourselves to find such resolutions.

What would happen if you had no answers to your questions? For some of you, it is a very scary experience. We have to know! We have to have an answer! If we don't know the answer, it means we are weak, dumb, unintelligent or not at the top of our game. You have seen people who have to come with answers all the time. It seems like there is nothing they don't know. They can talk about everything and come with a response and the correct answer about anything, all the time, on any subject at any given moment. I am sure you are not one of those people, but I bet you have a family or friend like that. Don't you?

If you look deeper, you will recognize that *knowing* is what is keeping you away from learning. You will say, like anybody else, that knowledge is power. We have all heard that. Actually, knowledge is not power. Rather implementation of knowledge is power! Getting to the power is from having inquiries versus having questions. When you have inquiries, you are digging inside an issue that is customized to you. If I just give you answers, we will not get anywhere and you will not get any long-standing value either. You *know* everything there is to know about losing weight

97

and having a healthy body and fitness. There is a multi-billion-dollar health and fitness industry out there, and people are signing up for the fitness programs every day and they buy fitness and exercise machines and equipment left and right, but at the end of the day, not many of them are getting to the fitness and weight they want! Why? Because knowing how to lose weight does not equal losing weight.

You know these people well. You know they have a *button* that is very sensitive. You know they are protecting that button. You also know pushing that button will upset them, and it will cause some resentments or unpleasant experience for them. But knowing that is not, has not and will not prevent you from pushing that button from time to time. Does it? Especially around the holidays; you push that button and they get upset, and you will say, "I am so sorry; I didn't know it would upset you!" Yeah, right! You knew it and you knew it would upset them, and you did it anyway.

So, *knowing* and *knowledge* will not make any difference if you are just looking for answers and a fast fix. Knowing the answer is not equal to the results that will come from that answer. However, when you have inquiries into the issues, and show interest to get to the bottom of what and how you have something to do with the presence of that issue, then you are getting ahead and you are making headway toward a breakthrough in that issue. So, I don't have that many answers, but for sure I have many questions that allow you to get to the answers, which will be a "fit" in your life and your situation. That way you will get the answers and they will stay with you forever, because you get it vs. *I gave it to you*!

You might have heard this famous quote by Kwan-Tzu:

If you give a man a fish, he will have a single meal.
If you teach him how to fish, he will eat all his life.

We can see in our world the people who are causing trouble, causing wars, killing, stealing and participating in other destructive behaviors are the ones who don't want to have inquiries into solutions and finding resolutions to their problems. They just want the fast fix and immediate answers, which most of the time causes more trouble for themselves as well as others around them. Don't be one of them.

5- Get involved

Getting involved with the issue at hand is another way that we know if we are on the field of our life.

Getting involved with the issue starts from being interested in ending our suffering! You can see it in yourself and in others when you are suffering, and/or when you see others are suffering about a particular issue and they don't do anything about it. Have you ever had any experience in this regard? You see they are in pain, physically, emotionally, financially or psychologically, and they don't make any effort to stop it or change the direction of where they are going. Unfortunately, they have trained us to not get involved. How? They are doing that separation by drawing an invisible line in the sand that says, "Don't go there!" or "This is your limit; do not pass it!" They have trained us for years by their speaking, their behaviors, their comments, their looking good, their success and their upset responses to our questions, and/or our interests to get *in* with them! I am sure you have some experience like that, especially with our teenagers, and/or close friends or family members. They just trained us to stay away and not say anything that might upset them or to do anything that might make them look at their unpleasant situation.

Have you found any examples yet? Now, I have to ask you this question, a hard question to answer. Well, maybe not, but let's try. Do you prefer to be liked, or do you prefer to be effective with someone who is struggling? Being liked is something that we are all dealing with. It is part of being human; it is a natural desire to be loved, to be liked and to have others be interested in us. We do anything to be liked or to be loved. We would sell our soul to be liked. We lie and we cheat to be liked. We don't say the right thing or do the right thing to be liked. You know exactly what I am talking about. You have done it, and I have done it! I have done it so many times that it makes me sick. I have done it in my marriages, in my business practices, with my family, and with the people who I call "friends." In the end, they did the thing that caused them pain and struggle, but it left me unhappy and feeling really small about myself because I did not get involved! I knew what to say or what to do, but I didn't so that they wouldn't think I was intrusive and they wouldn't stop liking me!

Wow! Even now that I am talking about it I feel small, and I am reminded of how I sold out on myself and my principles. I think by now you have a good idea when, how and with whom you have done this. Yes, with yourself the most. You are selling out on yourself more than you are selling out on anybody else. Actually, you start selling out on others because you have "sold out" on yourself. It is time to pick up the pieces and get back to the game. It is time to get involved with your issues, regardless of their size, dimensions or their history and attack them. When we get involved with yours, then we can get involved with others, too!

Start with telling the truth, and tell the right thing and do the right thing, and give up what others will think about you! I have news for you. It is both bad news and good news at the same time. People will always judge and evaluate you, regardless of what you do or who you become. Get with the program. Do the right things for you and get involved with your issues head on! Then you know you are on the field of your life, doing something about your issues. You are moving forward.

6- Play As a Team

You will be on the field of life when you are *playing as a team.*

Did you know you are member of so many teams in your life? Your family is one team, your own family like your spouse and your kids are another team, your co-workers, and/or your employees are another team. You might even be a member of societies, clubs or interest groups. Even further, your communities are other teams you are in with. These teams are getting bigger and bigger, like your country and the planet itself. In each and every one of these teams, you can recognize the level of your participation by recognizing the presence of your opinion versus the presence of your possibilities!

How can we do that? By watching how you are being attached to your ways, and being right about *your* way being the right way or the best way. Or by watching how you look for greatness in others and find what is so workable about their ideas and their ways. Their ideas or proposals might not be the best, but are you giving it a chance or are you just throwing it out as no good? You can see this phenomenon in your relationship with your spouse at home, or your business partner in your office. Either way, you are doing the same thing. In home or office, in a family event or company meeting, either way you are being the same way. If you are controlling, then you are controlling at home or in the office. If you are negative or resigned, regardless if you are at home or work, you will be negative and resigned. You can't help it! If you are a "lone ranger," you will not participate in games. If you are being a controller, you will not allow others to do something new. If you are negative, you will always find what is wrong and what is not working in everything. However, if you are a player, you find a place for yourself on the team. If you are open minded and see possibilities in others, you will allow them to be self-expressed and play full out, and if you are a positive person, you will find greatness and excellence in anyone or anything, because you are causing it and because you are welcoming it.

An observer can tell if you are on the sidelines of your team game, or if you are in the center and playing on the field.

7- Look At a Bigger Picture

When you are looking for a bigger picture you are on the field of life, your own life as well as other people's lives around you and ultimately the lives of your community, your society, your country and your world. It's a way bigger picture versus the small frame called "**my life.**" What an illusion! We think everything belongs to us; we say my life, we say my wife or my husband, my house, my god and/or any other things we are claiming belong to us. What is up with that? What is up with this control with which we are obsessed?

I am sure we have all seen and continue to observe what will happen to us when we just protect ourselves and to others when they are just looking for themselves; you can see the impact of this issue on our education system, health system and finance system. Do I have to say more?

Yes, this book is not about saving the world or saving our country from the dark hole of ignorance and corruption. It is about being able to shift our view of ourselves to the view of our country, as a community and as a whole, and that starts with us individually before expanding to others as a community.

A Larger Definition of Shifting Views

UBUNTU, *"I am because we are,"* is a distinction in the African culture and in the Swahili language. Swahili is the first language of the Swahili people, who inhabit several large stretches of the Indian Ocean coastline from southern Somalia to northern Mozambique, including the Comoros Islands, this includes Kenya, Zimbabwe, Rwanda, Burundi, Uganda and Tanzania.

An attempt at a longer definition has been made by Archbishop Desmond Tutu of South Africa:

One of the sayings in our country is Ubuntu – the essence of being human. Ubuntu speaks particularly about the fact that you can't exist as a human being in isolation. It speaks about our interconnectedness. You can't be human all by yourself, and when you have this quality – Ubuntu – you are known for your generosity.

We think of ourselves far too frequently as just individuals, separated from one another, whereas you are connected and what you do affects the whole world. When you do well, it spreads out; it is for the whole of humanity.

The first time I became present to this philosophy and distinction was when two of my very close friends who are like family to me (they were clients before we become family), Dawn and Kipp Denslow, adopted two beautiful girls, two sisters from Ethiopia in 2007, Baraket (blessing) and Ganat (heaven). That was the beginning of me becoming familiar with this gracious and amazing philosophy, and also beginning of me being "Uncle Behnam" again!

Dawn now owns a hair studio with the same name, "UBUNTU Hair Studio" in Solana Beach, California. I am proud to say she owns one of the very rare socially conscious businesses in the San Diego area.

The point of all of this is that when we are looking at the bigger picture, we are connecting ourselves to others and to the world. This might be different for different people with different interests in their lives, but we are all connected to each other .What we do impacts others around us and ultimately everyone on the planet.

8- Know That You Don't Know

At last, a player on the field of life knows that he or she doesn't know everything! There is a Persian Proverb that says:

Everything is known by everyone.

After so many years of learning, reading, observing, studying, being a student, being a teacher, digging within and distinguishing self-behaviors, in the end I realized that "I don't know anything!" and that is the best thing I have learned. There is nowhere to go. No place to arrive. Nothing to prove. Nothing to be right about and nobody to hate.

It was not that easy and it did not happen overnight, or even over a couple of years. It's taken more than 35 years so far! And, I think it will take many more years to get to the absolute peace of mind, freedom to be and to release the love within. However, the key is to love the process and enjoy the learning experience.

As soon as you say; "I know," you kill any possibility of learning something new about yourself, others and life itself. Like when everyone in the world knew that the earth was flat. Even the Catholic Church at the time threatened Galileo with death, asking him to change his theory about the earth being round. In more recent years, it is like the time that the most intelligent scientists KNEW that no one would have use for home computers. Or like the time that having watches and clocks work with a battery was just a silly idea and the watchmakers in Switzerland knew that this would not work. It's like when people laughed at the Wright brothers when they said they would make a flying machine; people made a joke about "they will make a bicycle fly!"

After two attempts to fly this machine, one of which resulted in a minor crash, Orville Wright took the Flyer for a 12-second, sustained flight on December 17, 1903. This was the first successful, powered, piloted flight in history … At that moment over the sand domes of North Carolina, the possibility of Neal Armstrong, as commander of the Apollo 11 walking on the moon on July 20, 1969, become reality. Within just 66 years, we went from flying bicycle to landing a man on the moon … and that is possibility in play.

Now, even going to the moon is not a big deal.
We are shooting for starts … literally!

Can you even imagine at this day and time, if we did not have access to airlines and airplanes or jets? No computers in homes, no electronic watches, and still fighting over the earth being flat or not? We can't even imagine life without them! These are all possibilities that became reality because someone was willing to look at what they didn't know versus what they did know.

Leadership always accompanies learning. They always go hand in hand. As President John F. Kennedy once said:

Leadership and learning are indispensable of each other.

We have touched the areas that you can use as alarms, and noticeable ways that we will know we are on the field of our lives and we are at play. Like being on the sidelines, being on the field has some benefits, too. There are some things we get by playing on the field. You will be getting something if you follow my coaching and play this game the way it is designed, not the way you want to play, or you know the right way or your familiar way of being, and the way of thinking that caused you to be stuck!

There are some payoffs or things that you are getting out of this part for yourself. Again, not good or bad, not right or wrong, it is just what it is. You be the judge of it and you look for yourself. As there were some things you got when you played in the *opinion* part, there is also something you get out of the *possibility* part when you are playing on the field of life.

What would we accomplish by playing this way on the field?

What are some things we are getting out of playing in possibility?

Where is the attraction in playing on the field of life?

What is in it for us if we keep playing in the domain of possibility?

1- Learning Something New

You are learning something new. Even about something that you thought you knew before. Something new about yourself, something new about how to be with others and something new about living life based on your values and principles vs. the way you think you should live, or the way you think others will approve of you and your way of living. Inside you, at this moment, are the power to do things you never thought possible. Such power becomes apparent and rises to the surface as you begin to operate consistent with your values and beliefs.

2- Being Open to Others' View to "See What They See"

By giving up your opinion and looking at possibility and playing on the field, you will be open to see the world around you from other people's views. You will be surprised to find out how much you are not seeing when you are not viewing life from possibility. Is there any possibility that we might not see what there is to see, really? Looking at the world around us without *opinion* is like looking at the world around us without any color and dark sunglasses.

Opinion is like sunglasses that add a little bit of color and protection. It is exactly that way in real life! We add a little color to what we see, like the things that are not there before we add them to the reality of situation, and we add protection by adding our opinion, and that is the protection of getting related to what is real.

We are afraid to be open to others' views because what if they are right? Then, we have to be wrong. Who wants to be wrong? So, what will we do? We stick to our ways again. So by playing on the field of life and the field of relationships, you will have an opportunity to look at the world you have built around you to protect you, and also you can see that world from the view of the people with whom you are in relationship.

3- How to listen without judgment and preconceived notions

When we are open to others' views and can see their views of life and their views of the issues at hand, then we can listen without any judgment. Power of communication is in the listening not the speaking. In my lifetime, I have seen so many people who are fascinated with the sound of their own voice. They are just so mesmerized with what they have to say without any interest to the impact of what they are saying to others, or the impact of what they are saying to the topic at hand.

Just imagine the impact you can have on your relationships by being open to the views of those people with whom you have the relationships, and to listen to them without any judgment. As I mentioned on the last point, you start protecting yourself and attacking with your words when you feel you are being attacked. Listening is the same. You can counterattack with the way you are listening. How? By not giving the speaker and what he/she says any credibility. You need to listen openly to what they are saying, because they might be correct, or that they might have valid points.

It is the same phenomenon exhibited in our relationship as a coach and coachee. The power of my coaching will be there if you give it credibility and value. Are you listening for "gold" or are you judging? Are you listening for contribution or are you evaluating? The power is in your hands! I always say this to my clients who are salespeople, "The way you are listening, and the way you are open to your prospect's view will make or break your sales. It is up to you!"

It is far more powerful when you are on the field and listening versus trying to make your point from the sidelines.

4- How to Speak to Others' Views and What They Hear

When you are on the field and playing the game, and you are listening to what is being said and why that is being said, you can powerfully and effectively speak back to it. However, at first, you have to be *present* to what is going on. Are you open to what they are saying? Are you looking for a solution to the issue, and are you open to listening to what they are saying like it is the truth? Because it is the truth for them!

When you are not running your opinion about what they are saying, you can hear what they are saying and you can respond to the way they are speaking, not the way *you* are speaking. When you step into their view and you know what they are seeing, then you can respond effectively to what they are seeing and saying, not what you want them to see or say. This is a very powerful tool for anybody, regardless of what they do. In personal relationships as well as professional relationships, it is always powerful when you listen and act based on what you are listening to, not what you want.

5- Respect for Yourself and for Others

On the field, you will gain respect for yourself and for others who are in the game with you. There is an old saying, "Respect is not to be given but to be gained!" It is so true! I always said myself, "My love you already have, but my respect you have to gain."

Nobody can give you the respect you desire unless you respect yourself first. There is no self-respect when you are running your opinion and participating in gossip. You won't respect yourself, nor will others respect you. They might participate with you and become engaged in the opinion game and gossip game, but they are not respecting you. They know that if you are gossiping about another person in their presence, then you are for sure doing the same thing about them in the presence of others.

There is a state of grace and dignity when you do not run your opinions and you deal with the facts. You respect yourself by doing that, and others will respect you for the same reason. Even in this coaching relationship between you and me. You will gain more respect for yourself by not running your opinion immediately, and actually go through the entire process, and in the end form your opinion.

6- Relationships, Friendships and Intimacy

It is clear that when you are on the field of life and playing full out you will build relationships and definitely have lots of strong and deep friendships. You must have heard this quote from Jeremy Taylor; "Love is friendship set on fire." It is true. Without friendships there are no relationships and ultimately no intimacy.

When you can't hold back and don't have everything be about you then you become more attractive, because it is not all about you. When you show interest in others and their interests it is very attractive and welcoming. People want to be around individuals who pay attention to them and show interest in their interests. Try that in your relationships and friendships and see how that will work! I promise you will be really happy with the outcome.

7- Knowledge and Understanding

By playing on field, you will gain more knowledge and more understanding of others. Without knowledge, nothing will move forward. Without understanding of yourself and others, nothing will move forward. Understanding, sometimes, is the hardest thing to do because we are wired to "be right and do it our way" and that makes the understanding part difficult.

By playing on the field and giving up being right, being open to others' views and listening to them, you will gain more knowledge and you will have more understanding of how do you operate. When you have that understanding, then you can understand others. But not before you understand yourself first!

8- Peace of Mind and Freedom to Be

Imagine if you had such freedom to be with what is there to be with about you and about life itself that it gave you the peace you have always wanted. The access to that peace and freedom is to understand ourselves and others, accept ourselves and others and accept what it is about us that we love or we don't love. We can then make a powerful choice to do something about it or not! Either way we are free, because it is our choice and no one else's.

For us to get to that enlightened point we have to be involved with our LIFE. We have to play on the field and not operate from the sidelines.

Possibility

And, the biggest price of all is possibility itself!

Ultimately, with endless opportunities and no boundaries around your life and your world you can invent and create anything, anywhere with anyone. That is the power and the beauty of possibilities.

Possibility of self-respect, possibility of knowledge and understanding, possibility of self-love and loving others, possibility of relatedness and relationships with others, possibility of peace of mind, and the possibility of freedom to *be*! Freedom to be with yourself and with others without your nasty opinions about yourself and others, as well as others' toxic opinions about themselves and others, which means you.

When you are free of self-righteousness, free of opinion and free of judgments, you are free to live the way you want without the weight of your own and others' opinions!

When you are on the *field of your life*, you can create any possibility around your own goals and results, as well as for others around you.

When you look at possibility and keep generating your views from possibility vs. opinion, you can and you are able to do anything! I am not talking about you generating the possibility of having a million dollars for tomorrow and you will get it tomorrow. It is most likely that you won't, but if you keep letting go of your opinion of yourself, others, and what is possible, most probably with honest work, strong work habits, and good planning, you will have your million dollars within a few years. This world is full of people who have accomplished great things by standing in the *possibilities* they have dreamed about and kept generating every day, day in and day out.

I am not a millionaire and, quite frankly, I have never cared enough about it to pursue it. I am a firm believer that if you care enough about what you do and take care of others while you are doing it, you will get some financial security in your future. However, I love what I do and I love the fact that I am working with amazing people who trust me and my organization to take care of them and coach them through accomplishing their dreams and fulfilling their goals. The point I am trying to get into is this … *I was not always like this*!

If you told me 20 years ago, "You will speak and write English for a living," I would laugh at you and say, "Are you out of your mind?" But, I saw that possibility a long time ago, around 16 or 17 years ago, when I felt the passion to make a difference.

I wanted to make a difference in my own life, as well as the lives of others. I was sick and tired of that opinionated, self-centered, self-caring jerk, who was just trying to survive and trying to make it so he was looking good and he could fit into some stereotype success picture. Does this seem like some people you know or have seen? I was tired of him, and I was tired of all same results he was producing over and over again! The same issues in relationships, same productivity in work, just mediocre and just surviving, sometimes just barely make it! This guy had a big mouth and lots of opinions and judgments! He knew everything and he was right about the *knowing*. I knew I had to kill that guy inside me so the other guy could show up! Later, I realized killing that guy inside me was not the answer. I had to love him. He needed my love, he needed my compassion, and he could definitely use my kicking ass, taking-names attitude to get him out of his miserable being. And, here we are! I love me, I respect me, and I even like me. Not from the point of view of being self-centered again versus loving myself and being true to who I am. I am a loving, caring, sensitive guy who does not take crap from anyone! One of good friends,

Susie Fields-Carder who is one of co-founders of Your Beauty Network in Carlsbad, CA calls me "A biker who likes champagne!"

For me to become this guy I always knew was in me, I started loving myself and doing what I love to do. The point is that lots of people have opinions about my change of direction in my career, from a general building contractor to a public speaker, corporate trainer, and productivity coach. What a shift! You cannot believe how many people used to laugh at me, point out to me that I am a foreigner with a thick Middle-Eastern accent, and without that many years of experience. On top of it, I was broke. One thing that made me keep going was the declarations I made, the decisions I made, and the stands I took. Who I am is the possibility of people's greatness and excellence. And for that to become real, I had to let go of my own opinion about myself, my opinion about others opinions about me and about life itself, and my attachment about how things should work out, or should be this way or should not be that way. I had to accept the facts and have a strong relationship to reality of my situations and what it takes to build this type of business.

It was one of the hardest things I have ever done, especially letting go of attachments to others' approval. It was hard when even some of my own mentors would tell me that I can't make it, or it will be real hard for someone like me to make it in this industry. I looked at them and I thought "I will" and kept going because I saw that possibility, clear and strong. And here I am, after several years in business, building Primeco Education into a strong operation with a presence in three different states, providing our programs and services throughout the United States and Canada. I am getting closer and closer to that vision and to that possibility! People come

116

and people go. That is the way life is, but you should stay firm about what you believe about yourself and keep going in the direction that will fulfill your purpose and your vision. On this road, you will deal with so many people's opinions and judgments. Just hear it and take it on. If you hear something useful keep it and if it is nonsense just let go of it. Keep your eyes on that possibility that you are.

This is what we are going to do in the process through which I am leading you. All these conversations about OPINION and POSSIBILITY were for you to get it that you have a say in the matter of how this adventure will impact you and your results in your life! You have a say about how what you have and will learn in this process will impact other people around you. These "others" are your spouse, your significant others, your life partners, your children, your family, and friends, your boss or co-workers or anyone else.

For you to get a 100 percent benefit of this coaching process, you have to give up your opinion all the time. Every chapter, every paragraph and every line. You have to give up taking it personally. You have to give up that you don't like to dig in to your negative and dark side. I promise you will get so much benefit and value if you become coachable, and follow the coaching! It means, does the process and practices the way it is designed not the way you think it should be, or the way you think you should do it. If you could do it by yourself, you would have done it by now. Give it up and let's get to more work!

I am here with you, side by side, shoulder to shoulder, and will walk you through whatever we have to walk through. I am your coach! I have lots of understanding, patience and compassion, but no mercy. You can go through this entire book, dig inside yourself and come out of the other side with your neck up. I just created the *space* for you to do it and showed you the directions. You had the courage and interest to go through it and follow the directions. That by itself makes our relationship intimate.

For us to get the full benefits of our coaching process in the end of any chapter, I will ask you the following questions. These questions are designed to make you think and for you to become responsible for what you have learned and how what you have learned will make a difference in your life now.

I am not interested in just giving you some information that you will pile up with the rest of the information you have consumed before. As we have established this before, knowledge is not power, the *implementation* of knowledge is power! So, I am explaining the reason and the wisdom of the questions under them just once and just in this chapter only so you can understand why I am asking you these questions and the relevancy between them.

You must write your answers clearly, simply and truthfully under each question. Do that, because there is a process at the end of this book called "The Big List" that is totally relevant to all these notes you are writing. You should not be worried about what will happen in "The Big List" now. Just think about the questions I am asking you right here and now; the rest of it will come together later. This is one of the pitfalls we always fall into! We want to figure things out fast and right now ... Just trust the process.

You will see the wisdom of this step-by-step process and you will learn a lot about yourself when you follow it.

Make sure you take time and be responsible for what you have learned about yourself and write them down.

1. What do you realize about yourself?

What did you learn about yourself by reading and applying the last three chapters? What was the realization about yourself in regard to this topic of Opinion and Possibility and the way you play in life? Usually, the nature of this realization is the "bad news," but if it is a "good thing," how? For example, you might realize you are an opinionated person, and you always judged and evaluated people. That by itself might be the bad news, however, it is a good thing that you got to face it and *own* "it," so you have power over "it" not "it" having power over you! So get into it and write it down:

_____

_____

_____

_____

2. What are you willing to add, change, or alter?

Now that you realized a few things about yourself, what are you willing to add, change, or alter about your life based on that realization? If you are not adding something new, changing something old or altering some behaviors and train of thought, what is the point? If you want something different for yourself and your life, you have to do something different. Start jotting down the changes. The scariest thing is the one you don't want to write down the one that you know has to be done. For example; if you realized that you are opinionated, what you would change is your view of people. You alter that way you relate to others. You will not judge them immediately before knowing them.

_____

_____

_____

_____

3. What are you promising yourself?

Now that you know what needs to be added, or changed or altered you have to make a promise to yourself that you will do something about it! This promise is one of the most important promises of your life because it is a promise to *you*! A goal without a promise and deadline is nothing but a good idea, so make a promise and keep it. Don't make a promise just because you don't know how to keep it. Just throw your hat over the wall and go get it! Write down your promise based on the changes that need to get done for the transformation of what you realized about yourself. For example:

I promise to not judge others immediately OR *I promise to not act on my opinion and spend time and find the facts.*

---

4. What are you willing to do to keep that promise?

Now that you have made the promise, you have to come with a series of actions that will guarantee the fulfillment of those promises! It is black and white. It is something you will do, not just think about it. You will take these actions, and you will do them to keep your promise. This is not conceptual; this is real! This has time, location and format. For example:

121

As soon as I judge someone, I will apologize for it and I will clean it up!
OR
I will keep myself away from opinionated people who do not care about the facts, and just want to gossip.

_____

_____

_____

_____

5. Who will you discuss this with?

These are people who you like to talk to and share with about your transformation. In some cases, these are people you have judged, evaluated and formed some opinion about! As hard as it is, you will gain so much respect for yourself, and they will develop so much respect for you when you clean up your mess with them and acknowledge what you have done. Clean it up and make a new promise to them. In that moment, you will be powerful and extraordinary.

_____

_____

_____

Once you have answered these simple but powerful questions you will be ready to move to the next chapter.

CHAPTER FOUR

INTERNAL CONVERSATION

THE CHATTER THAT TIES YOU DOWN!

You are building your life daily, hourly and
moment by moment through your thoughts.
With them you are molding your future.

In this chapter, we discuss CONVERSATIONS. Not just any ordinary conversation, but a very unique type. Before getting into that, we have to step back a little and talk about the difference between this type of conversation and other conversations we have every day. The biggest difference is that we have this conversation with ourselves. Yes, you never have this conversation with anyone else! That alone makes it interesting … and dangerous.

Because it is not a conversation that we would have with someone else, it is not a COMMUNICATION. Communication is between at least two people and has a purpose. For example, if you are talking to someone and say, "I am upset with you for what happened last night." What are you doing? You are talking to that person about the issue with the purpose of resolving the upset with that person. You might ask, "So, what is the difference between that and having conversations with other people? They are all communications." No they are not! As I said before, you might have conversations with many people with no intent or purpose whatsoever. Have you ever chatted with someone for hours about a job, the weather, fashion, politics and everything under the sun without any goal to achieve anything or accomplish any purpose? Yes, you have. There

125

is nothing wrong with having conversation with others. It is healthy and it is normal, but it is not communication. Communication has a purpose to accomplish an end goal and to get somewhere with the person with whom you are having the conversation. Yes, all communications are conversations, but not all conversations are communications. We use conversations to communicate.

The Language of Communication

Let's go back to the same example I used in the beginning of this chapter. Imagine that you are talking to someone, communicating some upset you had with this person. You say, "I am upset with you for what happened last night." Prior to this actual conversation, you might have had upsetting *conversations* with yourself about the issue, and you have been smart enough to get into *communication* with him or her after. That conversation you had with yourself is what I call *Inner Chatter*.

Let's get deeper into this for a minute. All of our conversations and communications are arising in language. The language that most of us are using shows up in the form of dialogue. For me, some in English, some French, some German and some Farsi. You get the point. Other people use other forms of language, such as "Sign Language" for the deaf or "Braille Language" for the blind. Either way, all of them are languages and they allow dialogue between people.

There is another very big language that everyone in the world uses regardless of their nationality, age, religion or any other difference. Body language! Yes, body language is the most common language used by the human race. You know what I am talking about. When you like someone, you have a certain body language around him/her, as this person does around you when they like you or even when they don't like you! When you are in your office meeting and you are bored, or you remember your resentments, notice your body language? How about when your spouse is really ticked off with you? What about when you are talking to teenagers? Have you noticed their body language? We all do it, and we can all notice it! What is so common about that body language? Body language quickly tells us if a person is upset, angry, resentful, on the edge or indifferent.

Something is causing all these attitudes, the biggest language of all. Body language causes us to do and say things we may not want exposed. Attitude and internal chatter cause our body language, our upsetting conversations, and our angry behaviors. It is our internal conversations or what I said I call our *Inner Chatter*. If you get present with your inner chatter, you will hear it right before you say that thing that you want to take back so fast! If you pay attention, you can hear it right before you do that thing that you will regret later! If you go back and review all of your upsetting situations, they all start right after you heard your inner chatter, and you did what *that* voice said!

By this time, you have recognized to some degree the voice in your head. This voice sometimes sounds like your opinions, your gossip and sometimes your complaints! We have talked about this "Internal Conversation" in the last couple of chapters, but in this chapter we dig into it and really getting familiar with how this thing works and how it impacts our lives, our relationships and our effectiveness.

You might ask yourself, "What sound are you talking about?" Stay quiet for a moment and listen to yourself in your head. It is there. It sounds like you. Sometimes it is upset, sometimes it is opinionated, sometimes it is disappointed, and sometimes it complains about everything and everyone! You have to hear it to believe it! You have to stay present and calm to recognize it. Funny thing is when this voice is *in play* it is very loud and very obnoxious, but we cannot hear it! Why? Because we are not paying attention to what we are saying, and usually recognize the damages of what we have said only after we verbalize the message. We listen to that voice more than we listen to what is about to come out of our mouths.

Have you ever been in an upsetting situation or an argument and said something that you wish you could take back immediately? Have you ever listened to that loud voice in your head and did that thing it screamed at you to do, right or wrong, and within hours regret what you have done? Yes, we have all done that! This voice is loud, but we cannot hear it until we calm down, get present and become aware of what we are listening too!

This voice is not your friend. If you pay attention, each time that you get yourself in trouble, personally or professionally, you have listened to that voice for a couple of seconds before the actual trouble started. Regardless of about whom, where and how this inner chatter is being used, there are common elements. The inner chatter can be extremely nasty, condescending, belittling and justifying! It is almost never nice or empowering. Neither to you nor to anybody else. I know what you are thinking right now, "I am a nice person. I don't think that way about others." Or maybe you think, "I am a very positive person and I love people." Okay. Let's dig a little.

You have to be able to separate your thoughts from your inner chatter. How? Thoughts are thoughts. You have little control over them. Thoughts are coming and going as you go about your day. But sometimes you have some inner chatter about the topic or the person that you have that thought about. For example, you think about relationships, your own. You like it and you are having a great time in that relationship. Very good thoughts … good for you! Everything is going fine and you have a great time with yourself and your thoughts. Suddenly, out of nowhere, you hear yourself saying, "What if he doesn't like me?" or "What if she finds out that I am a loser?" or "I will mess it up, I know I will, I always do!" Have you ever had that chatter with yourself?

Maybe, you are going to a job interview and you are collecting your thoughts and you are doing your positive affirmations, and suddenly you hear it in the back of your head, "You are not going to make it!" or "Who are you kidding, they will not hire you!" Perhaps you are going on a blind date, without any picture of how the other person looks like or sounds like. You are all excited and your positive thinking approach is in play. Then, out of nowhere, you hear yourself saying, "I am fat!" or "I am old!" or "I know he/she will not like me!" or "I am wasting my time!" or "Who wants to be with me!" or "The last several dates didn't go well!" or some other nasty, belittling, condescending and justifying comments you can come up with. Get the picture? Did I mention that this voice is *not* your friend?!

Tune Out the Negative Inner Chatter

Have you ever been in a situation in which you listened to your inner chatter and decided the outcome of that event or situation before they played out and things turned out totally different from what you pictured or decided they would be? Like when you decided that someone was a jerk but he or she turned out to be pretty nice? Or you decided that someone is out to get you and/or hurt you, but it turns out that the person is a nice person after all? Yes, you have! Because, you listened to that nasty, unfriendly inner chatter and you did what that voice (that means you!) asked you to do. You were RIGHT for a moment, about that person or about that situation, however for a little moment only. Then you got embarrassed for what you did, and because of the fast decision that you made. You might have even said something nasty to that person before you knew the facts. Embarrassing.

Right at that moment, your inner chatter started being belittling and condescending toward you. Maybe it told you that "You are an idiot!" or "You always mess things up!" or some other nasty and very harsh words that you and I use to put ourselves down, but I can't repeat here. If you are present to what is going on around you, you will notice that each time you consulted with your inner chatter you came out of that meeting being RIGHT about the topic of that consultation or the person you, and YOU were talking about! You almost never come out of that inner chatter being WRONG. Interesting, huh?

This inner chatter is running in your head 24 hours a day, even when you sleep. It is loud, and it is not friendly. Let's do a little exercise to see the reality of how this chatter is keeping you away from being loving and caring towards you and others. How this chatter keeps you away from everything that you would like to have or accomplish in your life, personally and professionally.

I want you to draw a circle like the one below (Figure "C) in the middle of a page. Take a piece of regular sized paper and draw this small circle (around two inches in diameter) in the middle of the page, and in the middle of this circle write "Conversations and Communications."

CONVERSATIONS

COMMUNICATIONS

Figure "C"

In this exercise, we attempt to capture all of your main inner chatter about yourself, others, your family, relationships, your body, your job, working, society, money and any other topics. You will see how busy and unproductive your head is! During this exercise, I ask you to capture your inner chatter about a specific area, and then write what the voice says down around this circle, between the outside line of the circle and the edge of your paper. You don't have to do it organized or neat. Just write things down anywhere you want as long as it is not in the circle and it is between the outside of the circle and the edge of your paper. Ready?

We are going to start from you, because you are the most important person in your entire life; without you nothing else matters! Yes, you are *that* important. I am not kidding. But, this importance is far away from being selfish and self-centered. It is the importance of your love for yourself as a great person and a very unique human being. I am not a religious person; however, I have a strong relationship to spirituality. I believe every human being has been created in a very unique way. There is no other person on this earth like you or me. There is nobody that looks like you, sounds like you, speaks like you or even lives like you! That alone makes you a very, very unique individual. Out of 6.4 billion people, you are the one and only you. If that is not making you feel special then nobody, no money, no fame or any other thing will make you feel special! However, do you think that way about yourself? No you don't! If I asked you what your inner chatter says about you, what would you say?

The following examples are things I have heard from people over the years. I have not made anything up here. These comments are as real as you are. I have not looked for a negative or condescending remark, but 99 percent of the time the way we relate to ourselves and others and issues in life is negative, nasty, belittling and condescending, like these answers.

I ask you to look at your inner chatter, but tell the truth! Maybe for the first time, tell the truth about what you say about yourself and others, and life itself. I am sure you have heard, "The truth shall set you free!" But they forgot to tell you the next line, "But it will piss you off first!" Tell the truth and know that it is okay to get upset. You will be free! You will be free to be with your own humanity and your own responsibility in regard to the quality of the life you have created for yourself and others.

Come up with your own answers, write them down and only then look at the examples I have put down here. If they are a match with what you see about what you are saying in your head, write what you hear in your head down around the circle on your paper.

When you think of yourself, when you listen to that nasty inner chatter talking about you, what is he/she saying? When you look in the mirror, when you cannot come up with the right answer, when you get rejected, when you are angry at yourself for your choices, when you are mad because of your actions or reactions, and when you have not taken care of yourself, what is the voice saying? What are you saying to yourself about yourself?

Myself

I am not good enough, I am not smart enough, I am not fit enough, I can't do it, I hate myself, If I just had … If I just could … If only I were … I am fat, I am ugly, I am not sexy, I am stupid. Nobody likes me. Nobody wants me, I can't win, I am not loveable, I am not capable, I am a loser, I don't have it, I am tired …

Make sure you write everything you hear down on the paper around the circle. Don't be worried about any order. Just write!

Now, let's see what your nasty inner chatter is saying about your family, your parents, your siblings, your grandparents, aunts, uncles and cousins. Those people with whom you spend the holidays. Yes, those memorable holidays that you are still upset about! Write your inner chatter about them mixed with the first group that you jotted down. You can mix them up in any order, all around that paper.

My Family

I am not stupid! Don't tell me what to do! You are not the boss of me! Why can't you just support me? I can't be enough! Enough about you! Just shut up! I am alone here. You don't trust me. Would you just control your kids! I hate you. Be nice. Give me a break. You are driving me crazy! Listen to me! You think you are better than me? What else do you want from me? You don't believe in me! You are lazy! Why do I have to do that?

Now, what you are going to add to the whole thing is your inner chatter about your relationship. This is your intimate relationship, the significant other, the spouse, the lover, the life partner. The one that you love and hate! The one you want to kick or kiss, depending on the situation, the one that you don't know if you want to stay with or run away from. You know what and who I am talking about. Yes, that one!

Start writing your inner chatter around that paper in addition to the pervious notes.

My Relationship

It's a lot of work! They run away! I am not ready! They let themselves go! I am not perfect yet, I will be told what to do. You are not the one. I can't stand that thing you do! You will hurt me, I don't know! Stop spending my money! I will lose my power! I won't be supported. Would you take care of yourself? I have done that before. It will tie me down, I cannot be myself. I can't believe I am here with you! I will lose my independence. Should I stay or should I go?

Is it getting really busy and crowded on that paper? Not enough yet. We are not done. We have a lot to go!

Now, let's look at what that inner chatter is saying about other people. These are people who are not your family or spouses; these are regular ordinary people around the neighborhood, around your community and your country. Don't forget to keep writing on that paper around the circle!

Other People

They are stupid. I don't trust you. You want something! I can't believe you said that! I have to protect myself. They are out to get me. Yeah, right! You are not real. You are full of it! Can you be dumber than this? You are

135

cheap. Go away and stay away! I am better off alone. You are not worth it! How can they do that? You are weird! Leave me alone! Stop dominating me! Something is wrong with you! Just stop talking!

Now, let's talk about money. What is that inner chatter of yours saying about money? Keep writing! Don't give up. You will see the results of this exercise soon.

My Money

I don't have it! It is hard to make. It is hard to keep. I am surviving. Give me some! I don't deserve it! Can't live without it! I don't make enough. It is not who I am. I have no idea! It is scarce. I can't save it. Why can't I make it? I am not getting enough, It has power over me, I don't know how to make it, I don't like poor people, It is a proof of my success, I want to be around rich people.

Are you getting tired? Don't stop now! I know there is no room on your paper any more. It doesn't matter. Pick up another pen with another color and write in different color.
This is a good one ... your job, your boss, your workers, your employees, your co-workers, your job itself, your work place, the office equipment, your working time, all of it! Good, bad and ugly. Let's get into that. You write your inner chatter, and I will help you by giving some examples from other people.

My Work and Job

I am not appreciated. I have to do it all. Nobody knows what I do. You don't know what you are talking about! You can't make me. This place sucks. I hate this copier. It is boring. Can I do something else? I am not supported. Here we go again! I hate the hours. This is not it. I can't wait to go home. Nobody can do it like I can. It is never enough. Another meeting? Can you say thank you? If they would just listen to me! Take this job and ...

And now your body and fitness, a sensitive area, isn't it? Let's get into that! Keep writing you know the rules.

My Body and Health

I am old. I can't do it. Why is this fat not going away? It takes time, I don't have time, It is hard, I am suppressed, It doesn't look good, It's my parents fault, I wish I would look like that! I am tired. I do my best, what is wrong with me? If I had a second chance! They are looking better than me! I have to be fit. It is a very hard work! I prefer to go to bed! I have to do it. I am back to square one again!

One more area and this is the last one for this exercise. Society, community, the area or town or city you live in. Keep writing over everything you wrote before, and keep going!

Society, Community, City

They are off. They are lost. It is not safe. I don't want my kids to watch this! It is sick. I don't know what to do! Where are we going? How did we get here? Stop fighting! Stop the BS and lies! There is no integrity. There is no decency. This is too much! I don't trust them. When are we learning? I have to protect myself. Why can't we do something else? I wish it were different. We went too far! Can't we all just get along?

Now, look at your paper. By now it should be full of lines, full of your words and you should not have any space left to write! Isn't it? It probably looks like this:

I am tired   I will lose my independence   I don't make enough
Don't tell me what to do! I am not loveable   If they would just listen to me!
You don't know what you are talking about   You want something
Take this job and …   I can't believe   I am here with you!
        I don't trust you I am not sexy You don't believe in me
  You are not the boss of me!   I cannot be myself   You are full of it
You can't make me   How can they do that?   I don't have it
Go away and stay away!   Nobody can do it like I can   They let themselves go!
  I am not good enough   I can't win   I can't believe you said that!
        Would you just control your kids!   It is not who I am
They run away!   Stop dominating me!   Can't live without it!
  You think you are better? I am not fit enough   I don't know how to make it
Something is wrong with you   This place sucks   I don't have it
I am old   I can't do it   Why is this fat not going away?
  You are not the one!   I am not ready   They are stupid   It takes time
  I am not smart enough   Why can't you just support me?   I don't know!
I don't like poor people I would lose my power It is hard to make Give me some!
I have to protect myself   Be nice, would you?
You are crazy   I am a loser   Just stop talking!
Can I do something else?   If only I were….
    I am not perfect yet   You don't trust me
  I can't be enough   **CONVERSATIONS**   It's a lot of work
    I am not appreciate   **COMMUNICATIONS**   It is hard
I am better off alone   I am surviving I hate this
You are cheap   Just shut up!
    Nobody wants me   I have to do it all
  Nobody knows what I do   I am not capable
It is hard   It is boring   I have to do it I don't deserve it
    What else do you want from me?   I have done that before
They are out to get me   Give me a break!   I have no idea!
I don't have time   Enough about you!   Should I stay or should I go!
  I hate my hours Why do I have to do that?   I can't do it I am fat I hate myself
Can you be dumber than this?   This is not it! It is scarce I can't save it I
hate you! I can't wait to go home Listen to me! Would you take care of yourself?
It is never enough   It is very hard work. I will be told what to do. Why can't I?
    If I just had… Another meeting?   If I just could… I am alone here
I am ugly   You are weird   I am not supported I have to have it
  You are driving me crazy. It will tie me down Yeah, right! I won't be supported
It is my parents fault   I wish I would look like that!   I do my best
Can you say Thank You?   Stop spending my money!   I am not getting enough
  I want to be around rich people Nobody likes me I am stupid Leave me alone

Figure "D"

139

We just worked on you, your family, your relationship, other people, your body, your money, your job and work, and your society. Imagine if you would add all the other areas on top of that! We did not talk about sex, God, religion, government, social and political beliefs, and so many other areas or topics affecting your life, but that doesn't matter, because we together made a huge and important point.

The Impact of Negative Inner Chatter

When you look at that paper with a small circle in middle of it, what do you see? You see chaos; you see a very unorganized, busy and dark space! Don't you? This paper represents your head! It represents your mind when you are listening to your nasty inner chatter. You can see the impact of your inner chatter on your ability to communicate and actually be listened to.

Look at the paper again and tell me, if you want to communicate what you need to communicate and have any conversation with someone that will make any difference in regard to any topic, does that communication have any chance to get out of that circle? No! Look at the density and chaos of that area around the circle. You think your communication has any chance to leave that circle? No Way! No How!

You have to create some opening into this craziness and chaos. You have to blast through this tight and unworkable inner chatter in your head! Look at the next figure (Figure "E"). You have to make some channels to the other side! What is the other side? It could be anything you have a commitment to producing and to having. You look at the communication or conversations you want to have with someone about some important topic or very sensitive issues in life, or business then look at the inner chatter you have about that person, that topic or that issue. Next thing is to ask yourself what are you really committed to producing here in this regard. If you want to be positional about whatever you are being right about and take a firm unbendable stand, go ahead! It just leaves you more right, more alone and at the same time more ineffective!

If you want to get to the other side of this chaos, to a place over and beyond the craziness in your head that is being generated by all that inner chatter, somewhere that you can think straight and without opinion, judgment or your desire to win, you have to open up some access to the other side. How? By looking at your commitments to the matter and telling the truth. Do you have any agenda, or do you want to be effective in this regard? Do you want to win here or do you want everyone involved to win also? Are you committed to making your point, or are you committed to finding the best resolution? For you to get to some answers here you have to think harder and think outside yourself.

For any of us to go to that other side and to get to what we really want to say, which is deeply buried inside of what we are actually saying, we have to open some roadways. I call them "Roads to Purpose." These roads could be Commitment, Stand, Integrity, Workability, Effectiveness, Teamwork, Intimacy and/or so many other distinctions that will empower you.

It ... f of my success I can't stand t ... ng you do!   You are not worth it!
I a ...   I will lose my indepen ...   I don't make enough
Don ... he what to do!   I am not lo ...   If they would just listen to me!
You ... ow what you are talking ...   You want something
Take t ... and …   I can' ... e   I am here with you!
         ... t trust you   I am not se ... u don't believe in me
  You are ... e boss of me!   ... nnot be myself   You are f ...
You can't ... ne   How can they ... t?   I don't have ...
Go away a ... away!   Nobody ... it like I can   They let the ... go!
I am not goo ... gh   I can't wi ...   I can't believe you said ...
         Wou ... just control you ...   It is not wh ...
They run away ...   Stop d ... ng me!   Can't ... ut it!
You think you a ... r than me?   ... enough   I don't k ... to make it
Something is wro ... you   Th ... e sucks   ... 't have it
I am old   ... o it   ... this fat not ... y?
  You are not the one ...   I am n ...   They are ...   It takes time
  I am not smart enou ... Why ca ... just supr ...   I don't know!
I don't like poor peop ... ould ... y powe ... d to make Give me
I have to protect mysel ... ice, would you?
You are crazy   I am a l ...   Just stop talking!
     ... do something else? ...   ... only I were….
         ... at yet ...   You don't trust me

CONVERSATIONS
COMMUNICATIONS   It's a lot of work

I am not apprec ...
I am better off alone
You are cheap   ... st shut up!
 Nobody wants me   I have to do it all
 Nobody knows w' ...   ... t capable
It is hard   It is h ...   I h ... it I don't deserve it
   What else d ... ant from n ...   ... one that before
They are ou ... e   Give ... eak!   I have ...
I don't ha ...   Enough a ... u!   Should I sta ... ld I go!
 I hate ... Why do I have ... hat?   I can't do it I ... ate myself
Can ... mber than this?   ... his is not it!   It is scar ... ave it
  I ... I can't wait to go h ... n to me! Would you take ca ... rself?
 ... r enough   It is very ha ... told what to do Why can't I n ...
 ... ust had… Another mee ... I just could… I am alone here
 ... ugly   You are weird   I ... t supported I have to have it
 ... ou are driving me crazy It ... e down Yeah, right! I won't be suppo ...
It is my parents fault   I wish ... d look like that!   I do my best
Can you say Thank You?   Stc ... ding my money!   I am not getting enough

Figure "E"

Let's look deeper into these potential "Roads to Purpose." They are roads that will make a difference in your life and your life results:

Commitment

It would make a huge difference to look at one's commitment to the matter at hand. The commitment to one's agenda and hidden issues, or a commitment to do something that will open some doors and produce results that will serve everyone.

Stand

Are you making a stand to produce results that will serve everyone involved, regardless of being just you and them? Or, are you and the team, or you and the community! Where you are standing makes the biggest difference! If you don't stand for something you will fall for anything!

Integrity

Without integrity nothing will work. Take a good look inside and see if you are making up all the inner chatter to not be responsible for what you can do, and what you are capable to produce. Are you lying? Are you justifying? Are you hiding the truth so you can manipulate? Did you just want to win and be right? I am not here to judge; I am here to ask questions! Are you responding to these questions with integrity? Integrity is the source of power and joy in life.

Workability

You can bulldoze through the crowded inner chatter and open channels of communication, because you are committed to workability. When you operate from that point, you stop that inner chatter and you make things work with others. You have to have a bigger vision than just winning.

Effectiveness

When effectiveness is your desire and your will, you know what needs to get done! I can speak for myself. When I say that since I reviewed my past results I have produced in my life, I can see how ineffective I have been. I am not committed to that again. I am more committed to workability. So now I look at any issue or scenario at hand and see what the most effective approach insight is to any situation or relationship issue. I recognize that my inner chatter is very ineffective and very destructive! Integrity, commitment, workability and effectiveness are all integrated and related in order to make things work, anywhere, personally and professionally.

Teamwork

In personal life as well as business life we are working with teams. Our relationships, our families, our circle of friends, our communities and our work places are our different teams. When you stand for something together as a team, when we move together for a common cause, we are a team.

Intimacy

This particular road to purpose is the one that will make any relationship work. You can't have intimacy when you listen to negative inner chatter. Without intimacy your relationship will not work. So, what is there to do? Get present to the importance of your intimacy with others. That will allow you to break through those barriers made by your inner chatter.

Deal with Your Power and Possibility

Consider this … we are making all of this nonsense so we don't have to deal with our power and possibilities that would make us happier, more effective and more successful in life! Almost no one wants to be responsible for the qualities of their life anymore. Have you watched TV recently? It is disgusting! It is all about modeling, who can dance better, sing better or design better. It is all about stories, dramas and failures as human beings. It is all about fighting, killing and taking over the other guy. It is all about the drama we have made up in our heads about ourselves,

145

others, work and life itself – drama, drama and drama ... stories, stories and more stories. Maybe that was what William Shakespeare wrote in 1606 as part of his play *Macbeth*:

Tomorrow, and tomorrow and tomorrow creeps in this petty pace from day to day to the last syllable of recorded time, and all our yesterdays have lighted fools the way to dusty death. Out, out brief candle. Life is but a walking shadow, a poor player that struts and frets his hour upon the stag and then is heard no more. It is a tale told by an idiot, full of sound and fury, signifying nothing.

Does that sound familiar? I am sure it does, because all of us have dealt with the seeming futility of life, and some of us are still dealing with it.

As I have mentioned, I have been married three times. I am not proud of this record, but I am responsible for the production of it. Most important, it gave me my three beautiful children, whom are everything in my life! That said; let me share with you about my second marriage and divorce.

I will tell you about my marriage with one of my wives and how inner chatter caused our divorce, and how after that my declaration of my commitments saved my grace to support her in the upbringing of our children, and making a stand for not making her wrong and promising to her to work things out so our children have peace in their lives. I share this life experience as an example to make a point that you have all the responsibilities for what you make up as you move along in life and what you cause in your own life, good, bad or ugly.

My second wife and I dated for almost one year before we were married, and our marriage lasted five years, so we were together almost seven. This divorce had so many great impacts on my life, besides social and financial. It had a big psychological impact on me, and especially my being away from my three-year-old daughter and two-year-old son.

Like any other couple, we had lots of issues: family, parents, money and to build our future. You can appreciate that it was not easy for me as a new immigrant, and for her when we had two kids back to back, and my daughter from a first marriage, and on top of that my wife's sick father who was dealing with a killer cancer. We both worked hard to stay on top of the game and keep ourselves away from all the interpretations that human beings can and will make when they are dealing with problems. Now, add all the issues, gossip and high expectations that our families put on us on top of that! In my culture there is lots of gossip, lots of unrealistic expectations, and lots and lots of interpretations of what others said or did. Unfortunately, I could not keep my wife, my family and her family away from this absolute BS! Anything I said was interpreted in a whole different way. Anything I did was assumed to be covering up a whole different thing. Any expression of interest to someone else was an accusation of a different kind of interest. It got to be so much that it was overwhelmingly hard to deal with. At that time, I had no idea what was going on. I thought, "What the hell is happening?" I was absolutely committed to taking care of my family and do what it takes to make things work. Yes, I was willing to DO whatever it took. I worked hard, with long hours, and I buried myself in work, and committed myself to the DOING part of my life, because that was all I knew at the time to do! Yes, I had a lot of information. I read books, and I was an expert on knowing! Does it sound familiar!!?

I was working hard and listening to my inner chatter about the life, the marriage, the wife, my family, her family and everything I had to do to make things work. The experience was like being in the middle of the ocean, dealing with a big storm with nothing to hang on to! It was horrible! I am sure it was horrible for her, too. I am sure she was dealing with a huge amount of nasty interpretations of what my family was saying or what she was hearing. I am sure having everybody on her was not helping our situation either. Both of us hid in the middle of our jobs and business. We were just DOING, so we didn't have to deal with our BEING. I can speak for myself. I know I had to work hard and be a good husband, I had to work hard to be a good father, I had to work hard and long to be able to take care of my family, and I had to work hard to take care of everybody else, because that is what a good man would do in my opinion.

I was doing everything on top of my resentments to all the BS I had to deal with in home that arose from all the gossip, interpretations, high expectations, and looking good! It was all over the place with everyone involved that would make it unbearable to deal with, so what would I do to not deal with it? I took myself away. I took my love, intimacy and attention away. I became a lone ranger. No communication, no dealing with the reality of what was going on and no showing intimacy. This went on for a couple of years, and before I knew it she found intimacy, communication and understanding somewhere else. When I found out what was going on she had been in a relationship with someone else for nine months, someone at work who was listening to what she had to say. It is such a common thing that happens in any workplace and/or any friendship, because people who are not in the middle of the crap and fighting are safe, and don't have anything at stake. As a result, they listen, and that is very attractive.

When I learned what was happening, it was hard to deal with. It was a heartbreaking time, not just for the two of us, but for our two little kids and my eight-year-old daughter, who was observing the house breaking apart again. Like any other children, they made a lot of decisions about life and about themselves during these times. I want to stay about the point I am trying to make, listening to your inner chatter is dangerous, it is ineffective, and it will cause nothing but interpretations, upsets and resentments, which leads to breakups, divorces, firing, losing and separations with family, friends and anybody who you care about, personally or professionally.

Right after that divorce and separation from my kids (the two little ones from that marriage, because the eight-year-old was with me) there was a period of time that a rush of nasty inner chatter was pouring in my head! "I am not good enough, I am not handsome enough, I am not man enough, and how could she do that to me? How could she take my babies away from me?" At the same time the inner chatter was talking about "This is the way women are! I will not trust them again. People are full of s ..." I began to attack the idea of relationships. "It is all BS. It is a lot of work and it is not worth it! You have to give everything and they give you nothing! You have to put up or ship out!" After that, the attack was on the life itself. "Life sucks! What is the point of this nonsense? Why do I want to continue living with this disgrace?" and so much other nasty, disgraceful, distractive and loud inner chatter. That chatter caused me to

149

even think about killing myself! I never attempted, but the thought was there. It was a very hard time! The things that saved my life were my kids, because they would need me later. I also thought of my parents, because I didn't want them to deal with another lost son and my experience of surviving Iran revolution, Iran and Iraq war and making it here to the States, as well as my experience of being a warrior. I remember thinking, "Killing yourself for a woman or for a divorce? It is not worth it! You have a lot to offer and you have one life to live for yourself and your kids. Now, make a difference with it."

It took me couple of months to take responsibility for what happened. That is the point of this story I told you. I was able to separate what happened from the inner chatter I had been hearing about my situation. I took responsibility for not being there for my wife when she needed me, to listen to her, to not defend my position and my opinions, to understand what she dealt with. It was not a surprise for me anymore about what she did and why she did it. I would have appreciated it if she would have communicated with me, but she did not know how to, so she did what she thought was good for her.

Right after that, I promised her that I would never bad mouth my ex-wife to our kids, and I would always support her for raising our kids. I promised that I would never undermine her and her decisions with the kids. It was and still is a hard thing to do, but I have kept my promise and intend to continue doing it even now that our kids are in college. We still have our differences in parenting and in different areas, but I am keeping my promise, because it is MY promise, and I am responsible to keep my promise. I will not break my promises by justifying others' broken promises.

Get Ready To Take Control

Now you can see your ineffectiveness in your communication! By now you have a very good question, "How can I take control of this nasty inner chatter and be effective in my thinking and my relationships?" Very good question! By becoming responsible for how and why you have created these internal conversations. By getting to the bottom of what is in it for you doing that? Because there is something in it for you to keep generating and creating the chatter! Do you remember I was saying, "*When you are fully responsible for your life, circumstances will not determine the quality of your life.*" I was talking about this!

You have to own it! If you make up some nasty inner chatter about having inner chatter, nothing will alter or change. Same nonsense, different topic, different day! You have to own that it is a part of you, you have to live with it, and you will die with it. However, the freedom is in the acceptance of it and ownership of it. It is yours, it is you!

You have to learn to coexist with your inner chatter. You have to build a strong "muscle" to be able to turn it around when it is happening, but you cannot stop it from happening. You can turn it around and listen to a whole new and different inner chatter that you can invent at the same exact moment right after you hear the nasty inner chatter.

151

It is like being sick, like having cancer. You might have cancer, but you are not your cancer! You are your hope, your vision and your future. That vision, future and hope allow you to fight back, but you have to live with that cancer for awhile. You and your nasty inner chatter are the same way. You have to learn to live with it, but not let it take over you and your life. You will hear it, day in and day out, all the time, almost in each and every interaction, meeting and conversation, but you don't have to listen to it. If you are aware of it, then you can be in charge and be in control of it. Your control of it is generating from your commitment to have effective communication and produce some results in your relationship that will add to your happiness, joy and fulfillment.

Remember, your *muscles* about controlling this inner chatter are weak now. You have to practice and keep recognizing it so you can do something about it. For you to work on that muscle, I have some questions that your answers will allow you to remember why you cause the inner chatter and what you are getting out of continuing to create it. On the other side, see how much it costs you to keep doing it.

So let's get to these questions, and let's get your honest answers.

As I said in the last chapter, write your answers clearly, simply and truthfully under each question. Do that because there is a process in the end of this book called "The Big List" that is totally relevant to all your notes. Make sure you take time and be responsible for what you have learned about yourself. Write your revelations down, too.

1. What do I gain by having internal conversations?

What is in it for you to entertain the inner chatter? Why do you listen to the chatter so often? What is in it for you? There is always something there for us when we keep listening to the chatter. Gain is not necessarily positive or a good thing in this case; it is actually something that is really not to our benefit.

_____

_____

_____

_____

2. How do these internal conversations affect my relationship to others?

As you can see, there is some impact on your relationship to others? There are some damage to your relationships with the people around you when you listen to the nasty inner chatter about others. What are those damages?

_____

_____

_____

3. How do these internal conversations affect my job and productivity?

You can see the damage caused by listening to your inner chatter in your job and productivity. What are they? How does the chatter keep you away from being productive and being effective in your job?

_____

_____

_____

_____

4. How do these internal conversations affect my health and vitality?

How does listening to the nonproductive chatter affect your health? What is the impact and damage on your weight, size, health and vitality?

_____

_____

_____

_____

5. What other internal conversations could I have instead?

You are the one who created the inner chatter. If you can create and invent these kind of unproductive, damaging and nasty conversations in your head, just imagine what else you can create and invent. Anything! You can create anything you want! You have to look back and see why you want to create those negative and nasty conversations about yourself and others, as well as life itself. Then see if the damage is worth continuing. If not, create and invent something else; something that will empower you, and move you to a much more productive and empowering space in regard to your relationship to yourself, others and life, in general. You are the creator here!

_____

_____

_____

_____

6. Why do I want to have these new internal conversations?

Now, look and see why do you want to do that? Why will the new and empowering conversations in your head versus the nasty and ineffective ones benefit you?

_____

_____

_____

_____

7. What do you realize about yourself?

_____

_____

_____

_____

8. What are you willing to change or alter?

_____

_____

_____

_____

9. What do you promise to yourself now?

_____

_____

_____

_____

10. What are you willing to do to keep those promises?

_____

_____

_____

_____

11. Who will you discuss this with?

_____

_____

_____

_____

CHAPTER FIVE

CONSPIRACY FOR SUFFERING

BARRIERS TO PERSONAL EFFECTIVENESS

Who you are, what you do and the way you do it
all depends on who you are for yourself
and your point of view of life.
Keep relating to yourself as the power and
possibility that you can and will generate.

In this chapter, we look at how we cause our own suffering.

I am sure you have had this experience as much as I have. You have seen it in others, too. When you get clear about how we cause our own suffering and get present to it you can immediately see it for what it is and recognize it in yourself as well as in others. We choose suffering because it is dramatic, and there are people in our lives who will buy it from us. We are all-too-ready sellers!

How We See Ourselves

If we look closely, we can see how we have created drama and suffering in our lives. In the last chapter you learned to recognize your inner chatter and how you create distractive inner chatter about yourself, others and every other area of your life that affect your relationships. In this chapter, we emphasize the three main relationships that determine your self-love or self-respect, effectiveness in relationships to others, and productivity in what you do. We look and dig into how we see ourselves, others and what we do. Why?

If you notice, YOU are always here. In any upsetting situation, in any fight, in any breakdown in your life, in anything you do, anywhere you go or any decision you make, you are one of the parties involved in the fight, disagreement or breakdown, or you are the only one who put yourself in the situation and who ends up suffering. You just can't get yourself out of the hole! The way you relate to yourself is the main factor in your suffering or your freedom.

How We See Others

On the other hand, wherever you go there are also OTHERS! You cannot avoid them even if you try! They are at home, at work, on the freeways, on the streets, in restaurants and every other place. We live with them, we are married to them, we are have been born from them, we work with them, they raised us, we raised them, we love them, we hate them, we want to be with them and we can't wait for them to leave sometimes. We can't get rid of them. They are everywhere! Even when we sleep we think of them. We see them in our dreams or nightmares. How close am I to your experiences about others? Our peace of mind, effectiveness in life and relationships correlate to how we relate to others. We are someone's child. We are someone's husband, wife or life partner. We work for someone or someone works for us, and we call them employee and or employer. We are all in this world together; we cannot live without other people and we cannot even exist without them! Look, we are a son or a daughter virtue of your relationship to our parents. We are fathers or mothers virtue of our relationship to our kids. We are husbands or wives virtue of the existence of the significant other person in our lives, and the same thing goes for the work place! Without them, we are nothing. So, we are all in this together, so you best get used to it! As soon as you get this, the sooner you can minimize your suffering and drama about who those "others" are, and the way they relate to you.

How We See "Working"

The last piece is the way we relate to and see "WORKING." I am not talking about the work you do or your career or your business. I am talking about the whole concept of working and doing what you do every day to earn a living. I know some of you love what you do. Me too. But for a long time, working was something "I had to do." It was "hard," and I did it "in order to." Therefore, it is not about the work you do, but rather about how you relate to the work itself. Or the WORKING.

How You See Yourself-Others-Working Affects You

When you see your ineffectiveness in these three relationships, and how much you have to do with the way you have created the relationships, you can see the source of your suffering and the drama in your life, and the source of suffering around your results in life. When I say "results," I am not talking about how much money you earn. I am talking about the results in your relationships, results in your communications, results in your productivity and peace of mind, everywhere and with everyone! You are always there, they are always with you and you are always doing something with yourself, or with others. There is no way out of this!

Let's start with you, with ourselves and the way we see ourselves. There so many different ways we can possibly see ourselves or relate to ourselves. Don't be attached to good or bad, or the positive or negative of it. Just look and see which one is or is close to the way you view yourself. Let's look at some examples that I have heard from people over the years. I am not committed that these are the only ways you see yourself, but when you are mad at yourself, making yourself wrong and judging yourself, you are going to relate to one, two, or all of these.

How do you see yourself?

We start from first base: YOU

Enough or Not Enough

Something like "I am not good enough" or "I am not thin enough" or "I am not smart enough." Just fill the blank! "I am……….enough." Or, you might think "I am not enough" of this or that. However, you can agree with me that most of the time we are going to "I am not" faster than "I am …!" This way of viewing ourselves is always holding us back from going after what we truly desire, such as sports, jobs or even a very special relationship.

Good or Bad

Some people are always BAD. You cannot get them to see good in themselves! To what degree are you *bad* in what you do, or the way you talk, the way you think and in your relationships to yourself? We always carry guilt, shame and blame with ourselves, because it is the way to not be responsible for the thing we do or what we think. So what is the way out? It's to blame it on being bad and no good! Right?

Worthy or Not worthy

This is the other thing we do to ourselves. "I am worth it" or "I am not worthy of that!" It is the other thing we create from guilt, shame and blame. Funny thing is that you can see the connection and relationship between these together, like; *I am not enough of this so I am bad and not worthy of it.* Can you see that? They are invented by us to keep ourselves away from what we CAN do and who we can become.

Beautiful or Ugly

Do you wake up in the morning and see yourself in a mirror as an ugly person or as a beautiful person? Do you know that what you see in the mirror has nothing to do with what you see in your mind about what you see in the mirror? I have seen so many beautiful, gorgeous, handsome and amazingly attractive people who do not see themselves as fit, handsome or beautiful. You know what? The fashion industry, beauty industry, and

163

manufacturers of clothing, make-up, and every other thing related to those industries all know this negative self talk very well. They capitalize on it. With the help of the media, they make you see yourself as *Not Enough*. As a result, there is a struggle in teenagers and young adults to be like someone else, and to look like movie stars or singers. Have you seen TV these days? Just look at the title of programs. For example: *"Who Wants to Be the Next super Model?"* Do you ever think about why we don't have a program called *"Who Wants to Be the Next Super Scientist Who Cures Cancer?"* Of course not! That is not HOT! Because looking beautiful is more important than being smart. And the sad thing is that no amount of surface beauty will make these people see themselves as beautiful within! This is something that I have such a passion for, given that these kids, teenagers and young adults are our future. They are the future of our nation and the future of the world, and we allow their minds to be abused and manipulated.

Smart or Dumb

I am smart to do something so important. I am smart to do this or I am smart to do that. Or, we view ourselves as not smart enough to get something done or complete a project (like completing high school or college). Do you know the percentage of high school drop outs? Do you know the number of people who do not complete their college education? Can't you see people around you who don't complete their projects? Do you know what the American garage is built for? Not for parking cars. The garage is for stacking up and storing all of the half-finished projects! What do you think is stopping us from being complete what we start? I am not enough, plus I am not worthy with a little touch of being bad (because of guilt!) and, in the end, being dumb! And to cover these things up in our own heads, we go shopping and take the route that the fashion and beauty industry has put in front of us. Please do not get me wrong. I personally like to dress well and look good, however, that is not who I am! When you are whole and complete within, you do not need anything else to make you worthy. You don't need approval of others to be good, smart and capable, and you are free! That is one of the points of this book. I always say,

I like to look good, but I am not up to looking good!

Disciplined or Lazy

This has become a very big problem for companies, because people will not complete their work, and they always have something to say about why they have not completed their job. Do you see yourself as an organized and disciplined person, or a lazy person? My only question is this … if you are organized and disciplined why are your projects not getting completed on time? Why are you dropping projects all the time? Why is your desk full of stuff in the "piling system" versus the filing system? In your head you relate to yourself as someone who is not a disciplined person. We resist being a lazy person because it doesn't sound good. Lazy seems like a dumb person and that is bad! Therefore, we reject the idea of being lazy immediately, and we have a lot of excuses, justifications and reasons why we cannot do what we said we would do. The really sad thing is that we believe what we say!

165

Responsible or Martyr

In the end, do you see yourself as a responsible person for your life results, or do you blame others? Do you hold yourself responsible for what happened in your life, for the consequences of the choices you made in your life, or are you blaming life, parents or spouses? When we look closely, we can see that we are responsible for what has happened in our lives. I am not talking about getting sick or having cancer. I am not talking about accidents on the freeways. I am talking about our relationships, finances, health practices and communications with others. You can see this in yourself as much as others who blame everyone and everything for what happened in their lives! I am sure you have the same kind of people in and around your life as well as I who will not be happy, even if their life depends on it! There is always something wrong, like somebody is being meant to them, something is not working, and some issues are causing their unhappiness. Take a look at yourself. Be authentic. Be honest and say which one you are leaning toward and which one you entertain more often. I know being responsible sucks. It means you are the one that lives your life.

Yes, you might be greatly happy and positive, read many positive thinking books and attended positive-being seminars, but you still fundamentally relate to yourself in a certain way. That is the source of your ineffectiveness in life! That way of *being* is the source of your pain, and it is the conspiracy you have built to make sure that you continue to suffer. Suffering is optional. Know this and take it to heart. You were not born suffering; you have chosen it! If you believe that happiness is not an accident, nor is it something you wish for, but happiness is something you design you are responsible for your happiness and you are not blaming others and/or the world for what happened to you!

Access to that way of being that you have created for yourself is through the main criticism and complaint you have *about* yourself. You and I have lots of complaints about ourselves, but there is one very big one that was selected by us a long time ago and that has been running the show since its inception. This view is linked to so many things we have done, the experiences we have had, and we continue having. In fact, we are still dealing with it. Maybe less than before, after we have read so many books and attended so many self-realization seminars and classes! But fundamentally we are still dealing with what we created … the way we see ourselves and the way we relate to ourselves.

For me, it is "I am not smart enough." As you can see, I used the word "am" not "was" because I am aware of it now, but for a long time I was not aware of this way of being and how I related to myself. It still comes to visit time to time, but because I am aware of it, I can choose another way of being that I have created from my vision for my life. You will get to that point before you end this book. Just be patient and stay with the thinking process and inquiries.

Let me tell you about how I decided "I am not smart enough," or in the language of a six-year-old; "I am dumb." Right now, we say things about ourselves that are in the language of adults, but when we decided those things to be truths, we were far younger. You need to get back and really deal with the straightness and directness of that younger generation's language. You know, they say it the way it is! We just try to make it look better, softer or more approachable. In other words, the "politically correct" way to say it! We soften our words to take the impact away and protect us from understanding the depth of the issue we have caused for ourselves. Yes, it is sad, but so what? Let's get going!

I now take you back to what happened at the time that I made the decision that I am dumb. I was six years old. My older brother Behzad was seven and a half, and already in the third grade, while I was just beginning of first grade. One weekend my family members gathered in our house, and everyone had a good time and talked amongst themselves. My father, like any proud father, was bragging and talking about his kids. He acknowledged my older brother for being smart. He said, "Behzad is so smart!" What I heard was, "Behnam is not!" How about that? He never said, "Behnam is dumb," or "Behzad is smarter than Behnam," but what I heard was the fact that I am not. You can see as a child I did not know the difference between facts and interpretations of the facts. As a six-year-old, I was looking up to my father to acknowledge my intelligence, as he always did, but at that particular moment he was acknowledging my brother's intelligence, and I made a decision that carried with me for over 40 years.

I need you to know that I have corrected my damaging self-view and relate to myself as a very intelligent person at this time. I know now that I have caused that earlier decision for protection reasons. However, at that time, I did not know; so at that given moment right after what my father said about my brother, I made a decision. "I can't be smart, so I will become charming!" If I can't get others' acknowledgment and attention by my intelligence, because I decided I am dumb, then I will do it with charm.

Another thing is that I decided charm is not enough, so I added hard working and reliable, because if one is dumb tone must work harder and be really reliable to cover the dumbness! That worked very well. Obviously, I am talking from the view of a child. Up to this day, my family acknowledges me for my accomplishments as well as my charm, reliability and hard-working character.

On one hand, I was working harder and I did some suffering, but in the end I realized that I was the one who made this decision about myself; nobody else! That is why I call it a "Conspiracy for Suffering." I collected a lot of evidence over the years to prove I was dumb and not smart. I had suffered. I worked harder than usual and longer hours than usual to prove I am enough of something. If that is not dumb, I don't know what is!!! You are doing the same thing!

Now, let's see how you have criticized yourself through the years. Be true to the decision and tell it the way it is from the point of view of a young person or a teenager who made that decision, and just say it to yourself. When you make yourself wrong and judge yourself, when you are not generous and kind to yourself, what is the thing you are saying to yourself? What is that complaint that you never let go of? That nasty and belittling comment you made about yourself and have been telling yourself?

The way I criticize myself is:

As soon as you figure out what the answer is, write it down in the box below (Line A). Use very simple language; say it the way that a 10-year-old can understand. For example: "I am dumb" versus "I have some challenges to understand the meaning of what I read!" Or, "I am fat" versus "I have trouble maintaining my weight." Stay present and keep it simple!

A

Very good! Let's move on.

How do you see others?

Now that we are done with you, we move on to second base, OTHERS.

As I mentioned in the beginning of this chapter, wherever we go we deal with other people; at home, at work, on the streets, at parties and in each and every place we go, we deal with other people. Even when we keep ourselves away from people it is because we are dealing with them in our heads and having a dialogue with them via our inner chatter. Staying in this concept and in the tail of the same approach we did on the first part (the way you relate to yourself) we are ready to look at the ways we relate to others. As I mentioned, I am not committed that these ways are the only ways you see other people, but when you complain and criticize others you will go to one, two, or more of these.

Enough or Not Enough

Do you see others as being enough of something? For example, they are smart enough for you, pretty enough for you, fast enough or any other enough? You fill in the blank. As we all know, this is one of the most ineffective ways to deal with and view others. Look at the dating systems and relationship matching companies. Why do you think they are out there? Because when we were out there trying to find our match or soul mate, we had lots of high expectations that would be very hard for others to fulfill. We do this with employees also; we look at people to be enough or not enough of something!

With Me or Against Me

Do you relate to others based on how you perceive their position in regard to you? You can see this thing starting from a very early age during our elementary school years when we were picking our friends based on our feelings of whether they were with us or against us. Funny thing is that a lot of people still pick and choose their relationships, friendships, and even business decisions based on this feeling into adulthood.

Worthy or Not worthy

Are these people worthy of you, your time, your business, your trust or even your love? Come on, you know you do this! Looking closely into this, if the answer comes as a "NO" then they are gone, and we do not pay attention to who they are or what they say, because they are not worthy of our time, attention or any other thing.

Reliable or Sloppy

Can I rely on these people or not? Are they sloppy and unreliable in your view of them? This is another way we relate to other people and the ways we see them. Let's not forget that this is one of the biggest ways we pick and choose who we will hire to work for us. It is not as if they are coming to the interview saying, "Hi, I am sloppy. Please hire me." No. Rather, they say anything in their resumes to get hired.

Trustworthy or Crafty

Can I trust them? Or are they crafty and shady? We do look at others from this view also. You can see it in others' eyes in any business meeting or first dinner date. They can see it in your eyes, too. The one-million-dollar question is can I trust them?

Generous or Selfish

Are they generous? Are they selfish? This is another way we might view others, and one of the possible ways we relate to them.

Safe or Not Safe

Are they safe or they are unsafe to be open with? Do you view others on whether you can be safe with them or not? If you don't trust them and they are not worthy of your time, it is very predictable for you to not feel safe with them!

Funny thing is that we always see our worst in others. They become a mirror to *our* shortcomings as a human being, and the very thing that we do not like about ourselves. We will see and observe all of our own bad characteristics in people. This very concept has been talked about through centuries and distinguished by great minds like Sufi masters and the Buddha. This area of thought has also been touched upon by many other flag holders for transformation and enlightenment and has been discussed by great writers like Deepak Chopra, Neale Donald Walsh, Debbie Ford and many other writers who mentioned this concept in their books or materials.

These, as well as the rest of them that I have mentioned so far, are the forces that cause us to see others in a very limited and already framed view. It is limiting and disempowering to them as well as to ourselves, but that is not holding us back from doing so, or does it?

Now, let's write down the way you view others, the way you criticize or complain about them in *Line B*. As I said about *Line A*, use simple language, short and to the point; how do you criticize others?

The way I criticize others is:

It is so simple. I always use this example for my clients who say, "I never complain about others." I ask them what they call people on the freeway when they are in a rush and people are driving slow or cutting them off? Yes… it's "stupid." Uh, huh. Caught you! Funny thing is that they are calling you the same thing at the same time. Yes, you are driving on the same freeway!

So stop being such a *good boy or girl,* and tell the truth. Tell me exactly the way you see it, exactly the way you criticize others when you are upset and running your opinion about them. You know what I am talking about. Just write in the *Line B*:

B

_____

Good work! Let's move on.

How do you view working in general?

Now, we are going to look at the third part of this three-part connection. This last part is the way you relate to "WORKING." By this time, you know you are always there, and you are always with others, so there are connections, and you are always doing something to make a living and to survive! There is no way out of this triangle. There is a particular way you look at working that is not really powerful. Let's look at some potential ways you might look at working, business, your job or your career. The way you relate to working was developed a long time ago, maybe when you started your very first job, maybe the very first time you had started your own business, maybe when you heard from your parents that "working is hard" and/or "you have to work hard" or "nobody gives you anything for free." The point is that we all have some heavy and disempowering view of working!

No? So why is everyone not happy and joyful in what they do? Why are there so many management positions to motivate the workforce and to make sure things run on time? Why are we trying so hard to be more sufficient and more effective in what we do, or managing *others* to do? You can see this desire to be more effective in each and every shop, business, and corporation in our country, as well as any other place in the world. Why? Because WE are there, OTHERS are around us, and we are DOING something!

Hard or Easy

Do you see working as an easy thing to do or as a hard thing to do? I am not talking about the time that you got a raise and you were happy for a week, but then you got back to your "hard" work. Overall, in general, how do you relate to working?

Hopeful or Resigned

Do you go to work with strong hope and motivation, or are you totally resigned about your future in what you do? Do you see your work or job as a bright future, or something you are doing to get paid?

Happy or Unfulfilled

Do you go to work happy and excited, or are you going to your work, business, or job unhappy and unfulfilled, and you think there is no end in this?

Appreciated or Not Acknowledged

Do you see your working situation as something others understand and are appreciative of who you are and what you do, or are you dealing with the black clouds of "Nobody understands what I do" and/or "Nobody appreciates the hard work I do"?

Productive or Getting By

Are you being productive and are you on time in what you do, or do you just get by every day and look forward to the weekends? Do you relate to your job or work as a way to be productive, or is it just another thing to do?

Love To or Have To

Do you see the work you do as something you love to do or something you have to do?

Passionate or Just a Job

Do you wake up in the morning and can't wait to go to work because it is your passion, or it is just another job to do?

The way I criticize what I do is:

I promise you that I am not trying to look at the negative part of working only, but in my long career of working I have observed about eight out of 10 people who are not happy and fulfilled with what they do for work! Take a look for yourself and tell the truth. You might love what you do now, but there was the time that you were looking for a job that you would love to do. Why? At that time you were looking at what you do as something you did not like, and that which you were not happy about. That way of being is still in you. You are still trying to not go back to what you did not like.

You can live your life based on "Not failing," or you can live your life based on "Succeeding." You would be amazed to see that you can produce the same results, but definitely two different life experiences *while* you are doing it.

177

Now, be honest and express your biggest criticism about working in *Line C.* Just write a simple, to the point, authentic and honest answer.

C

_____

Very good!

Now write down whatever you have written in *Lines A, B* and *C* here in the following order, simply, to the point and straight, without any fluff and extras!

A. _____

B. _____

C. _____

Imagine that you are going around introducing yourself from these three complaints and criticisms you have about yourself, others and what you do. I know you never do that! But just for understanding the impact and the point of this exercise, just imagine you are. As a matter of fact, if any of your friends or relatives have read this book or have participated in our trainings or courses, you can practice this exercise with them.

It sounds really bad! Actually it sounds really funny, because if the other person had the same understanding and awareness you had, your introduction would sound something like this …

You would say something like:

> Hello, I am …

A. Not good enough

B. You are stupid

C. And I hate my job

The other person would respond with something like:

> Nice to meet you …

A. I am ugly

B. I can't trust you

C. And I have to do it by myself

I know it sounds silly! At this time you are either laughing or upset. If you are laughing it is because you get how ridiculous this self depreciation is and how funny it is. If you are upset, it is because you don't want to hear how you actually sound when you walk around introducing yourself. I know you don't say to people what you wrote in the three boxes. Most likely you introduce yourself as a happy, well-adjusted person who relates well with others and who loves what you do. Right?!

I am not surprised one bit that you and everyone else do that. I have done it, and I have seen everybody else doing the same! It is human nature. We pretend everything is "OKAY," and nothing is lacking in our lives. We make everything sound really good in our lives, relationships and our work because it is expected of us. From whom? Who expects this from us? Others like us! They are us and we are them; we are all on this ride together. We are all about looking good for others and trying to survive the pressure of being *like* others. We say we are great, we are happy; we say we relate to others, our family, our friends and so forth. We act like we are completely and totally satisfied and fulfilled in our marriage, relationships, friendships and workplace. On the other hand, we would not miss an opportunity to complain, gossip, bitch and nag to ourselves, to others and to anybody who will listen about our lives, relationships and workplace. Funny, huh?

Watch. Do you remember all the parties and family gatherings you have participated in over the last several years? What was common at those parties? You either complain about yourself, your life, your relationship or your work. Or maybe you have been on the listening end of someone else's complaints about themselves, their family, their relationship or what they do. Hey, don't judge. You do that, too. You also listen to others who do it. It is so transparent for you that you cannot remember that you have done it! This concept to us is like water to a fish or air to a bird. We cannot see it for ourselves. Sometimes we even complain about others complaining! We just won't recognize it.

Imagine if you told the truth about yourself exactly the way you relate to yourself from your review of your compliant and criticism. Same thing about the way you see others and your work. It would sound exactly the way you practiced that introduction on the last page. We are "pretending" at who we are. We are pretending about and covering up how we see others and what we do. Look at your resume. Look at any resume you ever received from anybody. What is common within all of them? Everyone says that they are a "people person" or "they are communicative" or "they are a good listener" or "a trouble shooter." Really? Then why within the first two months of their employment do they have problems with their co-workers or management? Or why within the first two weeks do they get into office gossip and politics, and why do they become part of the problem? When you interviewed them for the job they looked so happy and so appreciative for the opportunity, but after the first quarter they are not happy and they are pretty resentful! What happened? They lied in their resume, pretending to be someone they are not! Exactly like the person who interviewed them, huh?

Can you imagine if they were to tell the truth? It would sound something like:

"Hi, my name is Mike! I am lazy, I absolutely love to sleep in and I will be late to work frequently. By the way, I don't like when people tell me what to do, and I don't care for deadlines. Would you please hire me?"

Or the manager who interviews Mike says:

"Hello, I'm Jack, the manager of your department. I think you are an idiot. I am jealous of your higher education, and I am going to love pushing you around and pay you less than what you really deserve! By the way, I will ask you to work overtime and I then act like I don't know you did that! Okay?"

Or imagine a first blind date, a man and a woman. This person actually tells the truth about who he or she is. It might sound like this:

"Hi, I'm Susan. I am ugly. You look pretty unsafe and I'm freaking out! Before I forget, I want to get married soon, have four kids and stay home to care for them. I have $50,000 in debt, too."

The guy might say:

"Hello, I'm Richard. I am insecure. I think you're fat. I am absolutely unfulfilled in my life and totally hate the people I work for. I hate kids, too. I love gambling, and I drink pretty regularly."

How fast do you think these two people will run for the exit door? Can you just picture that interview!? How refreshing, like a breath of fresh air. But in reality, we would not speak like that, but for sure we are projecting it out there in the universe. We complain about everything under the sun, and we even think our complaints sound good and make us more interesting! We love to sound like the victim. We love to become a victim of the circumstances and blame others for what happened to us.

For the record, I am not saying everyone is like that, but I can tell you with confidence that a majority of people act like this. I can also tell you that even people who are working on themselves and participating in transformation work for years still complain and criticize themselves, but in some other ways. They complain in a very transformed way, very subtle. They make it sound very "Zen-like." I am also not suggesting that people are going to job interviews and lying; they just are not telling the truth!

This way of being is so deep within us that it takes over our passions, our dreams and our productivity. That is the reason I call it a "Conspiracy for Suffering." We do our best to get people to agree with us on how messed up we are, and we go out of our way to make sure that people don't understand how intelligent we are! If they get how smart we are we would have to be responsible for our power, and they might ask us to play bigger! Then what? We would have to play bigger and be more productive, be more detailed, and we would have to get what we want! Then we become that idiot who made ourselves wrong for so many years and caused so many upsets in our own lives, and we have to face the reality of what we have done. So, we pick the easy way out. We keep complaining and playing "small" in our lives. That way, others will not look at us as powerful, smart or productive. We think the pretending is easier, but we are wrong.

It is always easier to talk about who we are versus *being* who we are. Who you are is not your home, your checkbook, your car, nor the people you associate with. Who you are is your passion, your vision and your dreams.

Who you are, what you do and the way you do it depends on who you are for yourself and your point of view of life. Keep relating to yourself as the power and possibility that you can and will generate. Don't forget that you are the only person who is living your life, AND you are only person who creates your world!

How do you see the world around you?

Now that you get how your criticisms of yourself, others and what you do are affecting you, you can also see that you have created a particular WORLD around you that is not supporting your passion and dreams.

When I talk about a world, I am not talking about the world as a planet. I am talking about an environment, a space, a created and invented space, or world that you have created so you could continue complaining and eventually not be responsible for the quality of your life, or your communication and the relationships that you could have!

Let's look at this invented and created world of yours:

Safe or Dangerous

Is this world safe, or have you created an unsafe and dangerous world for yourself? Do you relate to the space around you as safe or unsafe?

Responsible or "It is not my fault"

Do you relate to your life and the world you have created as your being responsible for the results of your life, or are you blaming other people or other circumstances for the results of your life?

Full of Joy or "Have to make it"

Do you enjoy the world you created, or do you have to make it in this world of yours? Do you wake up to a world of joy, or do you wake up in a world of suffering?

Contribution or "They owe me"

Have you built a world in which you can contribute to others and others are a contribution to you? Or have you created a world in which others owe you something because you are here?

"I love what I have" or "It is not fair"

Do you live in a world in which you love to live, you love what you do and you absolutely enjoy what you have? Or, in your world, are things or others not fair?

Accountable or "They don't know my sorrow"

Are you accountable for what you want and you are getting what you want in your world? Or do you complain that nobody knows what kind of life and trials you have gone through?

Possibility or Resignation

Finally, have you created and invented a world for yourself that is full of possibilities, joy and opportunities? Or have you built a world in which nothing is possible, nobody is good enough, no one understands you, and where you are the victim?

Do you wake up in this world you created where anything is possible and do you plan your day, your month, your year because you know you are the only one who is responsible for creating this world every day? Or do you wake up just because you didn't die last night? Are you waking up to "What am I going to do now? It is hard, it is not fair, I am alone and nobody loves me?" or are you waking up to "What I am going to do now? What am I going to build to bring me one step closer to my dream? Who am I going to love today? How I am going to contribute to others around me today?"

The way I criticize the world I have created for myself is:

Now write down your answer in *Line D* for now. Tell the truth and let it be. Your chief/main criticism of yourself, others and what you do have created a particular world around you. What is that world?

D

I promise that if you tell the truth and are honest and authentic with yourself, you will see there is an absolute relevancy between the world you have created around you and your results in your life. If you are in the world of "It is not my fault," you can see why your relationships are not working and you are always in a fight with others! If you have created a world of "This is not fair," you are always unhappy, unsatisfied, and you are not content with anything. If you created a world of "danger" you will not have fun, you are not enjoying others, you always have your shield up, you will always be suspicious, and you don't trust people because it is dangerous. That viewpoint affects the joy, happiness and fulfillment in your life.

You and I cause our own suffering; we cause our own sorrows and pain! We cause our own lack of productivity, and we cause our own unhappiness by continuing to entertain these complaints and criticisms. Remember this … suffering is optional, and you have choices! You were not born with suffering, nor with smallness, nor with pain; you have added all these to your life by continuing to look at how you can complain about something. Oh, yes, I am the closest to myself, so I will start complaining from me first. Then I will complain about my parents, my siblings and my friends. After that, when I am old enough, I will complain about boys and girls, and then about my husband or wife, and right after that I will complain about my work or my business and, finally, I will complain about the world I have created for myself. In the end, "It is not my fault!" Is this right?

Do you want to be happy? Stop complaining!
Do you want to be effective? Stop complaining!
Do you want to be successful? Stop complaining!
Do you want to be fulfilled? Stop complaining!
Do you want to enjoy your life to the end? STOP COMPLAINING!

Get it? STOP, STOP, STOP complaining and take responsibility for your life.

Make a Choice

We become what we repeatedly do. We can choose excellence as a way of being, and practice it as a way of living. If we do, it becomes a habit. However, we choose complaining as a way of being and way of living. Stop complaining and you will have time and energy for anything!

Get rid of people in your life who complain and listen to your complaints. They are not your friends. Friends are those who do not listen to your complaints and your small talk. Friends kick you into gear to go after what you want and support you in accomplishing your dreams. I have the

privilege of having true friends and a life partner who believe in me and
hold me to account for what I say I will do. They don't listen to my
whining and complaints about how hard it is to do what I do with my
broken English and how hard it is to build a successful business when you
are a foreigner or any other reasons I can find to complain about myself,
others and what I do!

I had people around me who complained about everything and everyone. I
know one of those people for whom no one and nothing could make her
happy. She changed five offices in five different locations in one company
because the manager was "not fair, jealous, and not understanding her."
Five in a row! Five within six to seven years! Went from Los Angeles to
Irvine, California, to Albuquerque, New Mexico to Reno, Nevada and then
it was on to Boston, Massachusetts. All these moves happened back to
back, but each time I asked her to look at the problem, she brought it to my
attention that the problem is not her but rather her manager. Finally I told
her, "Sweetheart, I think that manager in Los Angeles keeps following
you, and keeps quitting her job to keep bugging you!" This is very good
example of someone who is creating her own world to be a certain way,
and she keeps suffering in that created world. No manager will ever show
up as understanding and fair. However, the person who suffers most is her.
I call this phenomenon "drinking poison and wishing for others to die."

We walk around saying "It should be this way" or "It should not be that
way" or we say "They should be this way" or "They should not be that
way." Look, *should and shouldn't* is all over everything and everyone. We
start from ourselves, and apply it to everyone and everything. What do we
get from doing that to ourselves and others? We get to justify our lack of

happiness and satisfaction! I call it, "We are *shielding* all over ourselves!" There is nothing in these complaints, but they are keeping us away from having a life we love. I am not saying don't go after what you want and what you dream about; just don't complain about the process. Deal with the issues in the way they are or are not. Deal with them, resolve them and move in a forward direction.

I put everything we talked about into a display **Figure "F,"** so you can see all of it together to help you to understand the relevancy.

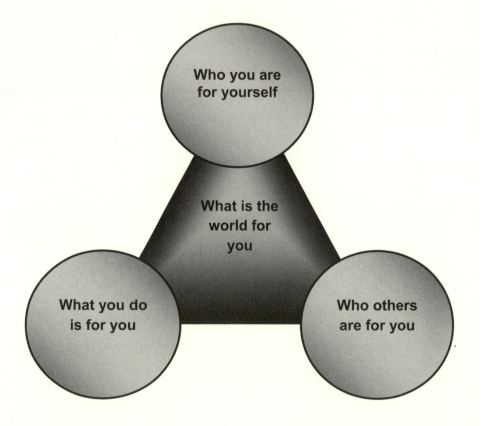

"Figure F"

As you can see, you and I have created this world for ourselves. We have invented this to protect ourselves, and then we forgot that we have done that and we start blaming others for our suffering! We are like a liar who forgot that he lied to himself. As a result, we continue to suffer and to cause our own suffering.

There is an old Persian story that I am reminded of:

A man went to the corner bakery to buy fresh bread for his breakfast (in the old days bakers started baking in the early morning and you could smell the fresh bread several blocks away.) Anyway, he went to the bakery and saw that it was crowded. It would take him a long time to get his bread. So, he became wise and came up with this idea to lie to people. He shouted, "People, the other bakery on the other corner is giving away fresh bread for free!" In no time, everyone rushed to the other corner to get their fresh and free bread. At this time, the smart guy went to the empty counter and asked for bread, but suddenly he thought, "Why should I buy my bread here when I can get free bread in the other bakery!!?"

These silly stories, as stupid as it sounds, represents how we lie to ourselves and believe what we say, and how after awhile we forget that we are the ones who made the stories up! Look at our life. Can you see where you have lied to yourself about your abilities? Where have you lied about your power and your intelligence? Where have you made up something about your beauty? When and where have you set your life up to be small? And, finally, how did you create a world of complaints and criticism around yourself and your life? When you answer these questions, you will see how you have created a conspiracy for suffering!

This conspiracy has held you back from being EFFECTIVE in producing results in your work, your finances and your health. The conspiracy makes you ineffective in your communications with others and people who you care about and who care about you. It makes you become ineffective in your relationships; in your relationship to yourself, in your relationship to others, and in relationship to what you do.

This conspiracy keeps you away from being PRODUCTIVE in your business, your career or your job. At the same time, it keeps you from being productive in your home and your hobbies, and life, in general.

Your *conspiracy for suffering* will take away your PEACE OF MIND in relationship to yourself, in relationship to others and in relationship to life itself.

You can look at the next display **Figure "G,"** and as a reminder, see how your world that you have created is holding back your effectiveness, productivity and peace of mind.

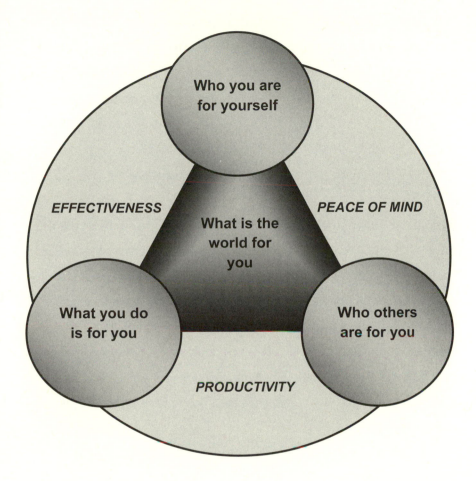

Figure "G"

Fall in Love with Life

You can fall in love with life again and start living it full out just like you used to in a time when you didn't care about what others thought of you. Like when you didn't care about what time it was, or how tired you were, or how hot or cold the weather was. As Norman Cousins said:

Death is not the greatest loss in life.
The greatest loss is what dies inside us while we live.

Do you remember how old you were when you felt free to live your life fully? Yes, you were younger and had less concerns, but then you became "mature." Who said getting older and getting more mature equals being dead? There is a child within all of us; there is a 10-year-old girl and a 12-year-old boy within all of us that will keep us alive! Let that child inside you inspire you and keep you alive. Don't allow him or her to dominate you, lie about you and complain about what you do. Just let him or her play with you, make you laugh, and cause you to become more playful and more creative.

You and I need to get back to the life we had before we started lying to ourselves. I want you to answer these following questions with 100 percent honesty and complete authenticity. You are answering these for yourself, and you better tell the truth. It is you who you are lying to if you don't answer honestly. And it is you who you hurt. This is the intimacy that you and I are building between us buy building trust that you are following the coaching I give you. Go through all these questions and give the answers to your best ability. Stay away from "I don't know" or "these questions are hard." Just get into them and write your answers in a simple language in simple sentences, and stay away from over analyzing and over intelligent answers! Also, stay away from psychology and self-therapy; look into your heart and soul, and say it the way you feel it. I have added a few explanations and give you a little coaching to direct your thinking to get the most of these questions. You need your notes and answers to these questions to complete your process in the end to get the most benefit out of this book.

1. The ways I have criticized myself, others, what I do and the world I have created are:

This could simply be what you wrote in your Lines A, B, C and D.

_____

_____

_____

_____

2. What I am gaining by holding on to these criticisms are:

As I have said in previous chapters, there is a gain and a prize in what you are doing. You are getting some payoff by holding onto these criticisms and complaints. What are they? The gain or the prize is not necessarily a good thing! Your being an irresponsible person in your life is a gain or payoff. If you are irresponsible you are not to blame; someone else is there to blame! Right?

_____

_____

_____

3. My excuses and reasons for holding on to these criticisms have been:

You are an adult, an intelligent and mature person, right? Why have you not let go of these complaints and criticisms sooner and ended your suffering earlier in life? If you notice, you continue to use excuses, reasoning or justifications to hold on to them longer! What are they?

_____

_____

_____

4. Where these excuses and reasons came from is:

Where, how and from who have you learned to use these reasons, explanations and justifications for holding on to your sufferings and not letting them go?

_____

_____

_____

5. What I am losing by these criticisms is:

The other side of gaining is losing! For any payoff there is a cost. What is this nonsense, drama and suffering you made up costing you?

_____

_____

_____

6. What I realized about myself is:

_____

_____

_____

7. **The changes I am making in myself and my life to have a great relationship to myself, others and what I do are:**

_____

_____

_____

8. **What I promise myself is:**

_____

_____

_____

9. **What I am willing to do to keep my promise is:**

_____

_____

_____

10. The people with whom I will discuss this are:

_____

_____

_____

You have done an incredible job so far! Good for you. I am very proud of you or anybody else, for that matter, which is brave enough to go through this hardcore digging to realize insights about him/her. We are getting to a point now where you can recognize how you think about yourself and your life. You can see by now how you have created your _own_ life. Stay with the process, because there is a great light at the end of this dark tunnel!

CHAPTER SIX

OWN YOUR LIFE RESULTS

INSPIRATION VERSUS DESPERATION

There is a certain solid peace within when you know
who you are, love who you are,
and can be whole and complete about it.

Are you happy, satisfied and fulfilled in what you do for a living, or are you just doing it?

Are you living your life with absolute freedom to be with yourself and your relationships with others or do you have high expectations for yourself, others and life itself that you end up in constant struggle against your unfulfilled expectations and pain that will be caused due to that?

What do you expect of yourself? What do you expect of others? If you notice, in most cases, what you get is very close with what you expect to get. You almost never earn more than you expect to earn, and you will rarely earn less. If you get present to it, and stop whining and nagging, you will notice that other people usually deal with you the way you expect them to. This is an amazing phenomenon. In the world of transformation it is being called the "Law of Attraction." So many great writers and philosophers have worked with and around this powerful distinction and tried to explain it, or make it black and white, so everyone can easily understand it. However, it is one of those things that are out there without any clear-cut explanations and facts. It is one of the ways that the universe works and produces results; by lining up actions with intentionality and putting them on the road of purpose which gets you to the end result that will be the fulfillment of your vision in life.

Improving Your Expectations

To improve your results, first improve your expectations of yourself, others and life itself. When you truly expect to earn more money, you naturally find a way to do so, by lining up your intentions and actions and becoming purposeful in your day to day living and production. When you respect others enough to expect the best of them, they will come through with a stellar performance, because you will expect that from them. They even become happier and more productive, because you hold a very healthy space for them. That means they can produce in that environment. We touched on this phenomenon in the last chapter. You are creating your world by entertaining and causing the way you are relating to yourself, others and what you do. It is this combination that determines your effectiveness, productivity and peace of mind in your life as well as the lives of the people around you. In turn, this directly effects what you do and how you do it.

Base your expectations not on what has happened in the past, your unpleasant experiences, your heartbreaking and painful relationships or your failures in some projects. Rather, let your expectations be guided by what you desire for the future, based on the vision you have invented and created, based on what you are designing and what you are expecting to happen because you said so. Set your expectations free of the artificial limits imposed by others, society, media or previous disappointments in your life or your profession. You have every reason to expect the very best for the future. When you do, you will most certainly find a way to make it happen. The key to this way of **being** is to not try to "make it" or to be like the other guy.

Nothing is the indication of a wasted life more than going through life just to make it, just to overcome some expectations you have of yourself or others, or making some statistics to prove "we are enough." It seems as though everyone in the world is trying to "make it," trying to become someone and/or something worthy of others' approval. As you can see in the last several chapters, our internal conversations and inner chatter are designed to make us not be enough and not be worthy. I know you might say "but not me ... I am a positive thinker." Well, good for you. You might be thinking positive in the moment that you are thinking positive, but in the moment that you have high expectations of yourself or others or about life itself, and those expectations are not fulfilled you are upset, angry and resentful. Suddenly, positive thinking is out the door and is gone.

One of the expectations we have from life is for it to be easier and go smoother. Sometimes we don't even know we are doing that. Smoother compared with what? But we still want our life to be smooth, and in most cases it is not. We want our life to present the way we dream it, almost with no effort. We want our relationships to be amazing without effort; we want our finances to be secure without hard work and/or without hard effort. I can tell you this much ... nothing can match the joy and satisfaction that comes from sustained and effective effort that we can put in everyday activities to fulfill our journey and accomplish our intentions. Our goals and results will be the byproduct of our effort to fulfill our vision; we have to accomplish our intentions and fulfill our purpose, not the purpose that is put upon us via others expectations of us or what we thing "it should be" but rather the one that makes our heart and soul sing.

Obtaining the Desire to Make a Difference

Every person, at some level, has a desire to make a difference in his/her own life as well as in others' lives, like getting things done, making things happen, completing a project and keeping promises to ourselves and others. Creating positive value through effort is a powerful and proven way to make that difference. Yet all too often we go out of our way to seek comfort and convenience, avoiding as much effort as possible to get things done, keep promises and complete deadlines. We make the tragic assumption that "the good life" or "happy life" is defined by an absence of effort and hardship of working hard and/or devoting life to a purpose, when in fact the opposite is true and meaningful. There is nothing emptier than a life committed and devoted to leisure, being comfortable and being relaxed all the time.

Don't get me wrong. There is nothing wrong with vacationing, having fun and relaxing, but after you have put in your hard effort to fulfill what you know needs to be accomplished in that time – that could be a month, three months or a year to complete your purpose and fulfill your vision of your life. Fill your days with honest and effective effort in whatever you do, either for yourself or for others, either in your own business or just for the heck of it, for everybody else you encounter in life. Make a difference in a positive way and your rewards will be great. You will experience the abundance of joy that comes from making things happen and getting things done. That said, we have to look at why we are not completely happy and satisfied with the way we work and produce results in life now.

In my career, I see plenty of successful people who are not happy with where they are in life. They have so many qualities that are suppressed under all the "looking good," "keeping up with Jones's" and "having their game face on" that they didn't even recognize themselves anymore.

I've seen them not enjoying their success because it came with a big cost. They made money, became famous, bought bigger houses, fancier cars and spent more time doing nothing because they thought it would make them happy. I am not suggesting making money and having a nice house or car is not good. Actually, if that makes you really happy you should go for it, but see to it that you do it while pursuing what you are passionate about and doing what makes your heart and soul sing!

In this chapter, we look at the question of whether you are moving through life because you "have to" or because you "love to." Are you inspired by who you have become, or are you desperate to become the real you and break through all these barriers you have put around yourself to protect you?

We will go through a series of questions to force you look at different areas of your life and the thoughts and decisions that made you who you are today.

Please complete the questions in the following section to the best of your ability. Look deep and come from a place of your commitment to learn something about yourself that has been hidden within you for years. This way of BEING that is hidden is that way of being that creates the real you. All the other ways you have built around you are those which you made up to protect the real you, maybe because you don't want to be known as someone who operates differently.

Let's get to work. Remember I am the coach and you are the coachee, and we are working together to achieve something.

What are your top five personal accomplishments in your life?

(Just list what you would call your personal accomplishments in life. Something you worked hard to achieve … something you worked long on and proved that you could do it. This could be moving to another state or country and making a good life. It could be finishing school, college or a university. It could be completing a project that was really hard. It could be saving your marriage or maintaining a great relationship for a long time. It could be your going through a tough career or career transition.)

This is where you want to be good to yourself and acknowledge your accomplishments instead jotting answers down because they might not be as good as the other guy's. Be generous and let yourself be acknowledged for your life. If I ask you what is wrong with you, you can write ten pages, but if I ask you what is so great about you, you have difficulty listing out your best qualities. Don't make yourself wrong or evaluate yourself if you cannot come up with five. Come up with two or three; we are not here to judge and evaluate. We are here to tell the story of your life the way it is and the way it is not. Same thing applies to the next question also.

1._____

2._____

3._____

4._____

5._____

What are your top five professional accomplishments in your business/career/job?

(Same as the first question but with an emphasis on your professional aspects of your life, this question is in regard to the things you do for living. Projects, deadlines, moving up in your company or a business you have successfully built or ideas that you brought to reality.)

1._____

2._____

3._____

4._____

5._____

What are the top two or three characteristics that your friends and colleagues would say reflect who you are and how you operate in life and business?

(If I ask ten of your friends, family or colleagues about your character or the way they describe your characteristics, what would their answers be? How do they see you? How are you known among friends and family? For example, do they see you as a hard worker, honest, charming, outgoing or shy, reserved, a Lone Ranger or untrusting? I am not necessarily looking for something positive or negative, good or bad, just the way you know that they know you to be. Tell the truth and don't hide anything. If you want to get the best value from this process it is necessary for you to write it down exactly the way you think people see you, not the way you want it to be or wish it to be seen.)

1._____

2._____

3._____

Here is a little insight into me. People see me as **charming, direct** or sometimes **funny**. If you ask ten of my friends, family or people around me to describe three of my characteristics, at least seven of them will say charming, funny and direct. Obviously, there are more or they would say other characteristics also, but these three will be in most of their answers. Later, I will tell you how I developed these characteristics. Now let's move on to the next question.

What are the top two or three characteristics that allow you to accomplish your intentions?

(Look at this as when you are facing hardship, problems and/or clear intention to achieve something or resolve pressing issues. What characteristics would you take on in those moments? They might not be like anything your friends and family know you to be, but it would show itself on the surface when it is necessary to deliver results or push through hard times. Look at the last time you pushed yourself to get things done or "get what you want." These characteristics are not necessarily what you would call positive. Sometimes we get what we want by lying or cheating. You know exactly what I am talking about, so stop playing innocent.)

1._____

2._____

3._____

Here are my answers for this question. **Hardworking, persistence** or sometimes **being tough**. Believe me, sometimes I don't want to work hard or be persistent but I can't help it. That is the way I am, good or bad, that is the way I know I can produce results and accomplish my intentions. Sometimes they are not good intentions, or sometimes they are. Results of what you want to have, do or accomplish are not necessarily just one way, good or bad only. They are a combination.

In my last marriage I stayed far longer than anyone else would say I should have stayed or they would put up with in that situation (so they said), but I stayed because I don't give up. I am persistent. I want you to see these characteristics as helping you accomplish your intentions or get what you want on one side and on the other side see how they keep you in some situations or environments that you don't want to be in or that you know aren't of benefit to you (but you just can't help staying because that is the way you are wired). You are a persistent and hard working person and you stick with a job that is not satisfying or with a boss who is not appreciative but you don't move on because you are "persistent" and "a hard worker" or you "don't give up" you can just imagine how miserable you are and will continue to be. Same thing goes for a relationship that you know is not for you, but you are not moving on or you are not telling the truth because you want to be that "hard worker" and that "never-give-up" person. On one hand you like it to be that way and on the other hand you hate to be that way, and you even complain about it with your friends, blaming yourself for being that way. However, when the next day arrives, nothing has changed. In this case, persistence is not a good thing.

Getting Unstuck

In the last chapter we covered conspiracy for smallness, barriers in self-expression and personal effectiveness. We talked about the complaints and criticisms that have made our lives hard and unproductive. We came to see that there is a close connection between complaints and the characteristics that allow you to achieve and accomplish things in life. You are a hard worker but at the same time you might complain about the hard work you do. I am persistent and don't quit easily, but I was complaining that my marriage was horrible and I was not happy because my wife was not the way I wanted her to be. Can you see the irony? It is like a vicious circle. You are in it and you want out but the only way you know how to get out is the exact way you don't want to **be** and it has caused you to stay in the vicious circle. This is one more example of the power of **being** and how our own way of being is transparent to ourselves.

In my last marriage we were together for five years. Two of those years we were married; before that we lived together for three. During these five years she left our relationship five times, an average of once a year. It is funny to look at the situation now, but it was not funny at the time. In fact, it was very painful and embarrassing, because I had expectations of myself to keep this relationship together.

For the record, I am not claiming that I am easy to be with and good either, I have shortcomings and issues that added to the issues at hand during the relationship, but the point to make is that I did not learn from her continuously leaving the relationship. It took several friends smacking me upside the head to get the message to let go. My wife at that time came back each time, apologizing and making new promises to never leave again. She promised to make things work, but within six to eight months after she returned each time, it was the same way as before and she left. Because I was a "hard-working, persistent, never-give-up" kind of guy, I was right back in the mess, doing the same thing that did not work before, time and time again. The end result was the same. I know what you are thinking. This reminds me of the following quote from Albert Einstein which has also been attributed to Benjamin Franklin.

The definition of insanity is doing the same thing over and over again, expecting different results.

I have to tell you the following short story from book of *Zen* to prove a point.

A monk was walking down the road. When he reached a small village he saw the people of the village gathered around a big pond shouting toward the middle of the lake, "Let go, let go!"

The monk looked in the direction of the shouting he saw a woman in middle of that big and deep pond drowning. She was going down and coming up. She was taking in water and struggling for her life, trying to keep herself above the water. She was holding onto a very big rock with both arms and would not let go. The monk shouted hard, "Let go of the rock!" again and again. Let go of the rock. It will kill you ... it will drown you! Let go of the rock!"

To everyone's surprise, the woman shouted back, "I can't! I can't!"
The monk and the people shouted back to the drowning woman who was still holding onto the big rock, "Why not?"

The woman yelled back, "It is mine!"

I was holding on to that mental and psychologically abusive marriage to be right about "I won't give up" and "I am persistent." At the same time it was killing me. If you look into yourself you will see where and how you hold onto things, situations, people or even jobs that are drowning you. If you explore the situation further, you may find that you have not let go of "the rock," because it is the only way you know how to be and the only way you know how to produce results. I am guilty of doing that in some jobs. I did not quit when I was miserable because that is "not who I am." I was proud of myself for not quitting, but suffered and blamed the company for my miserable way of being. Same way in my last marriage; I was staying there but blaming her. I felt happy that I was the hero and the one who wasn't giving up. I was sticking to my guns. In truth, we were both miserable. I am sure she was in the same cycle of thinking, trying to get it together but at the same time not being honest with herself.

You might ask now "how do I get out of this circle"? We will get to it soon, I promise. For now, keep working.

The point to get at this time is that you have developed some characteristics that caused you to fulfill your intentions and get things done or complete projects though these characteristics don't really represent who you are. They are characteristics based on decisions you made when you were younger, either on your own or by observing others. For you to get yourself out of this circle of torment you have to understand how you came to develop these characteristics and ways of being. Only then can you become responsible for your rules in placing these blocks in your own way without blame and without pointing fingers.

I want you to see how you have developed these characteristics that allowed you to accomplish and produce results in your life or business. Here I use some examples from my own life so you can see what I am talking about. At the same time, I want you to work through this process in the following format. Write the characteristics down, and then work on when each came about, where it was developed and who was there. Make it as real and as detailed possible. How did you make these decisions? Go back as far as you can to your childhood, to the time you made some life-changing decisions. This is one of those moments that you need to give up "knowing" and just look back to remember those incidences and discover what happened.

When you get one of them done and feel comfortable that you understand the process, repeat the practice for one or two more of your characteristics until you really get to the way you have developed those characteristics.

Please use the following format:

When, where and how did you build these characteristics?

Characteristic: _____

> A. When?
>
> _____
>
> _____
>
> B. Where?
>
> _____
>
> _____
>
> C. How?
>
> _____
>
> _____

I built characteristics that my friends and family recognized in me as being **charming, direct** and **funny**. At the same time, I built other characteristics that allowed me, assisted me and empowered me to accomplish my goals, produce results and fulfilled my intentions, for example, **hard working, persistent** and **tough.**

The first set started when I was 6 or 7 years old (I talked about this incident in the last chapter) and my father in front of family and friends said that my older brother Behzad is smart and I made it mean that I am not. Therefore, I had to prove that I am good for something, because I am not smart, but I could make others laugh; that was much easier than being smart (in the mind of a 6-year-old). I became charming and funny. I watched my father and my uncle being direct and no nonsense kind of people, and when you put that side by side with integrity and the hardworking characteristics they had, they gained respect in the community for the way they were.

I picked being charming and funny for not being smart and direct like my dad and uncle because it was the RIGHT way of being. As you can see, it was not my direct choice, it was not a bad choice, but it was not my choice. It was right in front of me to be chosen, given being SMART was out of question.

When I was a teenager and then a young man, I learned that my family kept acknowledging me for being a hard worker and being persistent in whatever I was doing. It felt good to be known as someone like that.

How I became TOUGH is a funny story. It is funny once you understand what really happened to get me there and realize the snap decisions we all make based on moments in our lives that can form who we are. Sometimes it's very sad to see how many years of our lives were spent NOT BEING something or someone. It is much easier to own who we really are compared to trying to be that person we have pretended to be.

Getting back to the story of me becoming tough, I was 12 years old, attending a private school with my brother and our friends. Some of us, including me, were part of dance group for a school party. My brother and I were part of a Brazilian Dance group and even had costumes. (My mother still has pictures from those golden days.) One day, I was walking from home to go to the dance practice in my prep school uniform; black shorts, white shirt, black jacket and a black Spanish style bow tie. Check it out! It was so hot as I walked down the street with my Brazilian Dance costume on a hanger on my back. Get the picture? I was walking on top of the clouds, being cute and happy. Suddenly, two kids, approximately my own age, on their bicycles pull over and cut me off. By looking at their clothing and their overall look they were not from my neighborhood. They must be from a poor Arab-populated village a couple miles away from our area, which was a higher rank staff of the National Iranian Oil Company.

To make the story short, they called me a sissy boy, preppy boy and other names. They beat me up, pushed me around and took my dance costume. Yes, I came home with my sad and long face to complain to my mother. At that time my cousin Hedayat was on mandatory two-year service in Iran Army and he was at our house during this short time off from the base. He was the tough one in the family and the one who was always in trouble because he would not take crap from anyone, the rebel type. He was in his uniform, handsome and so strong. He saw me and asked me what happened. And I told him the story while I was feeling sorry for myself as the poor victim of the event. He slaps me across my face and said, "How did you let them kick your ass and take your stuff away? Get yourself together," as he dragged me to the back yard. He taught me how to fist fight, but not just any fist fighting; he taught me street fighting, which as way tougher, nastier and there is no fairness to it. He taught me how to throw the first punch and take over the fight by being proactive; being offensive versus defensive and I liked it. I liked it very much. I liked the power, winning and being the one who stood tall and not being the one down on the floor.

Two weeks later, walking down the same road on my way to dance class, I was stopped by the same two boys. What do you think happened? I threw the first punch, and when I stopped swinging both boys were on the floor crying. They ran away! I liked the experience and definitely liked the excitement of feeling of being powerful. I became the one who always threw the first punch and won the fight. I began playing tennis, working out and lifting weights, so I could get stronger and have a more forceful punch. I became the tough guy nobody wanted to mess with. To this day, my high school buddies talk about my fights, and we laugh about them. Those feelings lead me to serve my country. I was very good at Army duties and at training and. I was so tough that I was recognized by my leaders and selected for special services training. I was proud to be a part of the Army, and it all started from failing to fight and the experience of being weak, followed by my decision to never be weak again.

Meanwhile, I got farther and farther away from that little boy who wanted to dance and play. That little boy wanted to draw, paint, dance and be happy. Tough guys who are hard workers who don't paint and don't dance. They should do tough stuff, like fight, play sports and hang out with other tough guys, right? That was when I started hiding my drawings and paintings, and I tried not to express myself too much. I loved poetry, both modern and ancient. I read poetry in secret and didn't share it with my friends, because it was not cool. I was the tough one, after all.

Now, look into yourself and see how, when and where you made life-altering decisions about who you are and or who you think you should be. Use this format, and be honest and truthful to yourself. Trust yourself and keep writing in your notebook.

Being tough, working hard, and being persistent, charming and funny made me successful and helped me achieve my goals. People respect me for it, friends like to be around me because of it, and they are the same good characteristics that to this day that make me who I am. I am proud of these character traits, but they are not ALL that make me ME. There is more to ME and who I am than just these character traits.

Have this concept in your mind as we follow the rest of this chapter and you will see where we are going so you can make more sense of this discovery process.

What was the common thread throughout all of these events?

The development of my strong character traits came about to protect me from getting hurt. Becoming tough, becoming the hard worker and even becoming the funny one protect me to this day. Years later, I recaptured my passion and interest in art, dance, poetry and writing, which allowed me to become the person I truly am today, that same little sensitive boy I once was who loved to express himself in artistic ways.

The common thread in all the events that brought me to the point of making the decisions about how I felt I had to be was *THREAT*... the feeling of being threatened by fear of "who you are is not enough for what is needed at that moment." It could be any situation or any event. If you look around and are honest with yourself you will see that all the major decisions you made about yourself began from "not being some other way." I am dumb, so I become charming; I am slow so I become a hard worker; I am weak so I will become tough. Can you see it? Especially when you are not happy with what you do and how you are because the whole thing is not authentic and does not have a strong foundation. That's because it is not who you really are. You might continue being the way you have always been but with the understanding of what caused you to become that way, an understanding of having a clear and free choice from any interpretations to BE who you really are without holding back from your absolute self-expression. Maybe this is the reason some people choose not to do what they do because they are inspired by it. Instead, they do it because they are desperate to do something.

What decisions did you make about yourself, others and life during the development of these characteristics?

The very first decision we make just as I made was "I am a failure" or "I can't do this" or "I am not smart" or any other disempowering decision that we have made about ourselves. Whatever we do after that means we have to get back to that moment of innocence and be our true selves again.

We can see this phenomenon in our children's eyes; when they are in the process of making those kinds of decisions about themselves, about you and about life itself. We owe it to them to understand this process and the impact our decisions made on ourselves so we are able to distinguish similar decisions for them. Maybe they won't make the mistakes in our decisions that we did.

How do you protect yourself and your results?

I asked you to hold on a concept I was talking about in the last several pages. It is that, in many cases, being the way we have decided to BE had us become successful, make money and be liked. The characteristics we develop may be very good ones that make us produce results or protect ourselves, our loved ones and our results.

In my case, being a hard worker and being persistent made me succeed in life, in my businesses and my projects. Being charming and funny helped me a lot in my presentations and opened doors of possibility with other people, because these characteristics are signs of confidence, of being a people person and being social. Being tough saved my life many times; in my military training, during the tough time of the Iranian revolution, in the time of political upraising in Iran right after the revolution. During the time of the arrests that came right after that, during the war with Iraq and throughout many other incidents, being the way I was saved my life. Not giving up on people and/or a project made me popular and made me a lot of good friends. The point is to not throw these ways of being out the door, because you need them to survive and to make things happen and produce results. But as I said before; these characteristics are not all we are within ourselves… there more out there in regards to who we are. Because for us to be whole and complete we have to learn to be with all of our characteristics; we can't just be with our love. Rather we have to learn to be with our hate also.

The Yin and Yang of Life

You can't love without knowing how to hate. They go together, like Yin and Yang. We love to pretend that all we are is just a good, loving and caring person. We do this by avoiding our own ways of being that made us a whole and complete human being. However, we can't be generous without being stingy, we cannot be happy without being sad, we can't just be loving if we can't be jealous, we cannot be giving without being a taker. When there is good there is always bad, too. When there is good there is evil, when there is light there will be dark, when there is faith there is doubt, too. This is a very deep concept that has been practiced and has been studied by many great philosophers, religions and disciplines over the centuries. You find this concept in any practice that empowers and promotes that being human starts with the love within and that without loving all aspects of yourself you cannot love yourself. Perhaps this is one of the best reasons that we as humans have such a problem stopping wars on this planet.

We kill other people in the name of God. How oxymoronic! We kill other people because they do not believe in our God and because our God is better than theirs. We ask other cultures to obey our God, and when they say no, we kill them. The number of people who are murdered and disappear during religious wars is staggering. Religions motivated by political movements result in jailing, torturing and executing the nonbelievers. Genocide, mass murder and flat out killings throughout history far exceed deaths caused by other reasons, such as illness, natural disasters and accidents. That is a topic for a whole other discussion. However, it makes one think. All those people who have participated in atrocities against supposed nonbelievers in their God or those who are participating in this type of behavior now believe that they are good people who are doing God's work. They feel as though they should be thanked and acknowledged for what they do. You can find them throughout history; you don't have to look far. Look within and you can find it there, too.

I know you are not a criminal or murderer... at least I hope not.... but we kill other people when they are not like us. You have done it. How? By being prejudiced, racist, judgmental, by not giving other people a chance to be themselves, by insisting that how we are is the way to be or to live. Why? Just because we think our way of thinking is the right way to think? And we think of ourselves as good people! Maybe you think this way and yet attend church every Sunday, to Mosque every Friday or to Synagogue every Saturday.

For the record, history is also full of people who believe God put them on this earth to do good for others. They believe in their faith and follow the steps of the prophets who teach them the good in their hearts. These people are still among us and doing God's work every day. You can see the benefits of their work around us. Mother Teresa, Mahatma Gandhi, Archbishop Tutu and Ayatollah Taleghani (of Iran) are some examples of these people.

Open Your Mind

We are human. We make choices and, unfortunately, sometimes the pathways to our choices and the way we view our options are very polluted. I was brought up in a very open minded and educated family; I never thought I was racist. I never saw or heard anything from my parents, my family or even friends as we were growing up that would make me believe they were racist, so I never considered myself a prejudice person … until 1991 when I had my constriction company in Los Angeles. It was then that we landed a new contract for remodeling a house in the West Hollywood area.

Stay with me here, because I want to make a point about killing off others without even knowing you do it and even when you think you are a good person. Let me tell you about my business.

223

The way our business was planned was that my partner got the lead and looked at the project. Between us we designed a proposal and estimate, and then presented it to the customer. If the customer accepted the price and the plan, I went to the person's home to have the contract signed. I also picked up the deposit and so forth. Based on time availability one of us had to manage the project. Okay, back to my story. We received a lead from a satisfied customer about a house in West Hollywood owned by two men. My partner did what he had to do; we estimated the work, planned it, and he presented the proposal. My partner met with the two men several times and they agreed to all the details. Now, it was my turn to go to their home and have them sign the contract, etc. I was the project manager for this job. When I arrived at the men's home I met with the two gentlemen. One wore a suit and tie. He was very professional looking and looked older than the other man, who was wearing shorts and casual shirt. He was clean and very fashionable. In my view, in my world, in my small world I have to add, I just thought two guys had an investment property together and they wanted to fix and flip it for profit, but when I looked around it seemed like they were living in this place. I thought they were just roommates. They asked me if I would like anything to drink and I accepted a glass of water. We talked details. I noticed that the younger man was not getting involved as much as the one with the suit.

To make a long story short, we signed the contract (at least the older man did). He signed the deposit check and handed it to me. Then he asked me if I want to look around the property and all the rooms, given this was a major remodel that would affect the whole house and they had to leave the place until we finished the project. As I walked with him around the house and looked at the rooms, we eventually reached their bedroom. There I saw a picture on the wall, a picture of the two men kissing. I was shocked. Frozen. (Someone should make a comedy movie out of this event! I can laugh at it now, but it was not funny at the time.)

At that moment I could not hear anything but my very loud and nasty inner chatter telling me run! The chatter was saying; "You shook their hands, you drank their water, you have to work for them." I was a wreck, but I kept a straight face, said goodbye and left. As I drove I was very upset and even angry. I decided that I was not going to work with gay people. I did not know that I was avoiding gay people. I just was not aware of the issue and the depth of it, given I was raised in a society in which being gay was a big no-no and nobody was talking about it. Heck, even if they were talking about it, it was mostly to crack jokes, say it is against religion and it is a very bad thing to be or to do. Gay was not in my world, so it was okay with me as long as they are not around me and my family. (That's why I called it my small world!) It was as if I were a fish in the water or a bird in the air. I was the fish and the bird; gay prejudice was the water and the air! The issue was transparent to me.

As soon as I got to the office I threw the contract on the table and I told my partner, "I am not going to work for these people. You have to do it!" He asked why and I explained. He laughed so hard that he almost fell off his chair.

He said, "What? Their money is not good for you?"

I brought to his attention again that "I can't work with gay people."

His response? "Cut the BS and get to work, because this project is yours."
Then he walked away. I was very angry because now I had a contract and
accepted the deposit. I was legally bonded. I ended up transferring the job
to one of my best foremen and one of my best crews to work that job site,
so I didn't have to be there. Clever, huh? (I know you are disgusted by
now ... me, too.) It took us about five months to finish the project before
deadline and exactly the way the plans were designed. It was a very perfect
execution of a very detailed project. Most important, I did not have to visit
the job site. Well done! The job was completed, payments were cleared
and everybody was happy. Meanwhile, I was thinking of myself as a pretty
open-minded person.

The next week, the customers moved back into their beautiful new home,
and I received a fax from them. They acknowledged our company and
specifically me for the way we handled working with the gay and lesbian
community and for getting their job done without any incidences that
would cause any upset with them. They thanked me for my professional
attitude. How do you think that made me feel? Very small. But I pushed it
under the rug like any other upset. Just push it aside and don't touch it and
it will go away! Uh, not! I put it aside; I was bothered by it, because my
conscious was awakened. I could not find anything to be upset about with
those guys; they were good to me, and I wanted to be good to them, but
something was holding me back. I was being *Right* about my Position! It
was the only way I knew to be. In that regard, about that issue, that was the
way it was for me, so I ignored my feelings. The couple sent us referrals,
too. Talk about feeling smaller! I think it was Albert Einstein who said:

Only two things are infinite, the universe and human stupidity, and I'm not
sure about the universe.

Years later, after I changed my career and started leading public programs,
I was back in Los Angeles. One of my participants was a young gay man
who shared with the class about his issues and problems of being gay in
society and the hardship that he felt by being separated, singled out and
being under the gun all the time. I felt his pain, I heard him clear, I know
the pain, I was there myself, maybe not from being gay but being different,
being Iranian, being darker skinned, speaking with an accent. I had to go
through so much crap and deal with so much prejudice myself that I could
actually understand. That was a moment of awakening for me in regard to
my relationship to gays, lesbians and homosexuality itself; it was an
opening to a whole new way of being. We all act as if we are open
minded; like we are not prejudiced. We would like it to be that way but it's
not. That's because we have not owned it yet. We would rather pretend vs.
owning our own crap!

We Must Walk the Talk

There was only one thing for me to do … walk the talk, do what I
preached and be the changes I want to see in the world. I went to the gay
couple whose home my former partner and I had remodeled and I knocked
on the door. They answered with a big question mark in their eyes. I asked
to come in and sit with them. I explained. I came clean and apologized to
them. We sat and laughed. We had wine together and joked. We laughed

like buddies who heard a very funny story. I hugged them, I kissed them goodbye ... and I was *FREE*.

Since then I have friends of all types, some straight, some gay, some white, some black, some are Latino, etc. I am proud to say my friends come from different walks of life, different religions, races, nationalities, genders and sexual orientation. As long as they are up to a bigger game in their lives vs. making other people wrong or judging and evaluating others, I can be friends with them. As long as they are direct with me and let me be the same way with them, we can be friends. As long as they own their humanity and let me be who I am, we are fine.

Now that you understand what I mean more clearly, look into yourself and see if you have killed off people around you. They could be friends or family members who are different from you, think differently, believe differently, do things differently and express themselves differently. After all, who made us the boss of everyone else so we get to tell others how to be?

The freedom of being human is to know you are whole and complete by being all of it – good, bad or ugly. Yes, that is what and who we are. Not bad or good, just human. Transformation is when we own all aspects of our own Being ... then start to alter our ways and our thinking so we can alter our way of being, the hardest thing for us to do.

As Plato, Greek philosopher who, together with his mentor, Socrates, and his student, Aristotle, helped to lay the foundations of western philosophy said;

We can easily forgive a child who is afraid of the dark.

The real tragedy of life is when men are afraid of the light.

We have a choice to use any way of being as we go through life. Yes, we have the choice in every given moment to choose how we will BE, like a tool box full of tools that you carry with at all times to fix problems. Which tools would you use for that particular problem? You will learn that some tools work with some problems and some tools don't work well with that issue. What would you do? You would use the tool that works the best for the situation, right? It will not work.

For a long time, my tool box was full of hammers – hammers of being hard-working, being persistent and being tough. It works for awhile but gets real boring and very ineffective after time. Once I realized the tools in my tool box (the way I deal with problems) weren't working very well, I did some positive thinking work. I painted my hammers pink. I thought if I was thinking positive about how hard I was bringing my hammer down it would make a difference. It didn't. Then I got different sizes of hammers in my box. It took awhile to get it through my head that it didn't matter if they were small or big, long or short, new or old, pink or black. They were all hammers.

Look into yourself and see what kind of approach you are using to resolve issues and problems in your life. Then look and see if they are effective or not. Remember, you can either be *Right* or *Effective*, but you cannot be both at the same time, so pick one. By evaluating the results you have produced in your life you can see if it is time to become who you really are.

Do these characteristics leave you feeling fulfilled and satisfied?

No, they are not! As a matter of fact, they are exhausting, boring and sad.

We want to be ourselves and be true to who we are, but all the heavy loads we put on our own backs is holding us back, because now we have to match up and be up to what we have made ourselves out to be for ourselves as well for others. The facade we built around us, like the image we have created about who we are, which is really far from the reality of who we are, is tiring.

We want to be that boy or girl we really are. We want to play, express ourselves and be happy. Instead, we have to do things, say things and even think certain ways to be a match with the picture we have created about ourselves. In many cases we do anything we can to match with the picture of the "perfect life" or the "perfect person" that different giant corporations or big industries are promoting to us via national media. In the end we are not fulfilled and satisfied, because it will be never enough to be the perfect person and live the perfect life. It seems like we have forgotten that we are perfect the way we are and the way we are not, and that in fact makes us perfect. There is nobody out there like you or me. With over 6.3 billion people on this planet nobody is exactly like you and no one is like me. Nobody sounds like we do, looks like we do, thinks exactly like we do, and nobody feels exactly like we do. That is what makes us very each unique and perfect!

What are you gaining by causing these characteristics to be present so often?

Why do we keep these characteristics ... these roles ... in place and play them every day? There are payoffs, prizes and there is something in it for us. We feel superior to others, the feeling of being somebody who we never thought we could be, hiding the fear, the inadequacy, and the anxiety of having to work hard to be someone matched with the picture of the perfect person! There is the illusion that we can hide who we are for a long time, the illusion of security and self worth. We are working hard to keep these characteristics in place because we think others want to see us this way and we need to be seen, related to and observed as someone like that person we created because we are addicted to that role. We are used to it. We made up the persona, we said it into being and we believed what we said. It's like we sentenced ourselves to years of living a lie.

What are you losing by causing these characteristics to be present so often?

We are losing something by holding onto these make-believe characteristics, the most important one is losing the opportunity to be ourselves and enjoy this one-time chance called "our life." We are losing the chance of being that kid we loved so much; within all of us there is a

12-year-old boy or girl who wants to play, love, be loved and have fun. Let that kid inside you inspire you and move you forward. Don't create some type of person you truly are not that will dominate you and make you do things you don't want to do. We are losing our chance to play and be ourselves by not pursuing our dreams and making something out of ourselves that inspires us. Give yourself permission to be happy, fulfilled and satisfied in life, regardless of the circumstances and obstacles in your life.

If you were not protecting yourself with these characteristics, what would you do instead?

If you were not in protection mode, or your pretending mode, or trying to be someone you really are not; what would you do instead? Would you do what you are currently doing for a living? Would you act like you act now? All together and "perfect"? Would you laugh more often? Would you express your love and appreciation to others more often? Would you dance? Would you start doing things you love to do? Would you play that music instrument you were always dying to learn how to play? Would you dare to play? Would you dare to sing from the bottom of your heart? Would you say what is in your heart, all of it, with holding nothing back? Would you dare fall in love again? Would you dare be YOU again?

Let me give you some examples of my own life in this regard. Take my ability to design programs and be a public speaker, for example. If you had told me many years ago that I would be designing and developing transformational programs and I would be leading them on stage for people in English, I would have said that you were out of your mind. I was just a tough guy who just wanted to play sports, act tough and just do what others were expecting me to do; just make it day to day and survive. I had to be true to myself and let myself expression and passion about enlightenment and transformation get the best of me. I could have just been that desperate guy who would do great construction work or I could be inspired to be myself and dare to act on it.

Follow Your Passion

My music is another example. For years I wanted to play a musical instrument, I wanted to play the saxophone, but I always thought it is very hard and "I am not smart enough" to play such a complicated instrument. I have to be a genius to be able to play this, I thought. I took a challenge from a young participant in one of my programs in San Francisco to make me act on it. She asked me to be myself and do what I was passionate about exactly the way I was asking them to do the same thing. Don't you love those kinds of participants who always challenge the leader? I am grateful for her challenge. I came back home to San Diego and hired a music tutor and got to work. I had to work against my loud and annoying inner chatter that was obnoxious saying, "I can't do this" or "it is so hard." My chatter was loud and not pleasant, especially when I made mistakes and played a wrong note; it sounded like a cat getting hurt. I was a 40-year-old professional and embarrassed, but I knew better. I knew that I could be my embarrassment or I could be my commitment. I knew in that given moment I could be my concern and quit or I could be my passion and desire; I could be desperate to leave or inspired to learn. It was my choice.

My writing and becoming an author is yet another example. After more than 32 years of studying, my interest in learning, and after over 16 years of presenting, designing, developing and leading programs that made a difference in more than tens of thousands of people's lives so far, I decided to get my first book done! Again, you might think I should have known better and should have done this much, much earlier, but I knew it made no difference. Knowing it was not enough to overcome the fear of failing and the fear of making no difference or concern of "who wants to read what you have to say?" The knowledge of what I knew was not enough. What made me finally move into action was getting inspired by being my own vision for my life again and living it: "Life fulfilled, passion, joy and laughter expressed, inspired by people's success, having fun and creating abundance." I knew I had a choice to be inspired by that vision or be desperate to express myself. The choice was clear.

Here is a very important key element. If you noticed, before taking on any of these daring activities, you have to give up something. It is the law of physics; no two objects can be in the same space at the same time. You can't argue with that. For me to be expressed, brave and myself I had to give up being scared, being concerned and give up "what will others think of me?" For me to start leading and presenting programs in English (as my second language, which I had very little idea about before coming to the U.S.). I had to give up the embarrassment to have access to my passion. For me to play saxophone and be able to express my musical expression I had to give up being dumb. I had to give room to my intelligence and my heart and soul. For me to get my first book out, working on it for the last three years and dare to write and express my message I had to give up the inner chatter that said, "I am nobody," "I will fail" or "what I have to say makes no difference."

I hope these examples made some difference for you to look at some areas of your own life and see where you stop being yourself and what stops you from going after what will inspire you.

What are the top two or three real characteristics that make your soul sing and are the source of your happiness and contentment?

1._____

2._____

3._____

If you were not concerned about anything, if you were going to swing out and be yourself, if you would dare to boldly and loudly introduce yourself to the world and say that this is who you are, what would you say? If you are not coming from protecting yourself, if you are not coming from desperately trying to impress others, what would you say about who you are?

Please write your answers in the spaces above. Mine is: passionate, sensitive and loving. That is who I am. I am the possibility of others seeing their excellence and their greatness and that is who I would put in front. I am a passionate, sensitive and loving man, father, program leader, business owner, boss and member of the community who is in love with making a difference in others lives and turning their desperations into inspirations and smiles.

You have to get deep inside yourself and tell the truth about yourself. You have to let yourself get moved by who you are, and remember that you have to give up lots of trash to get to your gold.

Please take time and answer the following questions. If you do not remember the purpose of the questions, go back to chapter three and read my explanations again. Remember, our relationship is coach and coachee; we have worked hard so far to bring you to this point and we are going to invent and create your life vision, maybe for the first time, in the next chapter. It is important that you take time and answer these questions in this chapter and the last several chapters, because they are relevant to each other.

Maybe I can inspire you by a quote from a master in his domain, Galileo Galilei:

> *Nothing can be taught to a man; but it's possible to*
> *help him find the answer within himself.*

Let's get to work and answer the end of the chapter's questions and inquiries.

1. **What do you realize about yourself?**

_____

_____

_____

2. **What are you willing to change or alter?**

_____

_____

_____

3. **What are you promising yourself?**

_____

_____

_____

4.   What are you willing to do to keep that promise?

_____

_____

_____

5.   Who will you discuss this with?

_____

_____

_____

You have done such great work so far. Good for you! We are about to start a very exciting and important chapter in our process that will assist you in gaining access to your *Greatness*, so that you can open the doors to your *Love Within*.

CHAPTER SEVEN

VISION AND VALUES

THE FORCES THAT MAKE THINGS WORK!

Inside you, at this moment, is the power to do things
you never thought possible. Such power becomes apparent
and rises to the surface as you begin to operate consistent
with your values, principles and beliefs.

Let's work together to create your life vision.

During the past several chapters, we dug into and recognized how much your current being is influenced by your past experiences and the decisions you have made about yourself and others. We learned that what you DO is often determined by who you have BEEN and that your decisions can be based on imaginary threats. We looked at how we behave with others when we want to be right about our point of view, or judge others, or make our way of thinking or living the <u>only</u> way.

How ineffective! My way or highway. We are not alone in this stormy, crazy world of "Inner Chatters" It can be a very unfriendly and unforgiving world, a very dark and lonely place, when we choose being right over being effective. Everyone experiences this craziness in some shape or form and some are in it so deep that it is unrecognizable.

There Is Light at the End of the Tunnel

Now let's look for the light at the end of the tunnel of life. We can learn to work with the forces that make things happen, to move us forward and to empower "source" us through the tough times in life. This is the source of who we are, what we love to do, our values and our vision for our lives.

Imagine yourself holding an electrical object in your hand, such as a coffee maker, laptop computer or hair dryer and you are trying to use it. What would you do with the two or three prongs at the end of the power cord? You would connect them to a receptacle on the wall, right? Without the power sourced by electricity, your electrical device cannot function. Even if you have a battery-operated device, you still have to charge it – and for that you must connect to a power source. No electricity, no function, which means it is no use to you. Your device is SOURCED by electricity.

What source is powering your functionality? What is sourcing your choices and actions? Go back and look at your notes. You will see that only things that have sourced you were your past decisions and experiences in life. You made decisions about yourself, about others and about life that were polluted by negative, painful experiences. When you plug yourself into to the receptacle called your PAST, you keep getting the same results that you don't like.

You keep missing the writing on the wall. We worry about what will happen to us and feel nervous about tomorrow or next week, because we let our past experiences determine our future moves. We think we are powerless, because we don't realize we have another option, called "Design your own Future." Consider this quote from George Bernard Shaw, from one of his plays written in 1893:

People are always blaming their circumstances for what they are.
I don't believe in circumstances. The people who get on in this
world are the people who get up and look for the circumstances
they want and if they can't find them, they make them.

There is another source of power we keep missing. It is the receptacle called the FUTURE. In this chapter, we will work on clarifying your VISION for your LIFE.

What is the first step?

Before you can build your future and design your "Life Vision," you have to forgive yourself for mistakes in your past. All your lies, gossip, hidden agendas and, most important, all of your mistakes. Forgive yourself for all the bad decisions you made. Release your heart and soul from the burdens of hate, anger, resentments, regrets, jealousy and sorrow that you have carried for so many years. Forgive yourself for any drugs, alcohol or destructive behaviors. Use the past several chapters to recognize your responsibility in creating those issues, then let them go by forgiving yourself.

Be sure to also forgive yourself for things that were not your fault, like accidents, family drama, violence and other hard and painful events in life. Forgive yourself for any blame or shame you may be carrying. Forgiveness is an act of grace and dignity, to you and to others.

How do we determine our values?

Look at your life in general and write down what you value about your life as a whole. The things you value are what become prominent in your life, so look for where you pay the most attention, where you direct lots of effort and energy, and where you make commitments.

When you value productivity, your work becomes more prominent. When you value serenity, your home becomes more important. When you value your family, you spend more time with them. When you value your faith, you practice it more often. When you value health, you pay more attention to your body. Value your ideas, your time and your money and they become more valuable. It is all in your hands and in your mind.

Value is not determined by a price tag or any other monetary system. The value of anything is the value we give it. What do you value most? What do you want to grow and become abundant in your life? Give more of yourself to the things you value, and they will flourish and become more present in your day-to-day life.

Our values show up in four key areas of our lives:

Personal

Our personal values define us as an individual. They determine how see ourselves and how we behave. For example: integrity, honor and respect.

Social

Our social values define how we relate to other groups of people in our lives, such as those from different races, religions or cultures. They determine how we connect with the communities around us and how we relate to the people with whom we interact most often. For example: fairness, diversity and equality.

Cultural

Our cultural values define how we relate to others in the world. They guide our behaviors around customs and traditions and determine how we relate to people with similar backgrounds. For example: family, tradition and celebration.

Professional

Our professional values define how we see ourselves in relation to the work we do. They guide our behaviors in work situations and determine how we relate to employers, co-workers and clients. For example: loyalty, teamwork and responsibility.

Let's begin by looking at the personal aspects of your life. Then we will move on to your values related to your career.

What do you value in your *Personal Life*?

In the following spaces list at least 10-12 personal values that are important to you. Don't look at the examples I below yet. First, write what is present for you in this moment.

1._____   5._____   9._____

2._____   6._____   10._____

3._____   7._____   11._____

4._____   8._____   12._____

Some examples to stimulate your mind are:

Intimacy	Health	Family
Security	Art	Honesty
Nature	Integrity	Freedom
Friendship	Relationship	Career
Contribution	Communication	Fun
Love	Beauty	Education
Culture	Peace of mind	Leadership

What do you value in *Business*?

Look at the professional side of your life: the job, the business, the work you do. What values are important to you in this area? List them below.

1._____   5._____   9._____

2._____   6._____   10._____

3._____   7._____   11._____

4._____   8._____   12._____

Some examples are:

Responsibility	Accountability	Service
Fun	Effectiveness	Honesty
Team Work	Leadership	Integrity
Education	Profitability	Sufficiency
Dedication	Stability	Organization
Excellence	Abundance	Communication
Reputation	Creativity	Workability

What important values did you miss?

Review these two lists. Do any additional values come to mind that are important to you, but that you have not written down yet? Take a moment to add them here.

_____

_____

_____

_____

Though you may say, "I didn't think about them at first, but they are important to me," or "I didn't have time," but it is no accident that you missed those last few values. What were they? Intimacy? Health? Communication? Contribution? They are important indicators of what is MISSING in your life right now!

It was no accident that you missed them because they are not present in your life. You miss "intimacy" when you complain about your relationships. You miss "communication" while you are in constant conflict with people around you. You miss the value of "contribution" when you are feeling alone and not connected to the world around you. I bet there is a correlation between the results and outcomes in your present life and the values you missed in your list.

This may also explain why we make lots of promises, but we don't keep them. We break promises to ourselves because we don't value what we promised to do or to become. We make promises looking at the core of our promises and <u>why</u> we are making them.

Imagine living a life based on a set of *values* and a *life vision.* To get there, we have to go through a process to discover why we are not living that way and what obstacles are in our way. Begin by asking yourself:

- What are the things you say you want in life, as value or as an experience?

- Where is the disconnect between what you say you want out of life and what you already have gotten, which is not a match?

- How can you commit yourself to having the things you say you want out of life be present for you?

- How can you experience a life you love to live?

Answering the following questions can help you get present to what is really going on in your life:

What promises to yourself and others have you broken?

I know you might think you have lots of broken promises, but just write the most important ones, the ones that still bother you. For example: losing weight, saving money, paying back debt, building a career or visiting family ... Be honest with yourself.

List your broken promises in the spaces below:

_____

_____

_____

_____

_____

What personal or lifetime goals have you never been able to accomplish?

Look at the things in your life that you have wanted for a long time and that seem impossible to get. Consider struggles you have been through to accomplish something that you have failed to do, things that seem far away and out of. Write them down:

_____

_____

_____

_____

What personal or professional aspirations or desires have you given up on?

I am sure you have given up on some dreams or desires because they seemed impossible or unreachable. List them below:

_____

_____

_____

_____

Which things on your "To Do" list keep showing up over and over again?

What is it that keeps showing up like a bad habit you can't get rid of? Like starting a weight-loss plan every year and within 30 days you have broken that promise. Or saving money, or fixing something, or going to a certain place, or doing something you have dreamed about doing. List them here:

_____

_____

_____

_____

We have created a life of broken promises and unfulfilled commitments.

What is common in all of your writing above is that you don't have the life you say you want because you have broken your promises to others and, more importantly, to yourself. Then you carry guilt, shame and blame for many years without realizing the weight those regrets put on your shoulders.

Why do we break our promises?

It seems very easy to make promises and keep them, but why are we not doing it? I am sure everyone who made promises to themselves and to others are good people with very honorable intentions. Then why are they breaking their promises? Here are some reasons that might reveal what is really going on:

- It was just a good idea. We have no real intention to follow through with it.

- It isn't an important enough goal.

- We are not truly committed because:

The promises we make are in conflict with our values. We may want to be nice to or agreeable with others or look good in front of others. Or maybe we have done it so many times that it's become a habit.

The promises we make are according to someone else's values. We may want to avoid conflict with them, or we adopt the values of others because we have never defined values of our own. Maybe we find this easier than standing up for what we truly want for ourselves.

The promises we make are not related to our values at all. They may be related to our goals and objectives, instead of our deeper values. We then lose our enthusiasm and commitment almost immediately.

- We have no one to hold us accountable.

Accountability is one of the most important reasons to recognize. Having an accountability or productivity coach is one of the best approaches you can have for developing yourself as a person who produces results in his/her life. What results? The results you promised yourself, such as your health, your relationships, your finances and your peace of mind.

Everyone Can Use a Good Coach

If you look at anyone you respect and admire in art, music, or sports, you will notice that they got to the top of their game with the help and support of a coach. Tiger Woods doesn't play golf in any tournament without his coach being with him. In basketball, Michael Jordan is a master of his domain, yet he always had a coach and he does not miss his practice. When he was making the movie "Space Jams," his contract called for a full-size basketball court by his trailer so he could practice his game when he was not busy shooting the movie. He also had the studio pay his coach to be there with him. You might think Michael Jordan could afford to take a break from his practice, given who he is. But he doesn't, because he is "committed" to his "values" and he makes himself "accountable" to someone else. His coach keeps him on his game. Michael Jordan's coach isn't better than him in the game of basketball; but he can see where Michael is not being who he said he would BE for himself. In his biography, he said:

I've missed more than 9,000 shots in my career. I've lost almost 300 games. 26 times, I've been trusted to make the game winning shot and missed. I've failed over and over and over again in my life ... And that is why I succeed.

Michael Jordan is not his failures in the game. He is his commitment. He did not quit because he lost some games, he held on to his vision of who he wanted to be in the game and for his team. Many of us quit after one or two tries because we feel like failures. Although we might fail in some endeavors, we do not become a failure unless we insist on it! The difference is in knowing that you are not your projects, your finances, or your body. You are your commitments, your values and your vision. You make those commitments, values and vision real by making promises and keeping them through a series of actions.

These are the questions worth asking and the inquiry worth having:

- How committed are you in your promises to yourself and to others?

- How many excuses, reasons and justifications will you come with to not keep your promises?

On the topic of "Promises to Keep" Jawaharlal Nehru, the first and longest-serving prime minister of independent India after declaring independency from England said:

*All thoughts which do not look towards action are abortion and treachery.
If then, we are the servants of thoughts we must be servants of action also.
People avoid action often, because they are afraid of the consequences, for
action means risk and danger, but it is not so. If you have a close look at it,
rather it adds to the zest and delight of life.*

What is the impact of breaking our promises to ourselves?

- Disappointment and damaged relationships with ourselves and with others
- Frustration and embarrassment that causes us to hide out from others
- Blaming others for our circumstances and our obstacles
- Loss of self-confidence and/or self-respect
- Quitting because we don't trust ourselves
- We give up and stop dreaming
- We see ourselves as a loser

What regrets do you have for the things you have said you wanted, but never achieved?

- Childhood dreams about sports or career?
- Health and vitality, such as your fitness and lifestyle?
- Future plans, such as education or traveling?

Write your regrets in the spaces below:

_____

_____

_____

_____

_____

What are the consequences of living life with regrets and disappointments?

- Exhaustion, being tired and worn out all the time and never having enough energy to "get it all done"?
- Loss of passion; no excitement about your life and having no fun or play in your life?
- Feeling like a failure; having a negative self-perception and disappointment about the life you currently live?

Write your consequences in the space below:

_____

_____

_____

_____

_____

Where is the disconnect?

Why do we make promises that we don't keep? Why do we say we value something, but our actions don't match with our words? Where and how did we get disconnected from our promises?

We get disconnected from our promises when we do not make those values OUR OWN. Perhaps we thought they were good values to have, or we were told to have them or we believe we are not good people without them. We can also break promises when we confuse our values with our goals.

What is the distinction between goals and values?

Goals are things we want to have or achieve. Goals are objectives, such as making money, taking a trip, getting married, building a business, becoming decisions about setting goals come from our motivations or desires. Our motivations and desires are generated by our values.

Values are qualities that define us and distinguish us from others. Values shape who we are and make us unique and memorable. They are the forces that give our lives meaning, purpose and direction. Ultimately, our values determine our choices, guide our behaviors and direct our lives.

Why are particular values important to us and where do values come from?

Take a look at your list of values from the beginning of this chapter. Write them on a separate piece of paper and keep it in front of you while you work on this segment.

By asking, "Why are these values your values?" I am not suggesting you they are not good values. I want you to think about why these values are important to you and not others. When was the first time you said to yourself: "This is a good thing to have or to be"?

We decide what values to pick and/or what principles to follow in two different ways. I call them "Direct Influence" and "Ontological Reasons." ***15**

Direct Influence on Our Values

Through direct influence, we choose our values based on what we observe, learn and are influenced by, such as our parents, family traditions, school, national pride, religious beliefs, profession or career, society and media.

Learn from our parents

Learning from our parents is the very first way that we decide what to value and how to be. By observing your parents doing things and following certain principles and values in their lives, you learn from them. Because you respect and love them you follow their lead, adopting their principles and values.

The opposite scenario also works to shape our values, such as observing destructive behaviors like alcoholism, drug abuse or other destructive behaviors. You decide "I will not be like them." Then you choose values and principles that keep you from becoming like them.

I began to value honesty and integrity, because I saw my father practice them and also watched my aunts and uncles doing the same things. I decided that, if I became honest and acted with integrity, others would respect me the way they respected my father.
Examples: Integrity, honesty, love, faith, patience, fun, giving, family, communication or responsibility.

Passed down through family, generations or traditions

Sometimes we follow our family's values from generation to generation without questioning them or choosing them for ourselves, because our parents, our grandparents, their parents and grandparents have followed them. This is not good or bad, right or wrong. It is just a fact. We have not made our own selections.

Traditions are the same way. They are passed on from father to son, from generation to generation and from family to family. We follow traditions they become part of our values and principles. We accept those values without making our own selections. In many cases, people have changed those traditions based on how they grew up, were educated, or adapted to other living situations.

Examples: respect, being nice, peace, honor, nature, hard working, pride, generosity, music, art or food.

Learned in school

We can pick up principles and values from things we learn in school. We arrive on time and do our homework because the teacher said, "Good boys and girls will do their homework and will be on time." From these experiences, we decide that being timely and organized are good values.

This continues in high school and college, as well as any private or specialized school. We can't help seeking others' approval and that often leads to adopting their values.

Examples: Organization, education, structure, leadership, fun, partnership, respect, exercise, friendship or hard working.

National pride

Some values come from being from or raised in a culture we love and are proud of. For example, hospitable and welcoming are two important Iranian values. Almost every Iranian will do anything to take care of you when you are a guest in their home, or even when they are just interacting with you. In interacting with the Japanese, you can see that they value respect and honor. Every nation can be known by its special values.

However, we often accept some principles and values because of national propaganda. In some cases government brain-washing techniques can cause people to hate other nations or races or groups, based on values that differ from theirs.

Examples: hospitality, history, culture, art, music, dance, nature, language, pride and self-respect.

Religious beliefs

When we go to Church, Mosque, Synagogue, Temple or any other place of worship from early ages, we adapt to what our parents or our religious leaders say or ask us to do. Again, this is not good or bad, right or wrong. It is just what it is. Many of us have done that and some are still doing it. The risk of developing prejudices against people of other religions applies here also. Many do judge people based on their religious beliefs separate from them because their values do not match. This has caused wars and killing based on religious differences.

Examples: God, religion, belief, faith, forgiveness, love, compassion or culture.

Profession or career

We select some of our values based on our profession or career, such as engineers, doctors, military and other profession. We become a certain way and follow certain principles.

Examples: orderly, perfection, precision, detail, intelligence, education, honor, respect, leadership and survival.

Learned from society

Growing up in different societies causes us to pick different values. Societal influences can even cause us to change or re-evaluate some of our values that came from our families, traditions, or religions. Society has a great impact on how we develop our values. Society can be like a stormy ocean that has no mercy on its victims. In a stormy ocean, you will get wet, you will get cold and you even might lose your life. People chose some values in certain societies because they had no other choices, or they are forced to give up values that they held before in order to become part of those societies.

A simple example of this is moving from a small town to a big, industrial city, or a teenager changing schools due to a parent's move or job change. You can see these value changes within yourself, when you have changed jobs, moved to a new town or gotten your first job after college. Peer pressure is another way that society influences us, as well as our kids, to select, change or alter our values.

Examples: working, making money, saving, investing, socializing, smoking, drinking, dressing up, being goal oriented or being a go-getter.

Following, reading and watching media

Media is another big influence that we cannot get rid of. It is everywhere! TV, cable stations, radio stations, newspapers, magazines, Internet – there is no way out. Big industries such as: entertainment, beauty, fashion, tobacco and alcohol, sports, pharmaceuticals and many others influence us via their ads and campaigns in the media. You can see this in our kids as they worry about what is the hottest thing to wear, or what is the coolest gadget to have, or what little actors or actresses they have to look like – their hair, clothes and behaviors. It's crazy.

Our kids don't realize that they are acting. This is not who they are; they are just pretending. They have been influenced by the same media that we have been influenced by; they are just deeper into it.

Examples: looking good, being liked by others, singing, dancing, drinking, being outrageous, being fashionable and being special.

These are not the only ways that we develop our values, but they are the primary areas of our lives. Therefore, our experiences in these areas determine what we value and why we value it.

<u>Ontological Reasons for Our Values</u>

We cannot help but hear our "Inner Chatter." That sucker is loud, crazy and has no mercy. Until we recognize our Inner Chatter and decide to not act on what it says about ourselves or others, we have no control over its nastiness and its influence on our decisions about what to do or how to be.

Ontologically, we select and act on some values or principles that don't reflect who we are, because we think we should. Our Inner Chatter also plays a key role in how Direct Influence shapes our values. Most of the areas of Direct Influence can be affected by ontological influences, such as:

To fix something or someone

Sometimes we embrace a value in order to fix a situation or a person in that situation. For example, you may begin practicing integrity because you were in a very dishonest situation. Or you become a hard worker because someone said you were lazy. You begin to value health and vitality because you don't want to be fat.

To do avoid failure

You might decide to become precise and do everything right because you don't want to fail in what you do. Maybe someone told you "don't fail" when you were young, or for some other reason, you decided that doing things right the first time is the way to go.

To do the right thing

Maybe under the influence of parents and/or religion, you decided to do "the right thing" all the time, or to not do "the wrong thing" because doing so was bad. Because of this, you started to value being straight and honest.

To prove something

People can pick values in order to prove something to themselves or someone else. We may value success in order to prove to our parents that can do it. In the process, we use education and accountability to become a "go-getter."

To say the right thing

Sometimes we want to say the right thing just to get what we want. We say we value things that we do not really care about or have any interest to follow, like loyalty, integrity, commitment or teamwork. We see this in corporations and businesses all the time.

To look good

People sometimes say that hold certain values just to "look good." However, who they are is not a match with what they say they stand for. For example, you might say you believe in being a team player, but you are always late to team meetings. Or you say value cultural diversity, but you don't have any relationships with people from different cultures.

To fit in

This ontological influence is similar to "looking good." We say and do things, acting like we hold certain values just to fit in with a crowd, society or some other group. While we see this mainly in high school, college and places where young people hang out, adults feel inner pressure to fit in, too.

To feel good

We might say we value something because it makes us feel good about ourselves.

Again, this doesn't mean our values are inappropriate or bad, or that we should not have them or value them, or that they are fake. It just means we pick them based on all the above influences and experiences. If we look closely at all of them, we can see that they have one thing in common. All these values and principles come from our *PAST.*

You will notice that regardless of what you value, such as communication, commitment, love, fun or honesty, by the end of the day you will have had some experiences that do not support what you say you value. This is because those values are past–based. You chose them to protect you, defend you, prove something, make you look good, and make you feel good or help you survive. The bottom line is that going about it in this way makes you work harder. It is not bad, but by the end of the day you are not happier or more enthusiastic about your life. Be honest with yourself about what you feel and experience regarding yourself, others and what you do each day. Is something always missing before you can feel whole and complete and have your values being present for you?

What are you experiencing when your values are past-based?

Tired	Upset	Resentful
Regretful	Angry	Frustrated
Indifferent	Resigned	Resistant
Jealous	Overwhelmed	Confused

Now that you understand that your current values were generated from your past experiences and past relationships, you can see why you have all these negative experiences. Even if you are value good things, you had no active role in picking those values.

Where else could these values come from?

Now that we understand how our past generates values, we can see that if we pick our values based on present experiences, they will immediately become our past. What other option is left in terms of time? Yes, the FUTURE. This is what I call having a *VISION* for your life and your business.

If we keep looking at our past to see what we can do differently, faster or better, we can never be happy and content because we will never be free from our past. Instead, we can generate the exact same values that we care about through the vision we have created for our future.

Personally, I could easily keep relating to my values from the perspective of making my life better than my past, because my past is full of struggle and hardship. Or I can look at my vision and make sure that it is what I am living for. I could look at my divorces and try to keep my relationship with my life partner from becoming like previous relationships, or I can look at my life vision and see how my new relationship can fit into it. I can give you many examples of my own life.

My absolute commitment and undeniable stand to fulfill my vision everyday has brought me peace of mind, freedom to be, freedom to express, inner peace and contentment. I know I always have a choice – I can plug myself into my past or plug myself into my future. This helps me be present to my life vision, which is:

Life fulfilled.

Passion, love and laughter expressed.

Inspired by people's success,

Having fun and creating abundance.

When I wake up each morning, I know I can be who I am from my past because it is automatic and takes no effort or intention. Or I can choose to be someone who can and will fulfill my vision, exactly like any leaders in history who inspired me and made a difference in the lives of others. They had the choice to be ordinary people who would dance to any tune that society or politics played, or just do what others expected. Go with the flow and don't rock the boat. Do what others do. Put your head in the sand. Keep going through life the way you have done in the past, like your family and society and the generations before you. But no – the leaders who made a difference in the lives of others are the ones who said, "NO. I have a vision and I am going to follow that."

Gandhi, Mother Teresa, Dr. Martin Luther King, Jr., President Kennedy and Nelson Mandela are some examples of these leaders in politics and social issues. Henry Ford is a good example of these leaders in business. Lance Armstrong is a good example of this type of person in sports. Each of them had the choice to stay small and be part of the bigger crowd or to feel bad about their social, economical or physical situation and circumstances. But instead, they picked values and principles that were an absolute match with the future they designed and that were generated from their life vision.

271

Gandhi told the British, "You will leave India without violence from the Indians." At first they laughed at him, but eventually they left. It took a long time but they left, without violence from the Indians. Gandhi's absolute belief in his vision kept him in his commitment.

Dr. Martin Luther King, Jr., said,

I have a dream, that one day a man will be judged based on the content of his character, not by the color of his skin.

In one of his books, Dr. King praised Mahatma Gandhi as one of world leaders who inspired him to challenge America's racial inequality with a "No Violence" approach.

There are so many inspiring stories. Look for yourself and find a world leader who inspires you. What were their views on life and the world? What was their vision for their own life? I promise you will get inspired to do the same – maybe just for your own life to begin with, then the lives of the people around you, such as your family and maybe your co-workers and other team members. After that, maybe you will inspire the lives of others in your communities and eventually your society and the world after that! It is possible. Can you see it? If not, it will not happen. If you can see it in the future, then have a better chance of doing it. This phenomenon is called many different things, such as having vision, seeing the future, visualizing, creating your future, or seeing it in your mind.

In the world of business, it is known as the "Merlin Principle." I am sure you have heard the myth about King Arthur and Marlin the magician:

Merlin the magician came to King Arthur when he was just an eight-year-old boy. Merlin told him, "You will become one of the greatest kings of England."

Arthur laughed and said, "Yeah, sure. I am just an eight-year-old, poor boy.

Are you kidding me?" Merlin said, "Let me show you what you have done!" He took the young Arthur thirty years into the future and showed him what he had done for England from the age of eight to the age of thirty-eight. Merlin brought Arthur back to the age of eight and Arthur did what he saw he had done in the future. He became one of the greatest kings of England.

Yes, it is a very cute and entertaining story, but there is great wisdom in it also. See your future and start to live it now – not someday, maybe, if it is not too hard. If you notice in my own life vision every sentence is past- or present-based, as if it has happened, I already have experienced it, or I am in that future now and living it now. I am not waiting for it to come to me and happen to me. I am going to it and living it at this given moment. This is surely the reason I do not get upset as much as before, I do not pick fights as much as I used to and I am more present to others' magnificence and greatness than to their shortcomings and flaws.

As we continue through this process, you will get clearer about what your values are and what your life vision is.

How do we truly determine what our values are?

Start by writing two different lists:

What is important to you personally?

Simply write down what is important to you. This list could include some of the values you wrote down before, but this time look at them from your future – not from your past. This time don't pick them from a place of fixing or proving. Don't pick them with a feeling of "I have to" or "I should." Don't select them to make you feel good about yourself or to try to fit in with someone or something. Instead, pick them from a place of what is important to you and what you would like to have present for you. Look deep into your heart and soul and let yourself get moved by it. Make a short list here:

1._____   5._____   9._____

2._____   6._____   10._____

3._____   7._____   11._____

4._____   8._____   12._____

What is important in life in general?

In the same way consider what is important in life. These two questions are similar in some ways, yet not the same. Access to your heart and your soul and see what is important to you that you want to see in your life more often. Maybe things that you want to see more in society, or in schools. Maybe some qualities that you care about seeing in other people. Maybe that space, that experience of truly living your life.

_____

_____

_____

_____

Roy Edward Disney was a longtime senior executive for The Walt Disney Company, which his father Roy Oliver Disney and his uncle Walt Disney founded. He said;

When your values are clear to you, making decisions becomes easier.

As soon as you have made these lists, you will be ready to look at what constitutes VISION. Use them as a checklist to assist you in designing and creating your own vision.

What is *Vision*?

What are the characteristics of a vision? What separates something inspirational from a true vision? How can we distinguish a *Mission* statement from a *Vision* statement?

A *Mission* statement is where many businesses and corporations clarify what they do. Their *Vision* statement describes who they are BEING while they are DOING what they do. Let's go through what Vision is:

Seeing a future and fulfilling dreams …

Can you envision a future? Are you fulfilling a dream? Or are you just trying to fix something you don't want to see anymore? Vision represents something in the future and something you are dreaming about.

Being "at cause …"

If you are not "at cause" in relation to something, you will be on the other side, at the effect end of it. Look at your complaints in life. Most are generated from being "at effect," and thinking you can't do anything about it or feeling powerless around it. Vision moves you to be at the cause of a movement that makes a difference in your life or the lives of others.

Having fun with it and are turned on by it …

Fulfilling your vision is fun. It is not something that you will not like to do or to be. It turns you on and you enjoy doing it. It is obvious to others that you are having fun with it.

It is a bigger picture and you can't do it alone …

Fulfilling a vision is a big picture. It is bigger than just a task or a project. It might involve different projects and so many different tasks that you can't do it by yourself. In fulfilling your vision, you will enroll other people to embrace the possibility of getting those projects completed, because your eyes are on the big picture. This is something way bigger than just you and your space. It affects others around you.

Is not limited to you, but it will include you …

Fulfilling a vision is not only about you; it is about others also. It is about everyone around you: your family, your co-workers, your teammates, your community and each and every person with whom you. While your vision is bigger than just you, be sure includes yourself. You are the cause and others will enjoy the effect around it.

Why are you doing this and how will it turn out?

The answer to this question could be part of your vision. Why are you doing what you do? How will all these things you are doing turn out in the end? Is it just about money and a feeling of security? Or is it for a bigger cause and a bigger plan that will make a difference for others around you, as well as for yourself?

It takes you to work and it will inspire others ...

A powerful and empowering vision will take you to work every day. You will not be tired going to work to DO what you need to do to accomplish and fulfill your vision. You will not complain that it is hard work. You will not bitch and nag, because you are inspired and moved by the cause. That will inspire others around you, because they can see themselves in you. I always believe "you can live your life based on not failing. Or you can live it based on succeeding. Both produce the same results, but offer two different life experiences."

Notice that nearly all of the above are common in the world leaders who inspire you. They describe anyone who inspires you to follow them or respect them for what they do. Notice that your experiences around these people are different. By taking notice of this about yourself, you will have many great experiences to draw from when you are inspired and motivated to accomplish something bigger that just something for yourself. That is the magic of being around someone with a vision.

When you create and invent your life vision from your future, versus from your past, your experience of yourself and the people around you is altered into something more positive and empowering. This brings you inner peace and the freedom to be.

What are you experiencing when your values are future-based and come from your vision?

Energetic	Powerful	Happy
Fun	Calm	Fresh
Caring	Creative	Team player
Supportive	Productive	Organized

The following are some examples of "Life Vision" that have been designed by some of our clients through our work with them. I am so proud and honored to be part of the creation of these people's visions for their lives. I am inspired by it and can see myself in each and every of them. That is the beauty of the vision – any of these could be mine:

Living a life of love, joy and laughter.
Making a difference through empowerment, generosity and play.

Dreams accomplished.
Life of joy, happiness, fulfillment and contribution.

Boldly taking risks.
Living a life of passion, love and play,
Connecting and creating abundance.

Living a Vibrant Life Full of Love, Adventure and Play!

As you read these visions, as well as my own that I shared with you, you can't help but feel inspired, moved and motivated to live your life that way. You just can't control the goodness, the empowerment and the rush of love and fun. That is one of the biggest characteristics of a vision. As that domain arises (look at Figure "H"), you feel the possibility of doing something new and powerful, something new and amazing, something that nobody else dared to touch and create, something so inspiring that it scares you to death, or something that makes a difference. Maybe it's something you love to do and are motivated to do because it is part of who you are and it moves you to action.

POSSIBILITY
INSPIRATION
MOTIVATION

Figure "H"

As soon as the first domain arises in your heart, mind and soul like the sun that comes up on the horizon, immediately something else arises next to it. It is as powerful as the vision itself (look at the figure "I"). It is despair self-doubt and resignation.

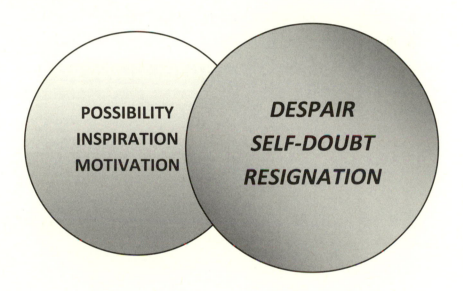

Figure "I"

Down through history, many people who stood for what is right were killed or jailed for a very long time. Anyone who said, "I will do something different," had to face discouraging comments from very resigned people and your experience will not be different. Many times in the past, you, yourself, were one of those people who brought down others' ideas, laughed at them and made fun of them. We have all done that, including myself – until I was on the other side of the resignation and despair and I felt the awful feeling that came from hearing that from others. Remember the crab basket I mentioned earlier and the way other crabs will pull down any crab that tries to go for freedom.

- Gandhi said to the British, "You are leaving," and they laughed at him. Eventually he was killed.

- Dr. King said, "I have a dream," and he faced much hardship from society. Eventually he too was killed.

- Mother Teresa said, "I will protect and serve the untouchable in India," and people said good luck.

- President Kennedy said, "We are pulling out of Vietnam," and he got killed.

- Henry Ford said, "I will transform the way we manufacture cars," and people in the car industry laughed at him.

- Lance Armstrong said, "I will win the Tour de France, back to back," and people said sure you will. But he did it <u>seven</u> times back to back.

- Nelson Mandela said from his prison cell that there would come a day when blacks and whites in South Africa would live together in peace and people said he was crazy.

Do you want more examples?

You are no different and the people around you are no different either. Resignation and despair is so deep within all of us that possibility and inspiration have no chance to shine for long, unless someone stands firm and makes a commitment to make all those possibilities realities. In your case – in your life – you get to be that person. You have to protect your vision through hard work and daily inspiration. You have to move your commitments forward by inventing practices and actually planning to make them real. You have to remember that most people don't know better than to plug their power into their past. They will continue to do things they are comfortable doing. They will continue to be someone with whom they are familiar, because change is hard. Don't take others resignation and despair personally. It is not about you.

Invent Your Life Vision

Let's get to work to invent and create your life vision. This is exciting because until this moment you have done almost everything from your past. Now, for the first time, you will invent yourself from your future.

The first step is to pick the top five values you love the most and you want to present in your life most often. These values represent the essence of who you are. Add the top two or three things that you listed as really important about life itself. Write them on a separate piece of paper and have them in front of you

Review this new list, keeping in mind the characteristics of a vision. Use this list as your reference in checking to see if you are on track in inventing your vision.

It may also be helpful to have the examples of "Life Visions" in front of you, so you can see how the sentence structure works. They are written in past tense. They look like the bold statements you see in magazines or news stories. They are solid and inspiring and they sound like they are from someone courageous and brave – someone who dares to dream and dares to talk about it.

Before you finalize your vision and write it down here, just start writing on a separate note pad. Practice and play. Don't try to do it right or get discouraged if it doesn't sound inspiring enough to you. Simply practice and play. Open your heart and soul. Say the things that move and inspire you. Don't hold back. Your list doesn't have to be long, and it shouldn't explain or describe because that would be a mission statement. You'll know you have the one for you when you feel inspired and motivated to engage in your own life and do something different about it as a result of the possibilities you get present to. You can't do it wrong!

Before this moment, you were just making it. Now you are about to invent something amazing that will move you forward and cause you to have all of your goals realized because you will be in action about them.

Keep practicing and do not stop. When you are done with your first draft, share it with someone close to you, such as a spouse, family member or friend. Ask them what they think. Don't get discouraged by the possibility of negative or belittling comments; just do it. Look to see if they can see themselves in your vision and if they get moved and inspired by it. Don't hold back. Be courageous and keep playing. Avoid making any interpretations about their comments. Stay present to your dreams and your vision and to what you want to create from that.

Get to work. Get your documents and note pad, and have fun!

My Life Vision is

_____

_____

_____

_____

Very good. I am proud of you. You have made an amazing discovery of yourself and the power within you. The beginning of mastery of love within is having a vision for your life that is caused by your own love and respect of yourself – not from trying to fix yourself. You should celebrate this moment.

Take a moment to answer the following questions. Be truthful and be as detailed as possible, because we will use these notes later.

1. What do you realize about yourself?

_____

_____

_____

2. What are you willing to change or alter?

_____

_____

_____

3. What do you promise yourself?

_____

_____

_____

4. What are you willing to do to keep that promise?

_____

_____

_____

5. With whom will you discuss this?

_____

_____

_____

What can stop you from becoming your vision and creating it every day, against all the obstacles in life? You will cause your own worst obstacles. How? By not being responsible, by not being accountable and by not practicing integrity as a source of power in making a difference in your own life and the lives of those around you.

In the next chapter, we look at these three powerful distinctions – responsibility, accountability and integrity – as the sources that will guarantee the fulfillment of your vision.

CHAPTER EIGHT

INTEGRITY, RESPONSIBILITY AND ACCOUNTABILITY

THE SOURCE OF POWER, MAGIC AND MIRACLE

*Extraordinary people are responsible people who
get both credit and blame for everything
that happens in their lives.*

Now that we have created our vision for our life, we must invent some new practices that will support us by having our vision and values be present within us and our lives, and be a part of our day-to-day activities.

What we can count on is that we are not fully disciplined and that our level of integrity has not been to this point sufficient enough for us to fulfill that vision. Our current life practices are not yet strongly in place, and they are not in the structure that we have planned over our lifetime. For example, consider all promises we have made to ourselves and to others over the years that are left unfulfilled.

During this time, we are not yet responsible enough to keep ourselves on track with our commitments and have little accountability to ourselves or anyone else when it comes to our dreams, goals or commitments. All the while, we do anything that is required of us for others. It is interesting that we are able to go out of our way to take care of others and please them completely only so we can appear to be someone they can trust and count on. The problem is that we don't always do that for ourselves! At the very least we don't do that for ourselves with the same quality, commitment or efficiency that we tend to extend to help others reach their dreams, goals and commitments.

Compare the promises we make to ourselves with those we make to other people. Which set of promises have we kept most often? To others, right? Maybe this is because we are not holding ourselves accountable to ourselves as much as we hold ourselves accountable to others. Maybe we keep our promises to others because they are our boss or superior at work, maybe because they are our parents or our kids, or even our best friends. There are even situations where we overly achieve at being a people pleaser because we feel we owe something to others or experience feelings of guilt. No matter. Any way we look at it, we are not doing the same things for ourselves as we do for others, and that is a big problem for our self-esteem.

For example: think about exercising, dieting, relaxing, reading, personal interests, personal development, relationships, social and occupational productivity levels and basic self-expression; these are all put on hold. We tell ourselves that we will get to these things "later" because we are busy doing something for others or we are just so entirely lazy and not responsible for what we really want. We are not being accountable to ourselves or anyone else for achieving our greatness and accomplishing our goals and dreams.

Beyond Your Limits

We almost never look at integrity, responsibility or accountability as forces that empower us to accomplish and to achieve when we are in a downward spiral of negativity. We almost always avoid them because they sound heavy and feel far too significant, and just seem too good to be true!

It is entirely possible that we take a look around the world and become resigned that no one takes any responsibility for the evil and bad things that are going on. Sometimes it can even look like no one in the world wants to be accountable for anything and nobody takes any responsibility for anything, almost as if everyone has forgotten about integrity. It can be depressing and very disappointing.

As much as I love to write about the world and express myself about what I see, this is not the topic of this book and it is not what we are trying to accomplish here. What we are trying to accomplish here will actually be relevant to what you and I can do and in some case will do in the world in general. However, we have to start from ourselves first, so as we become independently responsible, individually accountable and start practicing integrity as a part of our own self-expression. Only then can we spread it to the world. You will see it spreading to our family, in the work place, communities and eventually to society.

In this chapter, we look at how we can use these amazingly powerful forces to be the source of power, magic and miracles in our lives and use them to accomplish our goals and fulfill our future through engaging in a series of exercises. Through these exercises we will design to grant the fulfillment of our *Life Vision*.

Integrity

The first force we deal with in this chapter is *integrity*. Without this integrity, responsibility and accountability mean nothing. You cannot be fully responsible or accountable for your actions if you have no integrity. This force impacts every part of our lives and what we are doing. To make necessary changes in our lives, we must first gain true integrity in all we do.

Integrity is often looked at as moral, as making good things in the world and doing the "right" things. This view is a result of our making choices in life based on looking at them as "good vs. bad" or "right vs. wrong" or "true vs. false." Most of the time these choices arise from feelings of guilt, shame, blame or at our darkest moment when we have been accused of not having integrity. This is a very limited way of thinking and approaching our lives. In fact, integrity is a way to empower ourselves and others.

Who gives us the power and permission to judge and evaluate others' integrity? What gives us the right to base others' level of integrity on what we think integrity is or should be? We judge and evaluate others' decisions, their lifestyle or life choices and anything else we can push our opinions on, so we can impose our idea of integrity on them. When they don't accept our viewpoint, we become upset and resentful. We distance ourselves from them. When considering your idea of integrity, I invite you to separate your view of social law, religious beliefs and/or cultural beliefs from your idea of integrity at this moment. Look at integrity as a personal phenomenon.

Every person declares his or her own personal integrity based on personal beliefs, faith, values, principles and life choices. However, we all have one thing in common when it comes to integrity and that is ... without it things do not work well in our lives and in our commitments! Whatever our personal integrity is, when we do not practice it we do not accomplish our goals neither, therefore, our intentions. Integrity is not constrained or limited by rules, agreements, descriptions, in-order-to's or demands to get anywhere or to make ourselves or someone else do anything.

Integrity is the ability to be as good as our word, to declare power over our promises, to be true to our personal values and principles, to live our lives as our own people. Ultimately, being true to ourselves and being true to our self-expression is the simplest form of integrity. That is the only force in life that will bring us power, joy, freedom and happiness. We will fail if we live our lives and hold up to integrity only for others or to get others' approval, to please someone else or impress another human being. A life lived with integrity is a life that is based on your personal values and principles.

When I think of the principle of "living life based my own personal integrity" I can't help but think of a quote from Marianne Williamson that became really famous when used by Nelson Mandela in his inauguration speech as the first black president of South Africa. On that day he brought on stage the very person, the prison guard who tortured him in his prison cell for 27 years and forgave him. He told the guard, "You were just doing your job." He forgave the guard because he knows that the future of his country depends on the people's ability to forgive and forget, and building that country together again, which started with Mandela right then and there. Wow! He then read the following words by Marianne Williamson:

Our worst fear is not that we are inadequate; our deepest fear is that we are powerful beyond measure. It is our light not our darkness that most frightens us.

We ask ourselves, 'Who am I to be brilliant, gorgeous, talented and fabulous?' Actually, who are you not to be? You are a child of God; your playing small doesn't serve the world.

There is nothing enlightened about shrinking so that other people won't feel insecure around you.

We were born to make manifest the glory of God within us. It is not just in some of us it is in everyone, and as we let our own light shine we unconsciously give other people permission to do the same.

As we are liberated from our own fear our presence automatically liberates others.

To me this means that we can be powerful about what we think of ourselves when we are being ourselves and being true to ourselves.

You can use your integrity as a meter, like a sensor to distinguish and realize your degree of the reliability or truthfulness of your actions to your commitments and, ultimately, your word. To me, integrity is when we consistently produce what we promise to produce, do what we say we will do, or say what we tell others we will say. This rule applies to what we promise ourselves and to others. Regardless of the circumstances or obstacles in your way, personal integrity is one of powerful forces of decision making. Why? Notice that each time we get into trouble or cause upset with ourselves or others, it is when we don't follow through with our personal values and principles or what we stand for in life. When we sell ourselves and our integrity short for the sake of being liked, being part of the crowd and/or being ordinary, we short ourselves.

To put the power of integrity to work for us we do what we say we will do at the time we say we will do it. We stand behind our word with honor.

When we do not act with integrity, we leave our actions to justification. Reasoning each situation, spending energy on explanations of why and how we can't do what we say we will because of the circumstances or obstacles in our way is not having integrity as a focus of our life. In the event there is a real circumstance that cannot be avoided that prevents us from doing something we have promised to do, we must then approach the situation and create a new agreement, moving forward from there based on the new agreement. Communication is key to staying on track with our personal integrity.

Integrity is a powerful force in us. It is a way we can declare our word and live our lives free of any nonsense in our heads about what we have done or not done. Issues such as when and to whom we have lied, what we have hidden from others, trying to remember what we said to whom about different things when we participate in gossip are all very tiring and exhausting. Why put yourself through that when you have a choice to live and act with integrity?

I become much more powerful when I talk about integrity and the power of it at my lectures when I act with personal integrity. I am powerful when I hold people to their word and their promises because I am doing the same thing for myself. I walk the talk by acting with integrity. This is true when it comes to small matters and matters as large and important as coming clean with my taxes. I act with integrity in even the most seemingly insignificant matters, such as silly justifications I have used with to my family or friends about why I am not coming to a family or friends gathering. These white lies add up. We even justify them by calling them "white lies," because we are good people who never do any black lies, right? As long as it is white it is safe, acceptable and harmless! Sure, right.

You might think it is crazy to come clean about your lies and hidden agendas to others, even to family and friends. You might think it is not necessary, especially when they didn't even know what you had done or what you had hidden. The point is this … I knew the white lies I told, big and small, and that was enough for me to start coming clean about everything! I realized that my self-respect and freedom as a man was more important to me vs. money and comfort.

You must be the judge of your own life and practices. I am not here to judge, but I can tell you one thing … not having integrity or practicing it when you know you truly should the consequences of that action will always come back and bite you in the behind, sooner or later, with no exceptions!

When you clean up your integrity, it is not just a one-time act. It is something you will need to repeat time and time again to keep yourself in check. It's like the pile of laundry you face every week. If you don't do the wash it will ultimately begin to smell bad and make the whole house smell bad. You have to do laundry every week and you have to keep it up.

I had so many issues that I had to clean up. I had to become responsible for causing the issues. I had taken responsibility. I am no angel, but I am a powerful person now because I have cleaned up all of my messes, and if I make more messes I will clean them up as I go. I will keep doing my laundry! Don't become discouraged if your integrity gets out of alignment from time to time. Just put it back in the wash and keep moving forward. Learn from your mistakes and from cleaning up your mistakes with integrity and keep yourself away from repeating the same mistakes as much as possible.

The responsibility of having impeccable integrity is in causing your life verses being at effect of life. As I always said;

Be responsible. Nothing is happening by accident. Find the cause if you don't want to be in effect.

Rate Your Integrity

Now, look at yourself and rate your integrity in respect to your personal values and principles. Then come back with a series of promises that you must make to yourself and others (that by keeping them will bring your power back). Sometimes the issues that you need to confront are not a big deal and you can get them checked off your to-do list with a simple apology and asking for forgiveness. You would be surprised by just how far that simple apology might go!

You are the best judge of your own level of integrity. Get to work and write down where, how and with whom you have to clean something up, make new promises or declare your intentions. I know you think by just working hard, better or different and little bit of hiding and misrepresenting you can get away with not having high levels of integrity in your life. I will make this promise to you, you will be disappointed and upset when everything comes to light if you think this way. The price of cleaning up your mistakes, issues and lies slowly or not at all is a hundred times LESS powerful than if you were to get to work and restore your power by tackling these issues right now, head on.

It takes time, it will not be easy and it will not be very fun, but considering the alternative don't you think it would be more beneficial if you got to work on cleaning up your integrity now? We don't live forever. Get going!

In which areas of your life is your integrity not a match with your life vision?

Weigh all areas of your life. Where and how have you not shown integrity? Look at these areas and jot down what part of it has to do with integrity. Only then will you be able to work on the problems.

For example:

- Area: my health. I know I have extra weight, but I am still eating fattening food.

- Area: personal finance. I owe money to friends but I come with excuses for not paying them on time and at the same time I spend money on unnecessary things, like:

_____

_____

_____

_____

With whom is your personal integrity not consistent?

(I am talking about your agreements or promises with people and your relationships with them.)

Is there something you have left unsaid to someone whom you love or care for on some level? Check everyone that you have some form of relationship with, such as spouse, partners, parents, siblings, friends or any other relationship at work or play?

Look deep inside your inner mind; do you have some lies to clean up or some upsetting issues to deal with?

_____

_____

_____

_____

If you need more space use a separate note pad or recreate this on your computer.

Integrity is the first of the three forces that allow us to fulfill our vision and live our lives based on what we want them to be. For you to fulfill your life vision you need to have very powerful integrity; it is necessary for maintaining relationships with people with whom you will create partnerships and who will help you accomplish your goals and projects!

Responsibility

The second force of power that causes magic and freedom in our lives is *responsibility*. It is vital that you become absolutely and 100 percent responsible for the quality of your life!

Responsibility begins when we make a stand for our own choices and take full ownership of our lives and what happens in it. I mean everything we have done and everything that we have caused; all of it, not just part of it.

When we are responsible, we show our willingness to own every thought we have and own up to every action we take, good or bad, right or wrong, happy or sad, enough or not enough; we did it, nobody else, just us. When we get this straight in our heads we realize that "we are the ones who make it or break it." When we are willing to be the one to write the story of our lives and we come from the point of view that everything we do, everything we say and everything we generate in our lives are our own creation and invention. Only then we can rewrite the story of our life and write it in a way that will actually empower our future instead of suppressing it. And we must give ourselves permission to do so … to live a great life of abundance.

When we can look back into all the upsetting, sad, dramatic events of our lives and see how we were responsible for the outcome of each event we are free; we are free to be alone with ourselves. I am not suggesting that upsetting events don't happen in our lives on their own or at the hands of others, but what makes the events more upsetting is when we drag them along behind us throughout our lives like a sack of pain. Our

301

interpretations of these events and what we make them reflect about ourselves, others and life itself allow the upset and anger to continue in our lives. A bad situation that we lived through may not have been our fault, but the choice to rehash it over and over and to allow it to affect us negatively most certainly is. This is where we need to take full responsibility.

Remember back to one of the earlier chapters when I shared about my marriage that dissolved and all the drama that surrounded it?

When I look back I can see where I didn't take responsibility for the quality of my life and my marriage. Everything was about making it look good to onlookers and not about how to survive the upsetting events. This attitude cost me my relationship. No drama, no pointing fingers, no accusations; it just was what it was. It didn't happen in a vacuum.

I became responsible for my actions and for the red flags I refused to see! Believe me, we all refuse to look at the red flags in life. All those pretty red flags.

Why? We don't want to take responsibility for what we have put up with or the choices we may have to make as a result of recognizing the flags. The point is that we have to be responsible for the quality of our own lives. Stop looking past the red flags. Address them. Take responsibility.

Responsibility As Possibility

In responsibility as possibility, we do not blame, apply shame or assign fault. No "you did this," "you failed us," or "it is your fault," pointing fingers and looking for someone else as the cause of our problems.

Notice, when you are pointing your finger toward someone or something else (besides yourself) there are always three fingers pointing back at you. I know this is an old adage, but it applies.

How do we take responsibility? Simply notice what we have done in our lives and the messes we created. In the moment that we take absolute responsibility, we notice it without any judgment against ourselves or others. We become free to choose to create something else that fits us and our purpose better! When we choose what fits our commitments and our desires of a better, more fulfilled future of being free and self-expressed, we are happier and can achieve so much more in life.

I always use the following story as a good example of how we can take responsibility of "what happened in my life" without invalidating and watering down the facts about "what took place."

I remember years ago I led a two days public seminar. The attendees were there to get something valuable out of the program, personally and professionally.

I could not help but notice one of the participants, a woman between the age of 35 and 45.

The reason I noticed her immediately was because of the way she was protecting her body with big, baggy clothes. She wore sweat pants and a big sweatshirt. She wore a baseball cap pulled down to her eyebrows, covering her straight hair that fell around her face. She was hiding. Don't ask me why, but I immediately had a sense that I was dealing with a victim of some sort of domestic violence or maybe even rape. It wasn't just because of what she was wearing, but more by the way she handled herself and who she was around other people. She was aloof, a loner. She did not look up. And she seemed completely inside herself.

This woman did not talk for the first half of the day; she did not participate or raise her hand to ask any questions or dig inside any issues of her life. I made the move, because I was committed to making a difference in her life. I made a promise to myself and to the participants that I would give them my best, and that I would do anything for them so they could have more freedom in their lives and access to more personal effectiveness.

I asked the woman to stand up and talk to me. She did, and that was a great opening for me to get inside her world. I asked her; "Why are you here? What would you like to accomplish out of these two days?"

She said that she was there to work on her relationship issues and learn why her relationships with men never worked. She explained that she had two failed marriages within the last 15 years and a lot of unhealthy relationships aside from the marriages. Unfortunately, my guess was accurate; she also was a victim of rape when she was 15 years old, almost 30 years prior to this seminar.

The woman was aware of the impact of the rape on her quality of her relationships with men; it was obvious and she had so many years of therapy and psychological work around the issue, and I knew that she needed to not work on that anymore. I listened to all the stories and all the details of what happened to her since she was a teenager. She said that during that time she did a lot of drugs and drank alcohol to get even with the world to cover up her pain.

Also, during that time, she was in an abusive relationship and she stayed in it because she thought she was not worthy of love and respect. This was the recurring themes in all the other dramatic, upsetting and sad stories that made up her life. She clearly already knew everything about the impact of these events in her life. She was also aware of why she didn't respect herself and why she had done what she had done through her life. However, her knowing all of these truths did not make any difference in the quality of her relationships with men. Nothing, zero; same outcome, just different men, different times.

After almost an hour of working with her, one on one, walking her through the decisions she had made in her life, something huge happened. For the first time I saw that her eyes were locking into mine!

She was relating to me – a man – without any judgment, fear or protection. Out of our work together she learned that she was not taking responsibility for "what happened to her."

We all agreed that she was being violated and that she was subjected to a violent act and what happened to her was nothing that any of us can even

305

get close to understanding. No one even remotely, under any circumstances, suggested that she was responsible for "what happened" to her at that moment in terms of the actual act of violence and rape!

However, this woman understood that she was not being responsible for the decisions she made SINCE the violent acts. These ranged from internal chatter that sounds like "men are violent" or "the only thing men want from me is sex" or "don't trust men" or any other decisions and thoughts she allowed herself to think.

On one hand, no one can blame her for coming to such decisions, but she had already been living in hell for the last 30 years because of the decisions she made **after** that act of violence, that rape. The act that happened is NOT what she was not responsible for. Very impressively, she got that; she got that loud and clear and the whole world opened up to her from that moment on. We all laughed and we all cried. It was great to see her remove her baseball cap and pull her hair back. It was amazing to see a woman come to life in front of our eyes.

The next day she was there in a beautiful skirt, a very classy blouse and a sweater, with her hair tied back in a very cute pony tail. She even wore makeup! Her high heels were the highlight.

This woman was transformed, alive and vibrant, even laughing. She made a promise to lose weight, learn more about herself and open the doors of communication with the gentleman she was dating. She understood how she was not responsible for the nasty and negative interpretations she had added to "what actually took place," which had nothing to do with the actual event of "what actually took place."

We can all come up with incidents, events or issues that we have not been totally responsible for in our lives. We are, however, responsible for our decisions and choices as they relate to the memory of the events. That is part of life; it is how we choose to deal with our issues that matters. We tell ourselves lies and then forget that we lied to ourselves about the events. Then we continue lying for years without being responsible for that which we made up. We believe our own lies. Wow. What we need is to free ourselves from the chains of our lies.

Let Freedom Ring

We are free at all times by default, by the design of being human. If all you do is experience feelings of upset, angry, resentful and regret it is because in most cases you don't want to be responsible for what happens in your life, or how you want your life to be. We are crying out loud because we do not get what we want. If we do get what we ask for, it is not delivered in the manner in which we want it delivered, because we don't want to be responsible for anything we do! Sounds crazy, but this is what not taking responsibility is all about.

By not making clear choices, not listening to others, or just continuing to do what we feel like doing, and by not considering the consequences of our actions, we get to where we are, a very unhealthy, unhappy place. You know what we are really upset about? Ourselves and where we are. Funny thing is that we put ourselves here!

We like to make decisions and choices; making decisions without thinking them through is a dime a dozen. We make choices when we are happy, content and feel safe or when everything is fine and dandy, but we don't like to be responsible for the consequences of the choices we make. Being responsible for the consequences of one's actions and choices is nothing less than absolute power.

If we take responsibility for our actions and view responsibility as possibility, there is no room for shame, blame and fault. What is powerful is to see what we have done and then look at what we want to do about it next. This is the key. I am not suggesting that we break our promises and our word to ourselves and to others and say, "I am responsible for it. I am sorry." And then keep repeating it over and over again. No! I am saying let's take responsibility by learning from our mistakes and be responsible for the damages of our irresponsibility and then clean things up.

Like I said earlier, some things we've done can be cleaned up with a simple apology and some by paying a debt or doing something for someone. We have to look for ourselves and figure it out. Buy a journal and write down your action steps, who you need to apologize to and what else you will do to straighten out the messes you've made in your life. We all know exactly what we have done and to whom we have done it and with whom we have done it.

Taking Full Responsibility Frees Us

When we are fully responsible for our lives and our actions without any expectations, the circumstances and obstacles do not determine the quality or value of our lives.

Our past will not determine how our future will play out! For example, we can be broke but not poor.

Being broke I could work on, because it was temporary – something I had to deal with and turn around in time. I was responsible for where I was; I knew I caused my situation. Being poor is a mindset that I never entertained. Being broke is a condition that has nothing to do with my happiness, nothing to do with the quality of my relationships, nothing to do with my smile, my happiness and my love for life … nothing!

Are you thinking, "Well, it is easier to say than to do"? Yes, I agree, it is not easy, but considering the alternative it was the best choice and will always leave you free. Free from holding something or someone else responsible for your happiness or the quality of your life!

Happiness is not an accident; nor is it something we wish for. *Happiness is something we design.* We have everything to do with our happiness and our own greatness … everything! Full responsibility for your life leaves you free and able to invent and to create your life in every moment, every hour and every day, good, bad or ugly.

Personal responsibility is an amazing gift we give ourselves and others; it is absolute freedom from having to fix ourselves, others, any situation and even life itself. Aren't you tired of fixing yourself? It is tiring, it is hard and heartbreaking to see so many people that view themselves as "not good enough" for themselves or for anyone else. Our happiness or our sadness, our success or our failures, our loss or our gain … they all belong to us when we are responsible for all of it, not just part of it! That is why responsibility is freedom. We did it, it belongs to us, and that is that!

I read the following quote somewhere, and I think it was a good thing to share with you. It is called "Essence of Responsibility." The first line is from Publilius Syrus, a Latin writer of maxims, who flourished in the 1st century BC. hE was a Syrian brought as a slave to Italy, but by his wit and talent he won the favor of his master, who freed and educated him. The second part is anonymous;

Anyone can hold the helm when the sea is calm …

But in stormy water it takes strength, commitment and responsibility to stay the course. We cannot adjust the wind, but we can always adjust our sails. And when it comes our turn to hold the helm … we must be strong.

Becoming Responsible For Who You Have Become

I want to share with you something that is very close to my heart and soul. I lost my older brother during the early years of the Iranian Revolution. I would like to get to the facts of the matter to make a point without getting into any political discussion and opinions, because it is not part of what we are doing here.

My brother was involved with some anti-regime activities that landed him and some of his friends in jail, arrested by the Iranian Revolutionary Guard around June of 1981. I was in his house for his birthday when he pulled me aside and talked to me about his concerns regarding one of his friends who had been arrested. My brother was very concerned about this guy's ability to endure pain and torture. My brother then asked me if I could meet him in the morning to move him from his shop and help to relocate him. He was concerned that his friend might turn him in as a result of torture tactics. I asked him if the afternoon was okay. He agreed. That was the last time I saw my brother. He was arrested that next morning at his shop. He was in a political prison for 18 months before he was executed on January 1, 1983, along with many other brave Iranians who stood for freedom.

I blamed myself for many years for not picking my brother up from his shop that morning. I blamed myself for not making myself available to him at an earlier time… I blamed myself for his arrest for years. Since 1986, when I came to the U.S. and became a resident and then a citizen, I can count with my fingers the times I was out on New Year's Eve to celebrate January 1st… I just couldn't. I was full of self-blame, anger and hurt.

I carried all that anger, upset, resentment and hate with me for a long time. You think that the anger did not affect my abilities to love, to relax and to be with others? And most important to be alone with myself? I was making myself wrong, I was blaming myself and I could not just be happy. How could I love anybody else when I was full of hate and anger? That explains my short temper with people around me, including my ex-wife, family members and friends.

311

I did not get my freedom back and get back to my happy self, to my playful self who loves art, painting, writing poetry and dance until I realized that my brother was responsible for the choices he made in his life. He even wrote in the last moment of his life on a paper to my parents before his execution with such courage and tremendous grace without showing any fear or asking his capturers any mercy the following:

I am responsible for what I have done, for what I have chosen and the freedom I am fighting for. I knew the risk and the danger when I chose that. I know I will live forever in your hearts. Thank you for raising me so well. I am sorry for the pain I have caused for you and my family. I am sorry if I have not listened to your advice through my life, it was not because it was not good advice; it was because I had to find my own way in the world. Tell my wife I love her and I am grateful for our love and friendship. Tell Behnam to take it easy and don't go crazy, you have a daughter to raise. The world will not stay this way, things will change. Don't worry for me, I am fine and content with my life choices.

Obviously he wrote more than just this, actually he wrote two pages and he ended with a short poetry from Master Hafez. I don't want to make it about his last words vs. about the power of responsibility and of taking on the consequences of your actions and being free, even when you know you have minutes to live. Here is what he wrote from Hafez-e Shirazi and the English translation of it:

ازربان سوسن آزاده ام آمدبگوش

کاندرین دیرکهن کار سبکباران خوشست

حافظاترک جهان گفتن طریق خوشدلیست

تانپنداری که احوال جهانداران خوشست

--خواجه حافظ شیرازی

The World

Once I heard from the free-spirited lily:

This aged world is only pleasant to the kind,

Whose conviction demands not being silly

To carry a load on their shoulder and mind

> *O Hafez, deny, hence, the worldly attribute*
>
> *Lacking that only you gain happiness and joy*
>
> *Lest for a moment you wear the worldly suit*
>
> *Worldly delights make you but an abject toy*
>
> *--Hafz-e Shirazi*

Given that we do not know the exact place of my brother's burial site, because it was a mass execution and most likely he is in a mass grave with hundreds of freedom fighters and heroes like him, we could not visit his grave and have a ceremony in celebration of his life and bravery. With permission from our mother, my brothers and I engraved this poem on my father's grave, who is buried in San Diego. Now, when we visit my father's grave we will also visit our fallen hero's grave, that of our brother Behzad Bakhshandeh.

Behzad was responsible for what happened to him because he was so clear about what the Iranian government said they would do to anyone who goes against them. They literally said, "Because we are representing God, if you go against us you are against God, and killing you will be okay." By the way, this is not the first time governments, kings, rulers or people in power have killed people, or committed genocide against other cultures in the name of God. It is an old, sad story, and it goes on even as I write these words.

When I realized that I was poisoning my heart and my soul by holding onto the old anger and hate I felt about my brother's death, I knew I had a choice to make. I could either continue hating and leave my heart in the dark, or I could forgive and be responsible for the consequences of the actions that impacted my life. I could let go of the hate and anger, opening my heart and soul to the light. For the record, my choosing the latter doesn't mean that I don't remember my brother or that I am not honoring his stand or not supporting his cause. It just means I took responsibility for what happened, what took place and, ultimately, the outcome of those actions. My viewpoint does not make what the government did okay with me nor were its actions justified. My decision simply set me free. Remember when I said don't drink poison, wishing others to die!? This is one of those times. I forgive myself for all the things I made myself suffer though, becoming free again, free to love and free to be present to be loved.

Now, look into your own heart and see where and how you can forgive someone or something that when you do forgive will open the doors of light and love back to your heart and soul. Believe me it is not easy, it is very hard, but again considering the alternative, why not? I can say that it is one of the best decisions I personally ever made!

Why I keep pounding into your head about integrity, responsibility and accountability is because without these powerful forces we cannot achieve what we want to achieve from creating and inventing our own future. So let's get to work and go through a couple of questions that will make you think deeper:

What are you not being completely responsible for and still blaming someone else or something else for it?

Look at all those incidences that you are blaming someone or something for and see where you can be responsible for the interpretations you have made up about it.

_____

_____

_____

_____

What do you need to clean up and with whom do you need to clean it up with?

You know exactly what these items are so just write them down and look at them later. Then decide when you are going to clean things up.

_____

_____

_____

_____

If you need more room to write use a separate notepad or computer and keep writing.

Well done! Now that you worked on integrity and responsibility, it is time to look at the third force of this powerful combination ... accountability.

Accountability

I don't know about you, but each time I hear *accountability* or *being accountable* I can't help but think of something heavy and hard, like something I can't do, something that is too far from reality, nearly unreachable.

I have the following quote from Shearson/Lehman Brothers:

Try to not get hooked on what happened with this company during the current recession and financial storm of 2008-2009, but get related to the essence of what they are saying without judgment.

I know it is hard, especially when it seems like they just don't do what they are saying.

Accountability is taking responsibility before the fact, rather than after the fact. It is taking a stand, and standing by it. When those who are accountable are right, they take the credit. When they are wrong, they take the heat ... a fair exchange.

Accountability is a way of working. Those who practice it have an unspoken respect for each other. And a visible disdain for the absent minded apologizers, mumbling excuse-makers, and trembling fence sitters who run from integrity as if it were the plague.

It is amazing when we become present in our own lives how we come to see just how much we are not being accountable for! Accountability and responsibility come hand in hand, when you practice responsibility you can't help being accountable and having integrity. This is the essential component of the three-force combination.

Opportunity for Transformation and Alteration

Our power and presence is created and built on a foundation of our word and promises we make to ourselves and to others. The well being of our "life vision" depends on how we relate to our "word" and the degree to which we keep our promises.

Accountability is the opportunity to live our lives by our own decisions and our own choices, rather than thinking things are just happening to us in our lives by luck or by accident or the way others think we should live or decide. There is also something to be said about the negativity that comes from thinking that our life is based on what others say or want for us, or by doing what we think we should do because of what we think society dictates. We should be creating and inventing our own futures rather than having it happen to us by simplistic virtue of time and nature.

Without our commitments, our promises and our intentions, we would only rely on our feelings and emotions. Look at all business partnerships, personal promises, marriage vows, personal commitments and contracts or agreements we've made over the years. How many of them end with broken agreements and promises? We can take a deep look at our own way of being in regard to keeping promises and our overall lack of interest to being accountable for the quality of our life that have a direct correlation to the quality of our word or promises.

Here a great quote from an equally great warrior, a U.S. Marine, William A. Foster, about power of intention. William Adlebert Foster received the Medal of Honor for his "conspicuous gallantry and intrepidity at the risk of his life above and beyond the call of duty" during World War II in the Battle of Okinawa in 1945.

Quality is never an accident; it is always the result of high intention, sincere effort, intelligent direction and skillful execution; it represents the wise choice of many alternatives.

Only our commitments and our intentionality would guarantee the fulfillment of our *Life Vision*.

Keeping Promises

When we make a promise to ourselves about something we know has to get done to help fulfill our life's vision and will involve us in something larger than what we originally want it is not just about us. Others are involved. Our words and promises become our actions and manifest as a series of actions that impact our experiences and our results in our own lives, as well as the lives of others around us.

We have no idea how much our actions impact the world. That means any action, any broken promise, anything we do, anything we say will impact our relationship with others. Our relationship with others will impact the quality of our lives and eventually have a dramatic impact on our *Life Vision*.

By keeping our promises, continuing our practices and delivering on our commitments, we create conditions and environments that support our commitment rather than our mood, feelings and what we selfishly want for ourselves or for our personal benefit. Only when you act in a manner full of integrity, responsibility and accountability can you say you have separated yourself from your inner chatter and are not a product of your feelings or moods. You are now a product of your commitments and declarations. Simply put; YOU become YOUR word.

I am going to share another intimate part of my life with you. I hope it will make a difference in your ability to see what I am trying to say about being accountable and what it takes to be completely responsible and accountable for one's performance as one's word.

Earlier, I spoke about working as a construction contractor and building residential and commercial properties. The very last project I built belonged to a couple, two people who are my dear friends.

It was my last project, because I was changing my career as a builder and contractor to a program leader and public speaker. I made up my mind that I would make a drastic change in my life. For years I was pursuing both careers simultaneously, involved in building projects and participating as a volunteer, leading seminars and programs on the work that was and continues to be one of the closest to my heart and soul; working with people and making a difference in their lives now and in their futures.

These friends asked me to build their house because they trusted me. They believed in my level of integrity and felt that they could count on me. The combination of that trust and a compatible price made the deal!

During 1996-1997, I started the project. It was a challenging and very complicated project. I liked the challenge and I liked to bring my creativity to the table to resolve the issue with originality.

Given my involvement in my other passion, working on my public speaking and program leading, I did not manage the job with the detail and the management that I was expecting of myself or that which my friends expected of me!

I was engaged in my love of what I do and I did not pay attention to the extension of time and budget. We went over budget and missed the completion deadline by about four months.

As you can imagine, it was not a fun spot to be in. I had to make some hard decisions. There were several choices; the normal thing that most contractors would do would be to walk away from the project and fight with the owner for more money and time. I could have chosen to stop the work, go to fight with the owners and end up in court for proving that I deserved to get paid for the extension of time and money. In the extreme case, I could have even filed bankruptcy in 1998 and washed my hands of my entire financial obligation. There was a lot to decide.

Since the couple and I had a good relationship, I chose to look at the cost and the ultimate pay off of my choices.

What Would You Do?

I could not help but hold myself accountable for my own performance and work. Even for what I believed was an unfair and unexpected increase of time and budget, I could hear my own justifications, my own reasoning and explanations. I knew deep inside that I was responsible for where I was in life. It is only me that is accountable for the outcome of my life and my experiences of that outcome.

We sat down and looked at "what we are committed to accomplish here," and it was so clear to me and to them that we wanted to keep our friendship and to finish the job as soon as possible. Our commitment was clear and our declarations were expressed.

The owners gave me a loan with a very low and fair interest rate. I also borrowed some money from my own family and friends, yet it still was not enough. I went to my employer for whom I was leading programs. Based on my honoring my word and my employer's trust in me he lent me more money to finish the project.

At the end of the day, I completed the project and walked away with my head up, my friendship saved and honor untouched.

Thirteen years have passed and I paid off my employer, my family, friends and most of the money I borrowed from the owners themselves.

I share this story with you because I want you to know your feelings and emotions can be raw and pretty intense at times, but you must keep coming back to what you have committed to do.

When we honor our word and our promises we become who we TRULY are. We are our word as an action, rather than an idea. Our relationship to the world around us will shift from suffering to clarity and we will produce results that seem unpredictable and unforeseen.

Before now, we were just trying to survive. Now we are keeping our promises ... nothing else. You will begin experiencing joy, self-respect and magic vs. fear and anxiety.

One my favorite quotes of all time is from Mother Teresa. Born Agnesë Gonxhe Bojaxhiu, she was an Albanian Roman Catholic nun with Indian citizenship who founded the Missionaries of Charity in Kolkata (Calcutta), India in 1950. For more than 45 years, she ministered to the poor, sick, orphaned and dying, while guiding the Missionaries of Charity's expansion, first throughout India and then in other countries. She won the Nobel Peace Prize in 1979 and India's highest civilian honor, the Bharat Ratna, in 1980 for her humanitarian work. Mother Teresa's Missionaries of Charity continued to expand, and at the time of her death it was operating

610 missions in 123 countries, including hospices and homes for people with HIV/AIDS, leprosy and tuberculosis, soup kitchens, children's and family counseling programs, orphanages and schools. In her quote about commitment she said;

I never promised God I would be successful … I promised God I would be faithful to my commitment.

In the moment you choose accountability as a way of living, accountability shows as an opportunity to become your word.

This is who we are.

It is possible to be scared to make promises and declare your intentions. Check this part of you. Is it because you are scared that what you declare might come true? In that case, you have to become responsible for the quality of your life! You always wanted to have a good life, a successful life, right? Then you have to change and alter it!

In a funny way, as soon as you declare your commitments, the universe gets to work in your favor and doors keep opening. I don't mean just have intentions and do nothing. I am saying speak out your intentions and do something about them. Who you are going to be when you are doing them is the biggest key to your success.

Clarity

It is amazing when we get clear about our life vision. Suddenly the universe, people around us or even people who don't know us yet get enrolled to our vision for life! The world wants to be engaged with us and help us out to get that vision realized.

That is what I call *"Conspiracy for Greatness"* and what we need to reach is our *"Mastery of Love Within."*

In the end, I leave you with beautiful words from William Hutchison Murray the famous Scottish expeditionist and mountain climber. He wrote this part in his book *The Scottish Himalayan Expedition*:

Until one is committed there is hesitancy, the chance to draw back, always ineffectiveness.

Concerning all acts of initiative and creation, there is one elementary truth, the ignorance of which kills countless ideas and splendid plans.

That moment one definitely commits oneself, and then providence moves, too. All sorts of things occur to help one that would never otherwise have occurred. A whole stream of events issues from the decision, raising in one's favor all manner of unforeseen incidents and meetings and material assistance, which no man could have dreamt would have come his way.

I have learned a deep respect for ones Goethe's couplets:

Whatever you do, or dream you can, begin it. Boldness has genius, power and magic in it!

We are almost to the end of this chapter, so take a moment and answer the following two questions. After that, we will go through our standard questions.

Where are you not being accountable for your results in the personal and professional aspects of your life?

Look where you are just not holding yourself accountable for your bottom-line results.

_____

_____

_____

_____

In what areas of your life do you need to implement accountability?

What areas of life do you need to pay more attention to accountability and put some structure, declarations and actions in place?

_____

_____

_____

_____

We now have a better clarity of the influences that integrity, responsibility and accountably have on our life vision and the impact of not practicing them on our results in life. Simply, we need to use these forces to continue accomplishing and achieving the vision of our best future. In the next chapter, we work on practices, action plans and structures that will allow us to practice our life vision.

Also, we will work on maintenance plans and procedures that will assist us in keeping our values and our principles in place and side by side with our vision.

You are doing so well. Keep working! You are almost to the end of your exercises here. It is very important to complete all these standard questions, because we need them all to complete our work in chapter nine.

1. **What do you realize about yourself?**

_____

_____

_____

_____

2. **What are you willing to change or alter?**

_____

_____

_____

_____

3. **What are you promising yourself?**

_____

_____

_____

_____

4.   What are you willing to do to keep that promise?

_____

_____

_____

_____

5.   Who will you discuss this with?

_____

_____

_____

_____

CHAPTER NINE

CONSPIRACY FOR GREATNESS

CREATING AND INVENTING PRACTICES THAT WILL SUPPORT YOU

In the physical universe,
the only task you can manage is the one
you are facing at any given moment,
so take each task to its full completion.
Suddenly, you have built a future.

We are now at a place where we can create and invent practices that will assist us in reaching our greatness. If we do not manage and maintain what we learned or protect and support our vision, we cannot move forward in a productive manner. In this section we work on inventing new practices that will support our getting rid of the old and ineffective practices in our lives. This is where the rubber hits the road, the real black and white.

First, let's do a fast review and summary:

- We defined how to get out of our own way and live in the now to discover personal greatness. We found ourselves as capable and far from insignificant, able to do anything. We started the inquiry into "what it takes to have access to our inner power." We looked at what is in the way of our being great.

- We found what it takes to be open to possibilities versus our own pre-formed opinion. Then we looked at what we will gain out of being attached to our point of view and being closed to others views. At the same time, we saw how much it would cost us to "Be Right" about our opinion about everyone and everything.

331

- Next, we were introduced to our "Inner Chatter" in a whole different and very intimate way. We recognized the fact that we are the genesis of all of our own nasty, belittling and condescending inner conversations about ourselves, others and basically every other thing in our lives.

- After that, we looked at how we have created some of our own drama that created our own suffering. We choose to suffer because it is dramatic and attention getting. We then recognized that we have suffered due to our own celebration of pity versus our true inner power and greatness. We learned how to generate our own effectiveness, our own productivity and our own peace of mind.

- In the next section, we looked at why we were not fully inspired by what we do and what it takes to own the impact of our own decisions in life. This is how we kept ourselves away from what inspires us to be fully self-expressed and fully functioning doing what we love to do and how we love to be.

- Then we got to the place where we have the ability to create our own "Life Vision" from inspirations versus from a place of just surviving ... looking at our values and principles as well as what is truly important. We invented a vision for our lives that will inspire us, move us forward and in the end, make us happy.

- Last, we looked at the practices and behaviors in our personal life that would not be consistent with our new vision for life. We figured out that if we want this new vision to be powerfully recognized we have to use three powerful allies to make it strong and stable; and integrity, responsibility and accountability.

At this point, we look at how to fully support this new vision to become a reality. This will real support us to help us move forward achieve our goals and accomplish our dreams. At first I want to look at one of the biggest obstacles in our way to do that and that is to avoid **failing.** We don't like to fail and we are doing anything to not face failing. I am sure you can recognize the emotion and feelings that arise after the experience of failing.

By now you can hear all the negative inner chatter about failing as I always say; your head is a bad neighborhood, you should move out!

Consider this, you never know whether you will fail unless you try. The way you will fail is if you are being negative about what you say to yourself and what you are about to do! One of the greatest quotes I have read in this regards is from Sir Winston Churchill:

Success is moving from failure to failure with no loss of enthusiasm.

Failure is a Part of Life

The one point that is hard to explain but simple to say is that failure is a part of the process to success. While failure is difficult, it is part of the game of life and one of the things that if used correctly will make you stronger. I personally have failed in life more than I have succeeded, but I am absolutely certain of who is at the source of my successes and failures, me and me only. The problem starts when we don't see that the task we failed at doesn't define who we are at the core. Why? Because you are not the project or the goal, you are someone who is a source of the project or goal. When we look at a failure it is how we choose to define it. Simply looking at only the failure and not how we failed we are surrounded by the "conspiracy for smallness" and are the source of our own suffering.

The other side of the coin is when we look and relate to the project or goal as fulfilling our life vision, the idea that nothing is wrong and we have work in front of us. You must have an *"I can do it"* attitude because we can accomplish anything with the abilities, intelligence and resources needed. This is true even in our relationships. We must stand up, dust ourselves off and get back on the saddle so to speak. This is what I call "conspiracy for greatness" and "mastery of love within."

I totally understand and can feel the pain of failure. I have been there. I have compassion and understanding, but look at any goal or project you take on from this view... am I worth fighting for? Yes, I am! There is no doubt! One must be patient and committed to new practices, projects or goals that we choose to do. This is how we will have our vision fulfilled. Remember, nothing will happen overnight; patience and belief in the vision are very important to this process.

The following short story, "The Miracle of the Chinese Bamboo Tree" by Judy Armijo, will show you what I mean by patience:

The Chinese Bamboo tree is planted after the earth is prepared. For the first four years, all the growth is underground. The only thing visible above the ground is a little bulb and a small shoot growing out of it.

Leaders know what it means to pay the price to prepare the ground, to plant the seed, and to fertilize and cultivate, water and weed, even when they can't see immediate results. They have faith, that ultimately they will reap the fruits in the harvest.

And what wonderful fruits they are – because in the fifth year, the Bamboo tree grows up to eighty feet!

You are as as powerful as that little Chinese bamboo bulb! Even if you are small outside, feel scared, even terrified to take on life and bring home the vision you dream about. However, you are, strong inside, both powerful and a fighter! I hope that you can see am relating to you as a coach. We can do anything we put our mind, heart, and soul into. Failure is not a negative, until you say so. As matter of fact, it is nothing until you say so!

First, start with inventing practices and actions that will guarantee the alteration of your life experiences.

At the end of each chapter, there are a series of standard questions for you to dig into. Write down your realizations and insights. Check yourself on what recognitions you have had and what changes you want to make to move forward in a positive light. Make the things you write as a promise to yourself and then keep that promise.

If you have not yet created a promise for yourself, you need to go back and do it. You are BEING responsible and accountable to what you say you want in your life. No more wishing, hoping and dreaming! Now is the time to move forward! Unfortunately, the world is full of people with great potential, never realized. Each one of these people that are sitting dormant, have kept their genius within and never recognized their inner-power, because the inner chatter said the task was too hard or it would take too long. You might be one of them, but not anymore. You are learning NEW information and now you KNOW that greatness comes from within. Like a garage full of useful stuff that nobody ever opens the garage!

Fill yourself with integrity and relate to the relationship we are now forming with responsibility and most importantly, accountability. Be sure that you have taken the time to write your notes at the end of the chapter so your ideas will be fresh and you will take them more seriously. Otherwise it will be hard to work on your true needs.

In this chapter I introduce you to coaching. This will help you at least in four different ways:
- The Big List
- Vision, Value and Practices
- Weekly Value Practice
- Visual Structure

Knowing this will help you to maintain what you have learned so far and continue producing results out of what you have learned.

The Big List

The Big List is designed to be a place review. Compile a four-section accounting of the actions you have promised to put into place after redefining yourself.

Section One - Insights and Realizations

Looking back on the sections you have completed, pick out the insights or realizations you have after completing these chapters and questions at the end.

It is vital that you have at least ONE insight or realization per chapter. It will be manageable. Try to keep it no more than two so the task is doable.

Where to look for Insights and Realizations is in the end questions of each chapter when I asked, for example:

- What do you realize about yourself?
- What are you gaining out of this criticism or complaint?
- What do you realize about yourself; what are you giving up?

While the nature of the insight is usually bad news it can be used in a positive way. This is to know and learn about yourself so you have a choice to do something about it. Tell the truth without holding back; allow yourself to feel and experience the impact and pain of the past negativity.

This is very important because you can have a tendency to avoid reality and not face the truth of a situation or situations. That is why I said the nature of the insight can be bad news; for example:

> 1 - I am lazy and just want things in an easy way.
>
> 2 - I am disorganized and just don't care anymore.
>
> 3 - I always blame others. I am a martyr.

In the examples of the Big List format I have provided you with just 12 spaces, but you are more than welcome to recreate that format on your own computer and keep adding to it if it is necessary.

Right now, write your insights and realizations in the first section of the Big List (Figure "J") below before going on to section two:

Section One

INSIGHTS & REALIZATIONS

1. _____

2. _____

3. _____

4. _____

5. _____

6. _____

7. _____

8. _____

9. _____

10. _____

11. _____

12. _____

Figure "J"

Section Two – Operational Promises

Operational promises are those promises you make to yourself. These will impact the above insights and realizations that you have listed. In other words, if you keep the promises you made based on the insight you wrote, then you have altered and transformed the nature of your insight. Operational means the promises must have work behind them. You must DO something about them. They are not just conceptual like a pie in the sky! They are real and manageable, that is why these promises are categorized as operational.

Your answers to the following questions are an example of an operational promise:

- What are you promising to yourself?
- What are you going to do about this issue?
- What do you see you need to handle or complete?

For example, if your insights were as follows:

1 - I am lazy and just want things in an easy way
2 - I am disorganized and just don't care anymore.
3 - I always blame others I am a martyr.

Your Operational Promises might be something as follows:

> 1 - I promise to maintain my health and well being
>
> 2 - I promise to take on being organized
>
> 3 - I promise to become responsible for my own actions and the consequences.

One important note is to start each sentence with "I promise" because in that way you are holding yourself accountable. These are VERY important promises, because they are promises you have given to YOURSELF… the most important person you will ever make a promise to.

If you choose not to keep these promises, your insights and realizations will not ever see the light of day! Make a note to yourself, what you know makes no difference in the quality of your life, it is what you do with your knowledge that will ultimately make a difference.

"Knowledge is not power; implementation of knowledge is power!"

Look at how Section One notes on each insight and realization are relevant and make a promise, now write it in the Section Two. The number of your insights and realizations should match and correlate with the number of your promises:

Right now, write your operational promises in the second section of the Big List (Figure "K") below before going on to section three:

Section Two
OPERATION PROMISES

1. _____

2. _____

3. _____

4. _____

5. _____

6. _____

7. _____

8. _____

9. _____

10. _____

11. _____

12. _____

Figure "K"

Section Three – Operational Practices

Operational practices are those practices that you put in place, the nature of which will fulfill on the previously made promises. As you move further down the Big List, you should have one operational promise for each insight.

These are operational, which means they are something you DO, both specific and measurable. This is a measurement of accountability to show the practice was completed, which means a promise is closer to being fulfilled.

These practice answers can be found at the end of the chapters where I ask:

- What are you willing to do to keep your promise?
- What actions are you taking to alter that behavior?
- What is your plan for the changes you want to implement?

Here are examples based on what we already used, if your insights were as follows:

1 - I am lazy and just want things in an easy way.
2 - I am disorganized and just don't care anymore.
3 - I always blame others.

Operational Promises example:

> 1 - I promise to maintain my health and well being
>
> 2 - I promise to take on being organized
>
> 3 - I promise to become responsible for my own actions and the consequences.

Operational Practices example:

> 1- I will exercise one hour a day five times a week and I will cut fattening foods out of my diet.
>
> 2- I will get an organizer and schedule my activities daily in my calendar and also organize my work area every day before I leave my office.
>
> 3- I will not complain about anything and clean up my upsets with people within a week after the upsetting incident.

Now look at Section Two notes; based on each operational promise make an operational practice and write it in Section Three. The operational promise should correlate with the number of your practices; Promise #1 and Practice #1 are correlated and Promise #2 and Practice #2 are correlated and so forth.

Right now, write your operational practices in the third section of the Big List (Figure "L") below before going on to the section four:

Section Three
OPERATIONAL PRACTICES

1. _____

2. _____

3. _____

4. _____

5. _____

6. _____

7. _____

8. _____

9. _____

10. _____

11. _____

12. _____

Figure "L"

Section Four – People to clean up with

In this section you need to simply look back at your notes and find who you need to apologize to or clean something up with. I am sure as you were reading all the chapters you have realized the messes you have made, the broken promises to others you have made, the lies you may have created, the misrepresentations and even cover ups. You know what I am talking about I am quite sure. This is how to begin healing the relationships with people.

These people are in the end of each chapter when I asked:

- Who you will discuss this with?
- With whom to you need to clean up this matter with?

This is very important, because as you remember we talked about the only thing we have with others is our relationships and with our relationships we have nothing to hang on to, with our parents, our spouses, life partners, friends, clients, colleagues and so forth.

You know who you owe an apology to or who you need to clean something up or even someone whom you owe money too. Isn't possible that there is someone you lied to or participated in gossip about. Make a list and make sure you write down what the topic of the mess that you are cleaning up is about and your personal deadline on when you want to have it cleaned up by. Be clear, precise and to the point, without an open date so you will stay honest with yourself. For example:

1. My mother: gossiped about her with Tom by the 20th of this month.

2. My wife about my broken promise of cleaning up after myself, I will do it tonight after dinner.

3. My friend Jane about the money I owe her. I will communicate with Jane before the 20th of this month to make arrangements to pay her back.

The above are simple examples, but as you very well know, some issues are big, hairy and downright nasty! You can clean them up too … just communicate more to get deeper and give it more time for people to heal. Sometimes we have done such a big mess that it caused other people to not want to talk to us forever. I am sure you can recognize some of these issues, and you might even be the one who doesn't want to clean up that issue or not give the chance to someone else to clean up with you.

You might say "No, I don't want to get into communication with that person at all" or "To hell with them!" or "I don't care." It's okay, as long as you are not upset about it and it doesn't bother you. You know better than anyone else that some issues are still bothering you and keep you upset. It is very possible that you even know very well when you have stepped on some people's toes and made them upset; you know you have said things that you shouldn't have said; you know there are   hidden issues that will be upsetting if it comes to the surface publicly. By judging and evaluating yourself and others that you have made some major messes in life.

347

You and I both know that our lives are full of upsetting issues and damaged relationships. I highly recommend you get into the habit of cleaning them up; get into it; it is not too late yet! While you are undoubtedly thinking "it is lots of work" or "it is too much, and I don't know where to start" do this exercise anyway. It is okay. You know how they say to eat an elephant? One bite at a time!

Start from the small items and warm up to the bigger ones. With the easy clean ups and move on to the harder ones. In any event, consider the alternative which is to keep separating yourself from life and keep hiding and keep suppressing yourself; it is worth it to clean these very difficult issues up.

Please get to writing on the Section Four by reviewing your insights, your realizations and your notes overall. Look at with whom and about what you need to get into communication and clean up your past with them and take some responsibility for your actions and your past behaviors (Figure "M"):

Section Four
PEOPLE TO CLEAN UP WITH

1. _____

2. _____

3. _____

4. _____

5. _____

6. _____

7. _____

8. _____

9. _____

10. _____

11. _____

12. _____

Figure "M"

Good work, I am proud of you. Very good job!

You have gone through such an amazing space in a short period of time that so many people would not go through in their lifetime, and I am not kidding! I acknowledge you for your commitment to the quality of your life and future by designing a whole new vision for your life and the willingness to look at yourself and own all aspects the good, bad or ugly, all of it; the whole you.

That is *the mastery of love within* and that is what I call your *conspiracy for greatness*. By you taking responsibility for your life and by taking on cleaning up your past to have a greater future you have started a conspiracy unlike any other conspiracies you have been involved with. You know what I am talking about, when you say "I can't" or "It is so hard" and find someone to agree with you about "yes, it is hard" or "I know you can't" then you are in a conspiracy for smallness. When you get to gossip or backroom conversations with others about someone else in secrecy, you are involved with some conspiracy for smallness in regards to that personal relationship.

But like what you just did, when you look within yourself as deep and intimate as you have and make powerful promises for change. Then move forward on life alterations, even willingly take on cleaning up your own life messes, then you are in a whole different kind of conspiracy, you are now involved in a *conspiracy for greatness.* That is an act of self-love and self-respect; that is the beginning of the next level, the *mastery of love within*.

Now that you learned how to work with your Big List, I ask you to maintain your awareness and progress by continuing to add to it. Each time that you have some insight about yourself, write it down, make a promise about altering that insight, invent and write down a practice that will make the promise real and get to work, while you clean up your mess about that you have done, simple … piece of cake!

Vision, Value and Practices

We are now going to distinguish another great structure to assist you with your conspiracy for greatness; I call it Value Practices.

Go back to Chapter Seven and look at your Value List. If you remember you made two lists, one was what you are valuing in your life and the other one was what you are valuing in business. Put both values side by side and look at them and become the judge of this question:

Which of these values are the ones that I am not practicing all the time?

Or from this point:

Which one of these values is not completely present in my life?

For example let's say you wrote that you value "intimacy," however, you are not practicing it and it is not present in your life. Your life partner or your spouse complains about not seeing you enough or concerned that when you are together intimacy is not being experienced. Like you are just there and going through the motions, as if you are not communicating and holding back! So if you say you are valuing intimacy but you are not practicing it and it is not present in your day to day life, now is the time to change that.

Another example; you might have wrote down was "Fun" as a value you care about, however all you do is work or do things that are work related. Your family and your friends do not see you enough, you are not going to friend's gatherings and parties, the last vacation you went to was years ago, so there is no match with what you say and what you DO!

Another example is if you said you value "Health" but you smoke and/or you are overweight! Get the picture here?

The bottom line is that who you are BEING is not matching with someone who is committed to practicing their values. We all can come up with a lot of justifications and reasons why we cannot practice our values and how busy we are in this fast passed life. We both know that we lie about what we value and that is one of the biggest reasons that people leave relationships, quit jobs, get fired or experience loneliness. People watch how we act in the face of our commitments and at who we have been BEING while we are DOING what we said we care about and we are committed to. It is not very hard to notice that someone is being bored while they work at their job and by the way, in their job interview they said "They love to do this." We can all see someone not being engaged with us while they say they love us and they care about us; it is not hard to notice if someone is just talking or they are really involved and engaged in their passion and what they mean!

Unfortunately, unless we have been completely honest about what is going on around us, not taking it personally, we will not see what is really going on! We will not even notice that "this person is not engaged" or "this person is not practicing something that is important to them," because this is a language of someone who is present to what others are present to, it is the language of our ultimate transformation; it takes us being open to what the other person is not open to.

If we are not open to others and reality, we call them names, make mean-spirited interpretations and our opinions and judgments start kicking in, then we lose compassion and our understanding. All we will see are the "jerks," we see "not interested in me!" or we see "liar." We say to ourselves, "whatever!" or "yeah, right!" or "we'll see." I am sure you have never done that! But you know someone else who has done that, right?

Consider this. At the moment we are in a conspiracy for smallness against that person, at that moment we are looking for evidence of how small that person is and why we cannot trust them or why they are not worthy of our time, love and attention. In some cases we gossip our thoughts with others around us. That is why I call it a conspiracy.

On the other hand, if we care about the people, we help them to be open to the values they are really saying they want but at the same time they missed having them in their lives. How we can do that is by starting from ourselves first. Walking the talk and holding ourselves accountable first, then we can do that with others.

Now I want you to look at those values and the lists you wrote in Chapter Seven and find the top five values that you are NOT practicing the most. Look at the two questions I asked in the beginning of this section:

Which of these values are the ones that I am not practicing all the time?

Which one of these values is not completely present in my life?

When you select those five values that you practicing the least and that are not currently present in your life, write them in the following chart called "Vision, Values and Practices." Write your Life Vision first and get present to it, then write those values in order of #1 to #5, it will look like this: *Value #1: Fun.*

When you have written your Life Vision and your five Values, then start writing under the right column first and that is "***New practices I am inventing.***" For each value come up with three practices that you have never done before or that you have completely put aside and have not practiced for a long time. See what you are resisting the most and that might be the one you want to do! Look at what is in your mind and is hard for you, and pick that one. That is Conspiracy for Greatness!

For example, it would look like this:

New practices I am inventing

Value #1: Fun

1. *Schedule one gathering with my friends per month*
2. *Sign up for dance class on Monday nights*
3. *Take my wife out on a date once a week*

Clearly, these practices could be anything and about any values you might choose, but remember this, it doesn't need to be something so hard! Simple things make the biggest difference in the quality of our lives as well as the quality of our life experiences, as well as the quality of our relationships with others.

When you did that then go the right column and work on the other side: ***"Old practices I am eliminating"*** because eliminating what is not working and helping us to have the experience and the presence of our values in our lives is as important as inventing new practices. There is a lot you can stop doing, such as stopping and eliminating negative behaviors which makes inventing new practices much easier to deal with, so these two sides will work hand in hand in empowering you to have the experience and the presence of your values in your life.

For example, it would be something like this:

<u>*Old practices I am eliminating*</u>

Value #1: Fun

1. *Stop lying about "I am so busy"*
2. *Stop screening my calls*
3. *Watching trash TV*

Put them side by side in the format I have provided for you, then you can see exactly what needs to get done and what needs to stop so you have what you want as a value in your life be present for you, so it would look something like this:

<u>*New practices I am inventing*</u>   <u>*Old practices I am eliminating*</u>

Value #1: Fun

1. *Schedule one gathering per month*	1. *Stop lying about "I am so busy"*
2. *Sign up for dance class on Monday nights*	2. *Stop screening my calls*
3. *Take my wife out on a date once a week*	3. *Stop watching trash TV*

This is the way you design new practices that will work as well as eliminating old behaviors that are not working so you can have a FUN present for you and your life as a value will exceed expectations. Your experience as a new person will shine out of your every moment and you will begin to see yourself as much happier, productive and fun person.

Get your spouse, life partner, your business partners, close friends and family involved with selecting and inventing new practices that will help you to eliminate the old and unworkable practices. Get these people engaged in helping you realize a value based life and the beauty of living your life by design and not just accidently.

As one of the greatest American authors, Jack London, said:

The proper function of man is to live, not to exist. I shall not waste my days in trying to prolong them. I shall use my time.

At this time, after selecting those top five values, write down the new practices and choose the old practices you are eliminating. Please use the following format which is designed for you to see both sides of the process at the same time. If you need to recreate the format (Figure "N") in your computer then do so to serve you better, but get to it now!

VISION, VALUES & PRACTICES

My Life Vision: _____

_____

_____

| **New practices I am inventing** | **Old practices I am eliminating** |

Value #1:

1. _____   1. _____
2. _____   2. _____
3. _____   3. _____

Value #2:

1. _____   1. _____
2. _____   2. _____
3. _____   3. _____

Value #3:

1. _____   1. _____
2. _____   2. _____
3. _____   3. _____

Value #4:

1. _____   1. _____
2. _____   2. _____
3. _____   3. _____

Value #5:

1. _____   1. _____
2. _____   2. _____
3. _____   3. _____

Figure "N"

Good job! And if you just jumped over this part and have not done the work required to finish it, get back to work and get it done, not for me, but for you.

When you get good at it and by practicing some new behaviors and actions, then pick another value. Basically what I am saying is that you don't have to stick with the first five values you have selected, you can choose another value when you get good at the ones you are working on, and it is a process.

Now I will show you another simple process that you can add to the above processes and get the full benefit of your week to be happy and fulfilled in your life.

Weekly Values and Practices

Every week, choose a value you care about and invent new practices to have the experience of that value be present for you during that particular week. By doing this you will add more happiness, fulfillment and self-expression to your daily life. Just make sure not to repeat the values that you have incorporated in the Vision, Value and Practices format, the first five that you picked. These are totally different values. They are your values but they are the ones that you are good at and you love to have them present for you, so we will manage that together.

The best thing you can do is to reproduce the format in your computer so you can have access to it whenever you need it to change and alter weekly.

First thing to do is to write your Life Vision right on the top of the form, because everything is generated from you relating to that life vision.

Once you do all this, complete the starting and ending date of the week, starting on Monday and ending on Sunday, and that will be the week you are targeting.

Then you select a value that you care about and want to work on in that week; could be intimacy, productivity, respect, health, and/or any other value.

After that invent just two new practices exactly like what you had done on the above "Vision, Value and Practices" exercise from before. Just two is enough, not more than that, because I don't want you to have an experience of "you have a lot to do!" Have fun with it and keep it simple and real.

When you do that then do the other side and select old practices that you will eliminate and get rid of so the experience of that value is present for you during that week. You have done this before on the above process, just repeat it and be truthful and honest! You know exactly what you need to stop doing, just do it! Again, keep it simple and real.

The only thing that this format has that the other one doesn't is the last question:

What I have to give up for this value to be present for me are:

You got that one right! Without you giving up something in your life, such as an old practice or old behavior or old belief you cannot bring something new in its place to replace it with ... simple, but very elegant and powerful.

Remember the law of physics? No object can exist in the same place at the same time. We cannot say we want health but we will not give up smoking. It just won't work. We cannot say we are valuing productivity but continue coming in late to work and then leaving early, it just not a match. We can't say we are valuing intimacy and closeness but withholding our communications.

I highly recommend that you look at what your inner chatter is saying about the presence of that value in your life, or how hard it is to work on it, or how frustrating it is to maintain it, then you know what you need to give up for that value to be present for you. For example, giving up the righteousness of "it doesn't work" or give up "I can't do it" or give up "It doesn't matter" or any other negative, heavy barriers you are bringing into this process. Give them up for the possibility of having that value be present for you. I know it will not be easy, but considering your alternatives, why not?

The next piece for you to work on is below in Figure "O":

WEEKLY VALUES & PRACTICES

My Life Vision: _____

_____

_____

Week starting from:_____ **and ending at:**_____

The value I chose for this week is:_____

A. New practices invented for this value this week are:

1._____

2._____

B. Old practices eliminated about this value this week are:

1._____

2._____

C. What I have to let go off for this value to be present for me are:

1._____

2._____

Figure "O"

Visual Structure

Now we look at another practice that will help us keep our vision alive and vibrant and in front of us. I call it a Visual Structure.

If we take on that we are disorganized and we will forget things even if we want to do them we have to become responsible for how to keep all these desires and projects in front of us. Obviously, it will be a lot to remember and so many things to put in place and keep in order. You know better than I do that we get discouraged fast and as a result we will drop the project or practice.

One of the ways I find it helpful to is to create a Visual Structure for the practices we do to keep our vision alive and in front of us, such as:

Life Vision Frame

As I said before, make sure to frame your vision in one beautiful frame. Place it in front of you on your desk at work or your on computer workstation. It will be helpful if you have another one in your living room also so you can share it with others and actual create a conspiracy for your greatness by exposing your vision to everyone in your family and friends and people in your circle.

Vision Board

Make a board or poster approximately 18 x 24 inches or 24 x 36 inches and start posting pictures of what you see in your life and your future on that board. Could be simply a note you are writing on it or a cut out picture from a magazine or newspaper in regards to what you want or desire for your life and your future out of you fulfilling your vision.

This could be a picture of a house you see yourself in within the next ten years, or the body shape or form you can see yourself to be in the next two years, money, family, relationship, career or any other area or aspects of your life.

By hanging this poster in front of you somewhere you actually keep your mind on the goals and keep reminding yourself about what your vision is about and what are you aiming for. It is not about just making money or having a tight body or a big home … it is about what those things will remind you of, like health, abundance, prosperity and freedom from just surviving.

Displays

This could be anything ... could be just a statue or small stuffed animal, or as simple as a sticky note in front of your computer. Things that will remind you of what you are up to, what you are working for and why you are doing it. I simply have pictures of my kids around me. Yes, I know, I should have them any way, and I do and they remind me of what this is about. I also have a little frame that has a little note in it that says: "It is not true, I just made it up." It is a silly thing but think about it, how many times have you made things up after someone said something and then you suffered for many hours or even days, but when you got into it and found out the truth you realized you had suffered over nothing? At least nothing as significant as you made it to be. This way I am always present to how much interpretations I make up.

If we look closely, we can recognize that most of our thoughts about ourselves, others and life itself are interpretations and made up junk, but for sure we are not present to it in that given moment. That is why these kinds of displays will help keep our minds straight and focused on what is important to us.

Inspiration

Have something around you that will inspire you to action or inspire you to think or motivate you to do something different every day. This could be simply a picture of a public figure you admire, a picture of one of your heroes, symbols that will inspire you or maybe just a quote from a great person. As a matter of fact I have series of quotes in picture frames right in my office in front me, and I look at them every day while I work with others. I have quotes from Buddha, Gandhi, Helen Keller and Dr. Martin Luther King, Jr., in front of me. These quotes help me to think straight and keep my mind and soul right on track with my life vision.

Don't Cheat!

Do not cheat on yourself by postponing these processes. The only person who will benefit out of this work is you, and that is why I call it "Conspiracy for Greatness" because as a society, we need to stop the pettiness and get on with what we have to do and who we have to become. This will lead us to have that wonderful life we love to have and live. That is why it is in the next step of this book we deal with the "mastery of love within." Only the magic and power of love that can heal our wounds. Most of these wounds were self inflicted, when we sold out on what was right for us, caused by moments lies we told ourselves to say "this one will be different." Over time, these actions cause scars; scars take even longer to heal as we deal with calling out our inferior feelings and ideas about ourselves. This is the time when we bought into the conspiracy for smallness.

It is time for you to stand up, and declare, not this time, not now and not anymore! This time we stand for our own futures and our own power as a dignified human being who is inspired to cause conspiracy for greatness. We will take the time and effort to get everyone we care about involved and engaged into our lives and living it full out because we are becoming the masters of love within.

You have to develop some power in regards to your relationship to discipline. Discipline to follow your dreams and your goals to the end, and to fulfill your vision.

I have the following quote from Buddha right in front me every day;

Endurance is one of the most difficult disciplines,
but it is to the one who endures that the final victory comes.

You are making very good progress and I am proud of what you have taken on. You should give yourself a huge hug and big high five!

In the next chapter we look at the power of acknowledgment and empowerment and the positive impact these very powerful practices have in our lives and our relationship to ourselves and to others.

CHAPTER TEN

Acknowledgement and Empowerment

ACCESS TO OTHERS' GREATNESS

One of the things that makes you distinct
from others is the way you leave people.
The question worth asking is this: Are they left
bigger or smaller than when you found them?

In this chapter you learn about power of acknowledgment, appreciation and empowerment.

Access to others' greatness is from one or all of these elements, which is what's missing in the world today. I am a firm believer that if we use acknowledgment and empowerment and if we find something that we can appreciate about others, we have accessed their greatness vs. looking to find what is wrong in them and for their shortcomings. We do that because we do not have compassion and appreciation for ourselves. We have already established that point in this book, so to access others' greatness requires us to acknowledge and empower ourselves first.

Recognize Your Own Greatness

I know it is hard. Sometimes we do not find anything great about ourselves, because we can't get past our shame, blame and faults. Sometimes we can't get past our body dimensions, our financial situation or our social state. By now you have the tools and strength to deal with all these issues and have access to your power and to your life as a possibility. Now that you have a vision for your life, which is more important and more exciting than just surviving, you need to gain access to the acknowledgment of yourself.

To start with, you can acknowledge yourself for:

- Taking on yourself and your life
- Looking at areas of your life that were not easy or comfortable to look at
- Starting to understand the way you operate and start to become responsible for how you have operated in life
- Taking some accountability in regard to why you don't have what you desire in your life and start a plan to get there
- Starting or continuing to love yourself and appreciate who you really are
- Starting to relate to others and to the world around you from a whole different and more empowering way
- And so much more…

As one of my heroes, Dr. Martin Luther King, Jr., once said:

Whatever affects one directly affects all indirectly. I can never be what I ought to be until you are what you ought to be, and you can never be what you ought to be until I am what I ought to be.

For us to be able to acknowledge and appreciate others we have to look deep inside and acknowledge and appreciate who we become when we let LOVE into our heart and soul. When we let in love we automatically push out hate and darkness. There is just not enough room for love and hate to exist together in our heart and soul; we have to practice one at a time, so why not love? That will give us access to forgiveness, to letting go of pain, sadness, resentments and regrets.

Cleaning Up Is A Necessary Step

Letting go of your ego is the first step in the cleaning up process.

If you look at "The Big List" in Chapter Four you have a list of people with whom you said you need to clean something up. Maybe you want to start with acknowledgment and addressing what they have gone through with you and/or about the issues they have with you, so that the list is a very resourceful list.

When we look we can find items worth of acknowledging in anyone about anything, the issue is are we willing to let go of our ego, our upset or our anger to see the good or not! The hardest thing is the willingness to acknowledge. I can share about my own life here. As I mentioned, my second marriage ended in a very nasty and belittling way, with cheating, lying and manipulation. I did not and still don't know who is telling the truth and when I will be lied to again, or what kind of games she will play. But one thing was very clear for me; I was not willing to put anything negative in my kids' minds about what happened. I let my kids and my former wife know that I am talking about these events in my book, so heads up, but my kids are almost 19 and 20 now, not 2 and 3 as when the marriage ended.

Now, back to the story. Even with having the kind of anger and upset that was in my heart, I always looked to find good and great in my ex-wife. I continued choosing my own greatness over my own ego and hurt, I found her greatness in being a very committed mother to our two kids. I might not agree with her parenting style or some of her decisions, but I always supported her in her decisions because I knew she was the best mother those two kids could have, and she has done a great job raising them. I had to let go of my darkness to see her light, and that gives me the opportunity to see my own light each time I do that. I make sure to acknowledge and empower my ex-wife and to let her know that I know what a great job she has done as a mother. As a matter of fact, on several occasions she acknowledged me for keeping our relationship peaceful.

Same way with my former teammates or any employee I ever worked with or any person I ever had some disagreement with or discussion about something sensitive. I continue to do my best to be sensitive to what they see and what they relate to when they talk to me. It is not easy but it is effective.

This could be with anyone on any topic. When we start with acknowledgment and appreciation of others for anything, maybe even something small, we assist them to put down their protection shield and relate to us on a whole different level, which sounds like a conspiracy for greatness to me.

Another use of acknowledgment and appreciation is to say what we need to say to someone to make sure our relationship with them is whole and complete and nothing left unsaid. It doesn't have to be anything negative or upsetting, maybe just acknowledging who they have been for us and how joyful it is to be with them. We are not that good at expressing our love and appreciation to our loved ones. This is especially true of men; we learned to just be tough and not expressive. This is one of the most common complaints I have heard from my female clients ... their husband or boyfriend is not expressive enough or they are holding back their feelings and emotions.

At the same time, I have heard from my male clients that they are upset at their wife or girlfriend because they are always pushing them to be more expressive and more in touch with their feelings. By the way, this issue has nothing to do with gay or straight ... even in same-sex relationships people have the same issues.

Again, we have to look and ask ourselves what are our expectations of acknowledgment or appreciation. Maybe they are acknowledging us and appreciating us but in their own way, but are we looking to find it or are we just attached to what we say acknowledgment should be?

Sometimes we are just too reserved to give acknowledgment and appreciation. It doesn't even have to be with someone we are upset with, sometimes even with people we love and don't have anything upsetting between us; like our parents, our siblings or our best friends. I think the hardship of expressing our feelings about someone and acknowledging them is sourced by our fear of intimacy and vulnerability. For us to be that way with people we have to really get close to our own humanity and become intimate with ourselves. That is scary in itself.

I can give you another example of this from my own life.

In early 1996, my father was diagnosed with lung cancer. The funny thing was that he was never a smoker in any way, shape or form. At the time he was in Iran, so my brothers and I (we don't have sisters) got together and brought him to the U.S. within three days. He started his chemotherapy and his radiation treatment, but the cancer was in its advanced stages and he did not survive beyond five months.

Almost a month before he passed, we all knew what was going to happen, but at the same time Father's Day was right around the corner. Everyone was thinking about what we should do for him on Father's Day given that we knew it would be the last time we would have him with us for Father's Day. People were talking about a party, gifts, food and every other regular and common thing that everyone would do for celebrating someone they love, like we all do and nothing wrong with that.

But what people really want from us, our parents, our siblings and our friends and family is our love, our appreciation of who they are for us, acknowledgment of what they have done for us and how they have supported us and loved us in any way, shape and form. For some people it doesn't come easy to acknowledge and express their feelings so they buy gifts, give stuff to each other or they are going out and trying to spend more money on someone to say, "I care for you, and I love you."

I was kind of the same way, maybe not so savvy but in some cases very reserved with my feelings, especially for my father, because I had a massive amount of respect for him. I remember the first time I said "I love you" to my father in a very straight way without all the extras around it. Let me tell you what happened, I don't want to go away from the topic but I think it is relevant to what we are talking about here.

Don't Be Afraid To Express Your Love for Others

The first time I did any program with Landmark Education was when I did the Landmark Forum in 1993 in Los Angeles. There were almost over hundred people in that course. I attended that class by an invitation from one of my very close friends, Ata Hassani, after my nasty separation and all the drama with my wife at that time. The program was three and half days and as I remember just sitting in the back row judging and evaluating others as they shared their life issues. The program leader helped them see different angles of their issues and in some ways taught them to be responsible for the quality of their lives. On the third day, a young man from one of the front rows stood up and started talking about his issues with his father. I was not really listening to it because I had a great relationship with my father, nothing negative, nothing abusive or inappropriate. He was a great father, amazing husband to my mother and a very respectful member of our community, so I had no issues with my father, and I was not paying much attention to what the man was saying. I was in my world of judging and evaluating; not like any of you have ever done that, right?

As I observed him I started noticing our differences. The young man was in his early 20s and I was 36 at that time. Judging from his clothing I thought he was either unemployed or a college student, kind of broke and not spending money on himself. I was educated and at that time I had my construction company. He was a white American and I was Iranian from the Middle-East; he was a single man and I was a married man with three kids. As he shared his life he mentioned he was gay and I was straight, so in my mind there was almost nothing in common between us. Even you might come to the same conclusion given the evidence.

As I said before, I was not really listening to him until he started digging into his relationship issues with his father and his father's disapproval of him being gay, and all the problems they had and all the hardships they went through and the damage that had happened in his relationship with his father. What was interesting to me was my realization of a common thing I shared with this young man, and that was that we both loved our fathers tremendously. With the help of the class leader the young man realized that maybe his father was showing his love to him the way he does, by trying to protect him from society who was not ready to accept him completely or for any other reason. The point was that the young man, regardless of how much he loved his father, almost never completely expressed his love to his father, given the issues they had from a very early age. He was not telling his father that he loved him because in his hurt heart and mind if his doing so meant he was aligned with his father's view of his sexual orientation or lifestyle, so he kept his love away from his father.

I didn't have the same issue with my father or any other issues with him, but when I heard the young man say, "I never told my father that I loved him," suddenly a light bulb went on in my head. "Me either!" It was shocking to me because as much as I respected my father and no matter how much I loved him, I never told him that. Interesting. This made me think more about where else I have not expressed myself, where else had I held back my love, with whom have I not shared myself with yet, and who is very close to me but has not had *me* yet?

I tell you all these examples to make a point … that we all do this. We are all in the same boat. We all in some areas of our lives and with some people in our lives holding back, not expressing our love and appreciation for them, especially parents because we assume they know. They don't! They need to hear it as much as we do. I was looking at what I did for years, buying gifts for my parents on Father's Day or Mother's Day, taking them to dinners, paying for some of their bills from time to time, fixing their home, giving them rides to places and trying to take care of them as much as I could and the way you do, too, but again, I never told my dad how much I loved him. Maybe because I was mister tough guy and I had to keep the façade. I don't know, maybe it was my culture or maybe it is the male culture; for whatever reason I was awakened and now I knew that I had not said that I love my father. I decided I would handle this issue and I would get into communication with my father. I would let him know how much I loved him.

I called back home to Iran. It was almost midnight when I left the class and I was home. At that time it was almost noon time in Iran given the time difference, so when I called and my father recognized it was an overseas call (you will hear some extra noises on the line when you are connecting to an overseas call) and given all of us three sons were here in the States and it was a very unusual time to call back home, he got worried and the first thing he said after he heard my name was "What is wrong?"

I said, "Nothing is wrong, Father. I just called to talk to you."

His response was, "At midnight?"

"Yes, Father," I replied, "it is very important for me to talk to you now."

He said, "Are you okay? Are your kids okay?"

I said, "Yes, Father, everyone is fine."

He asked again, "How are your uncles? Are they okay? Your brothers okay?" I know he was really worried about us, given the unusual time of the call, so I stopped him and assured him that everything and everyone was fine.

I said, "Dad, everyone here is fine, nobody is dying, nobody is in jail and nobody is divorcing anyone, so relax." Then I continued telling him about my experience with the class and what I discovered about myself. I shared with him that I realized that I am the biggest jerk in the world and I realized how much my attitude had cost me in my life.

He said, "How much did you pay for that course?" I knew it was a loaded question but I could not resist giving him an opportunity to take a shot at me (you know it is their way to say I love you, too), so I said $375. He replied "I could have told you that for free! I have said that for the last thirty years." We both laughed.

I told him, "Dad, you had told me that, but this time I got it myself and I think this time it will stick." I continued, "Dad, there is something else I wanted to tell you and that is what I recognized about my relationship to you." He was very quiet and listened without any comment, so I continued. "And what I realized is that I always showed respect to you, but I never told you how much I love you and how important you are to me."

There was a short pause and then he said, "Are you drunk?" and we both laughed again. At this time I assured him again that I was not under the influence of drugs or alcohol, I did not join a cult or become a member of any holding hands and singing Kumbaya group.

Then he started listening and I had a chance to really acknowledge him and let him know that I knew what he had done for me and my brothers and for our whole family. He quietly listened, and I could hear he was crying a little. I didn't say anything and he did not mention it either. He said he loved me, too, and he was proud of what I had done in my life, and he made sure to mention that I still had a lot to learn. I said "I love you, too, Father," and we hung up.

In that moment I knew that he knew how much I loved him and that our relationship started having a much deeper value and intimacy to it. I was very content and at peace with me and my relationship to my father; it was a very peaceful moment. Since that phone call, whenever we talked, when we were together, we still spent our time going to dinner and/or getting together with family, but we were both present to the love for each other and it was not that unspoken thing. It was out on the table, and he always encouraged me to continue my education in transformation and keep working on my personal growth.

Getting back to the original story, after we knew my father would not survive his cancer and we had a very short time, I decided to write him a letter and try to thank him for everything he had done for me as much as I could remember. At the time my father passed I was almost 39 years old, so there was a lot I could of say or mention, but I just trusted my heart that everything that needed to be said would come out and that would be a real authentic communication. I started writing, and it kept coming to me.

Here is the actual letter I wrote on June 16, 1996, to my father as his Father's Day gift:

My dear father,

For a long time, I thought about what I could give you for a sign of my appreciation and acknowledgment for all those years of training and generosity from you, years of training on how to be a human being. I gave you gifts and material things but never gave you myself. I want to say Thank You for all those years of support and unconditional love from you. I could not find anything to show my respect and love for you, but my words, and my words only.

Thank you for my life,
Thank you for being great,
Thank you for being my father,
Thank you for raising me so well,

Thank you for being there when I needed you,

Thank you for being there, always,

Thank you for buying me everything that I asked for, or promised that you will later,

Thank you for teaching me how to use tools and make things,

Thank you for being so hard on me for my education,

Thank you for giving me my brothers,

Thank you for bailing me out after I got involved in a street fight,

Thank you for loving my mother and being the greatest husband,

Thank you for teaching me how to dress myself,

Thank you for teaching me how to be interested in things,

Thank you for acknowledging me for my painting and art,

Thank you for staying awake on the nights of my school exams,

Thank you for staying awake on the nights of my illness,

Thank you for showing up at my sport events,

Thank you for coming into the swimming pool when you didn't want to and did it just because I asked you to,

Thank you for teaching me how to ride a bike,

Thank you for teaching me how to drive a car and letting me drive your car,

Thank you for taking me to beautiful places for vacation,

Thank you for teaching me how to respect others,

Thank you for teaching me the difference between good and bad,

Thank you for teaching me the difference between religion and fanaticism,

Thank you for showing me what it takes to be related to the god,

Thank you for teaching me how to love unconditionally,

Thank you for enforcing discipline and following rules in our lives,

Thank you for teaching me how to be a man,

Thank you for supporting me on my wedding expenses,

Thank you for showing me how to gain respect,

Thank you for believing in me,

Thank you for showing me how to raise a child,

Thank you for supporting me during my school and college,

Thank you for supporting whoever asked you for support,

Thank you for respecting everyone regardless of who they are or what they do,

Thank you for sending me out there to take care of my own life,

Thank you for being an example of integrity and honesty for me and my brothers,

Thank you for training me on how to be strong and straight,

Thank you for staying strong during my brother's captivity,

Thank you for showing grace and power after my brother's death,

Thank you for taking care of my mother during my brother's captivity and death,

Thank you for taking care of my little daughter when I left the country,

Thank you for bringing my daughter to me after five years of loving and raising her,

Thank you for teaching my daughter all the things that you taught us,

Thank you for always being proud of your family,

Thank you for always being proud of your country and teaching us to never forget where we are from,

Thank you for taking us to the village that you were born in,

Thank you for supporting me during my divorce even when you did not agree with it,

Thank you for being a kind human being,

Thank you for never smoking and teaching us the same thing,

Thank you for teaching me the difference between drinking for fun and getting drunk,

Thank you for always being strong and committed,

Thank you for always being forgiving,

Thank you for teaching me forgiveness and grace,

Thank you for teaching me that hitting would not making a difference,

Thank you for teaching me to be there for my family and friends in their happiness and grief,

Thank you for fighting your cancer,

Thank you for showing me strength and belief in miracles again,

Thank you for loving me,

Thank you for being my father,

Thank you again for my life,

And thank you for everything and anything I forgot to thank you for.

Happy Father's Day.

With love and respect from your son, Behnam

I sat by him until he read the whole letter. He finished it, smiled at me and said, "Thank you." Then he placed the letter in his brief case and we both knew that he got that my acknowledgment and our relationship was whole and complete, nothing left unsaid, love was present and appreciation was clear.

Days after that my mother asked me, "What was that paper you gave to your father? He is showing it to everyone!" After I explained it to my mother we both laughed because we knew my father was really enjoying the acknowledgment he received. I also taught my mother to do the same thing and to make sure she said whatever she needed to say, to acknowledge and to appreciate him before he left us. She said later that she did so and she was so grateful for my suggestion.

Soon after that my father passed away. In the last moment we were all there with him, one of my brothers and me, my mother, my sister-in-law, my uncle and some of other family members were at his side. He passed as I was stroking his head. Obviously, it was a difficult moment; I was very sad, very heartbroken yet at the same time very complete with my relationship with him and acceptance of his passing. I invite you to start acknowledging and showing appreciation to your loved ones before they pass so they can enjoy that experience of being with you longer.

My Thanks To You

Thank you for investing your time and reading my letter to my father and to read about my experience of it. The reason I shared this with you is to encourage you to take time and start acknowledging your loved ones and to make sure they know what they have done for you before it gets too late. Life is very short and very fragile, so don't wait.

There are so many people around your life that deserve an acknowledgment and to hear our appreciation. There are so many people in our lives that we can empower by using a different choice of words or even choosing an attitude or behavior so they get empowered by us and don't shrink or feel small around us.

They are not that far from you and it is not that hard to find them. It takes commitment to make sure people are being taken care of when they are around. During your reading this book I am sure you have found some names to contact, somebody to communicate with and somebody that you should start expressing yourself to, so get into it. Be a hero and let go of your upsets, resentments and angers; be a hero by making your life about acknowledging, appreciating and empowering others, by listening to them, by understanding them and by loving them they way they are and most importantly the way they are not. That is what makes you unique and amazing in this world. You might have heard me say or you will hear me say:

Make your life about others and your life will work.

The next thing you need to do is to reveal "what is next" in your life, in your future and what mark you will leave on this world. What is the difference you will make in the lives of others by practicing these newly embraced values and by realizing your vision?

You have done a fabulous job! Very good, very impressive and very beautiful; take on this life of yours and move it to a very empowering direction.

CHAPTER ELEVEN
WHAT DOES THE REST OF YOUR LIFE LOOK LIKE?

WHAT IS NEXT?

The most important thing is
to continue learning, to thrive on challenges
and to fight ignorance.

We are at the end of this book and the beginning of the rest of your life.

This marks the end of our basic coaching and training for you, your life and your productivity, in general, in the personal side of your life as well as your professional side.

The bottom line is that it is your life and it is your productivity. You can do it or not. You can follow the steps or not. Your call. And that is the beauty of this process. What will it be? Yes, you have a say in how it will go and how it will end; you have a say in how you are going to view yourself, others, life itself and how you will relate to those views and experiences of what you are viewing.

As I have always said:

You are either producing extraordinary results in life or have a great excuse why not.

I really don't have that much to say in this last chapter. We walked through a major process of looking within ourselves and we got present to all the conspiracies we have generated to stay small and not get involved with our own greatness, because this can be scary for us. It is frightening to know we can have anything we want from life if we stop dreaming and start believing in ourselves. All I tried to do in this coaching process is to make YOU believe in YOURSELF, for you to get involved with some other conspiracies, to get more access to your greatness, to develop the mastery of love within.

You have always been GREAT, you never needed to be something else or someone else, you just needed to be yourself and start loving yourself, and you have within you everything you need to be happy, fulfilled and loved, because when you love yourself you don't need to be someone else so others love you.

Edward Estlin Cummings, popularly known as E. E. Cummings, said it the best. He was an American poet, painter, essayist, author and playwright. His body of work encompasses approximately 2,900 poems, an autobiographical novel, four plays and several essays, as well as numerous drawings and paintings. He is remembered as a preeminent voice of 20th century poetry as well as one of the most popular. A very passionate and very successful human being, someone who got to know himself in a very deep and intimate way, he said the following in regard to being yourself:

To be nobody but yourself in a world, which is doing its best night and day to make you like everybody else means to fight the hardest battle any human being can fight and never stop fighting.

That is the fight I have tried to make you ready for, the fight against the ordinary out there in the world. You are an extraordinary human being who sometimes forgets how extraordinary you are. You are a diamond in the rough. My job is to assist you and help you to breakthrough to shine again. Nothing changed, you are still some piece of carbon, ordinary carbon, but extraordinary because you have been through so much pressure over a long time. All the suffering, shortcomings and problems that you and I went through brought us here in our lives. We are still a bunch of guts, blood and biology, but transformed to people who can take responsibility of where he or she is in our lives.

Before, we blamed others. Now, we take responsible for designing what we want.

Before, we complained and cried about why the world is not lined up to take care of us, but now we hold ourselves accountable for what we have done and what we love to do.

Before, we did what we wanted when we wanted, but now we look at what will empower us to make that beautiful 'Life Vision' realized.

Before, we conspired into our smallness, excuses and reasoning, and now we are conspired to the greatness of ourselves and the people around us ... and what a different world to wake up to and live into.

That is transformation! Some people think transformation means everything and every relationship is perfect at all times, with everyone in every situation. That is craziness! Are you kidding me? When you know you are ordinary then that is the beginning of being extraordinary, when you got completely in love with yourself, who you are and how you are and accept it without any condition, only then you are transformed to an extraordinary human being. Some think that enlightenment is sitting somewhere and just meditating and getting connected to a higher power. In some cases meditation is very good and very welcome in my own life, but enlightenment and transformation are way bigger than that and at the same time much easier than putting a sword through your face or putting a dagger through your tongue, as you might have seen some Sufi masters or Buddhist monks do when they get to the peak of their enlightenment high.

Enlightenment is just accepting who you are and how you are without condition and expectation of yourself and others. With that comes freedom to be an absolute self-expression, but the hardest part is the acceptance and relating to oneself as a whole and complete human being.

I love what Carl Jung said in this regard. He was a Swiss psychiatrist, an influential thinker and the founder of Analytical psychology. Jung's approach to psychology has been influential in the field of depth psychology and in countercultural movements across the globe. He said the following about the notion of transformation and enlightenment:

Enlightenment consists of NOT merely seeing luminous shapes and visions, but in making the darkness visible. The latter procedure is more difficult, and therefore, unpopular.

To me enlightenment is to own all of myself, good, bad or ugly, and love myself without condition, and then going after what is important to me without fear and without concern of what others might think and say. Just me, living my life the way I want it, and that is transformation. Looking at my own darkness and starting to own it by loving it; looking at my own shortcomings and accepting them as they are; looking at my body, size and dimensions and owning them as mine … that is transformation and practicing enlightenment.

I am not promoting laziness and "just doing nothing," because now we love ourselves. No, that is not what I am promoting. What I am promoting is that you are already loved by you. Now, find someone else to share this love with. I am saying now that you know how to be happy and fulfilled, by being responsible for your own happiness and by being accountable for designing your own happiness, now you can share your happy being with someone else without any reservation and concern, because that is who you are. Period. That is why we have structures, practices and action plans to assist with you developing those new muscles you have recognized during reading this book and exercising the practices and assignments. Like any other thing, if you do not practice what you learned, it will go away. Like a diet that you stop following and all the weight you have lost has come back again, so practice what you have learned and you will be okay.

Go after all those projects that you left half-done, go after your dreams that you thought you might not be able to accomplish, tackle it again, see what you can do for others around you, and find some projects that will empower others around you, your family and your community. Time to time, you will be stopped by your inner chatter that is going to undermine what you are up to and will say some nasty things to slow you down or make you quit. Don't listen to that nasty voice. Change the channel and listen to the other station you have built for yourself. *Your Life Vision.* That station is more fun to listen to!

Enjoy your life and make it be about serving others and making a difference. That reminds me of a famous quote from George Bernard Shaw, a superstar playwright and tart-tongued literary personality of the early 20th century; he was talking about the love and joy of life:

This is the true joy of life, being used for a purpose recognized by yourself as a mighty one: being a force of nature instead of a feverish, selfish, little clod of ailments and grievances complaining that the world will not devote itself to making you happy.

I am of the opinion that my life belongs to the whole community and as long as I live, it is my privilege to do for it whatever I can.

I want to be thoroughly used up when I die, for the harder I work, the more I live. I rejoice in life for its own sake.

Life is no brief candle to me. It is a sort of splendid torch which I have got hold of for the moment, and I want it to be burn as brightly as possible before handing it to future generations.

To Say Thank You

I want to THANK YOU for your time and generosity. Thank you for trusting me and following my coaching and doing what I asked of you and coached you to do. The power is yours and the work is done by you and for you, so the credit is yours also. I just pointed you to a direction and asked you to LOOK, and you did and you took that direction. If you get something out of this, well, good for you. More power to you. If you did not get anything, I am so sorry that I could not make a difference. Please forgive me.

I hope to be able to be your coach in my other books, events and seminars. Wherever we are, we are now connected through our vision for our lives and the possibility that is generated from those visions in the world around us, to ourselves, to our family and friends, to our community and our society and eventually to the world we love so dearly.

Now you have the tools to be yourself and be loved by yourself. I am holding you accountable for the quality of life you desire to live; only you have the mastery of love within you. At this moment, is the power to do things you never thought possible, such power becomes apparent and rises to the surface as you begin to operate consistent with your values, principles and beliefs.

In the end, I want to leave you with a very old Iranian poem from one of the greatest thinkers, philosophers and poets in human history, Omar Khayyam *7. His book of *Rubaiyat of Omar Khayyam* is the second most sold book in the world after the *Bible*. In the following, "Rubai," this ancient wise soul, advise us to live our lives without trying to think about the secret of life. He tells us to live life, enjoy life and don't try to figure it out. Live it and enjoy the time you have in this world.

Again, for keeping the integrity of the poem, I add the actual poem in Farsi and then the English translation:

اسرار ازل را نه تو دانی و نه من

واین خطّ مقرمط نه توخوانی و نه من

اندر پس پرده هست حرف من و تو

چون پرده برافتد نه تو مانی و نه من

-عمر خیام

You and I do not know the secrets of life eternal
You and I cannot read this secret script

Behind the curtain are discussed the fate of yours and mine
When the curtain drops, both you and I cease to exist

--Omar Khayyam

We can't manage what is going to happen to us, but we can manage how we will react to it. We shall live our lives for ourselves, our loved ones, and our dreams and for our values. Controlling life is sourced by the fear of what might happen … I don't know what might happen, but I know that I am alive and I am capable of loving.

You want to control something? Control your anger, control your resentments and control your darkness.

Don't be afraid of getting close to others, and don't be afraid to love them. Don't be afraid to be YOU. Love you so you can give the love away to others, and don't be afraid of your light.

Go through your great life and create some **Conspiracy for Greatness** ... for yourself and for others around you, now that you know how.

Be well.

And continue being great!

With love and respect,

Behnam Bakhshandeh

References

*1

The religion Zoroastrianism was founded by **Zarathushtra** (Zoroaster in Greek; Zarthosht in India and Persia). Conservative Zoroastrians assign a date of 6000 BCE to the founding of the religion; other followers estimate 600 BCE. Historians and religious scholars generally date his life sometime between 1500 and 1000 BCE on the basis of his style of writing. This would make Zoroastrianism the second oldest world religion, next only to Hinduism. It is a wide belief that Zoroastrianism is the very first monotheistic religion.

Zarathushtra lived in ancient Persia, modern day Iran. Legends say that his birth was predicted and that attempts were made by the forces of evil to kill him as a child. He preached monotheism in a land that followed an aboriginal polytheistic religion. He was attacked for his teachings, but finally won the support of the king. Zoroastrianism became the state religion of various Persian empires until the 7th Century CE.

When Muslim Arabs invaded Persia in 650 CE, a small number of Zoroastrians fled to India where most are concentrated today. Those who remained have survived centuries of persecution, systematic slaughter, forced conversion, heavy taxes and other cruelties. They now number only about 18,000 and reside chiefly in Yazd, Kerman and Tehran in what is now Iran. The Canadian 1991 census counted 3,190 Zoroastrians in that country. The actual number is believed to be much higher. According to the *Fezana Journal* survey, published quarterly by the Federation of Zoroastrian Associations of North America, there are about 11,000 Zoroastrians in the United States, 6,000 in Canada, 5,000 in England, 2,700 in Australia and 2,200 in the Persian Gulf nations.

"Zoroastrianism is the oldest of the revealed world religions, and it has probably had more influence on mankind, directly and indirectly, than any other single faith."

- Mary Boyce, *Zoroastrians: Their Religious Beliefs and Practices* (London: Routledge and Kegan Paul, 1979, p. 1)

"Zoroaster was thus the first to teach the doctrines of an individual judgment, Heaven and Hell, the future resurrection of the body, the general Last Judgment, and life everlasting for the reunited soul and body. These doctrines were to become familiar articles of faith to much of mankind, through borrowings by Judaism, Christianity and Islam; yet it is in Zoroastrianism itself that they have their fullest logical coherence...." - Mary Boyce, Op. Cit. p. 29.

Information collected from:
www.religioustolerance.org/zoroasta
www.avesta.org

*2

The substance of **Sufism** is the Truth, and the meaning of Sufism is the selfless experiencing and actualization of the Truth. The practice of Sufism is the intention to go toward the Truth by means of love and devotion. This is called the *tariqat*, the spiritual path or way toward God. By definition, the Sufi is one who is a lover of Truth, who by means of love and devotion moves toward the Truth, toward the perfection, which all are truly seeking. As necessitated by love's jealousy, the Sufi is taken away from all except the Truth.

Sufism has come to mean a wide range of beliefs that center on the quest for personal enlightenment in the union with God. Sufis are sometimes described as the mystics of Islam, but Sufism fits awkward in the categories of all religions. One of the few concepts that Sufis seem to agree on is that all religions offer a path to salvation or enlightenment and that true God realization, no matter how it is achieved, transcends the limitations and classification of any religion. Basically, a saint in any religion is equal to a saint in any other religion, because they are inspired by the same Divine source.

Initially, the term Sufi referred only to those who had achieved God realization, but it has since come to be applied to anyone who follows that particular spiritual path. The name Sufi comes from "Suf," the Arabic word for wool or "Saf," the Persian word for "pure." The dervishes or advanced students of Sufism wore inexpensive wool clothes as part of their life of renunciation.

No matter how it is explained, Sufism and any related movement is a spiritual force that is spreading. Jesus stated that loving God with all of your heart, soul and mind is the greatest commandment, and the second is to love your neighbor as yourself. In no religion is this held to be more absolute and uncompromising than in Sufism. Every minuscule detail of Sufi doctrine, in virtually all denominations, holds these commandments to be all-important. If in your own heart, through your own beliefs, you can also embrace and live by these commandments of Christ, your salvation and your union with God are in alignment. For those who do not find the alignment and continuity in your own religion to follow these commandments, Sufism may be a place to learn more.

To be a Sufi is to be no more than a student of a school. The Sufi way is one that is accepting (not just tolerant) of all other religions. For anyone interested in mysticism, the study of Sufism is an area of riches. Mysticism in many ways provides a bridge between individual religions by exploring the experiences of personal spirituality.

A good first encounter with Sufism would be through reading the works of the ancient Sufi poet Rumi, who is currently the best-selling poet in this country.

Certainly anyone with spiritual interests of any religion will find rewards in an exploration and further understanding of Sufism.

Information collected from:

Dr. Alan Godlas – University of Georgia

www.nimatullahi.org

www.Wikipedia.org

*3

Mawlānā Jalāl-ad-Din Muhammad Rūmi, known to the English-speaking world simply as **Rumi**, (1207–1273) was a 13th-century Persian poet and theologian. Rumi is a descriptive name meaning "the Roman," since he lived most parts of his life in Anatolia or "Rum," now located in Turkey.

Rumi lived most of his life under the Sultanate of Rum, where he produced his works and died in 1273 CE. He was buried in Konya, and his shrine became a place of pilgrimage. Following his death, his followers and his son, Sultan Walad, founded the Mawlawiyah Sufi Order, also known as the order of the *Whirling Dervishes*, famous for its Sufi dance known as the *samā* ceremony.

Rumi's works are written in the New Persian language. New Persian (also called Dari-Persian or Dari), a widely understood vernacular of Middle Persian, has its linguistic origin in the Fars Province of modern Iran. A Dari-Persian literary renaissance (in the 8th/9th century) started in regions of Sistan, Khorasan and Transoxiana and by the 10th/11th century had overtaken Arabic as the literary and cultural language in the Persian Islamic world. Although Rumi's works were written in Persian, his importance is considered to transcend national and ethnic borders. His original works are widely read in the original language across the Persian-speaking world. Translations of his works are very popular in South

Asian, Turkic, Arab and western countries. His poetry influenced Persian literature as well as Urdu, Bengali and Turkish literature.

His poems have been widely translated into many of the world's languages in various formats, and BBC News has described him as the "most popular poet in America."

Information collected from: www.wikipedia.org

*4

Shams-e-Tabrizi was an Iranian Sufi mystic born in the city of Tabriz in Iranian Azerbaijan. He introduced Rumi in the west to Islamic mysticism, for which he was immortalized in Rumi's poetry collection *Diwan-e Shams-e Tabriz-i* (*The Works of Shams of Tabriz*). Shams lived together with Rumi in Konya in present-day Turkey for several years and is also known to have traveled to Damascus in present-day Syria.

According to Sipah Salar, a devotee and intimate friend of Rumi who spent forty years with him, Shams was the son of Ala al-Din and was a descendent of Kaya Buzurg, an Imam of the Ismaili sect, who disassociated himself from it later. Shams received his education in Tabriz and was a disciple of Baba Kamal al-Din Jumdi. Before meeting Rumi, he traveled from place to place, weaving and selling girdles for a living.

After several years with Rumi, Shams left him quite suddenly and traveled to Khoy, where he settled. Shams Tabrizi died and was buried in Khoy. His tomb was nominated as a World Cultural Heritage Center in UNESCO.

As the years passed, Rumi attributed more and more of his own poetry to Shams as a sign of love for his departed friend and master. Indeed, it quickly becomes clear in reading Rumi that Shams was elevated to a symbol of God's love for mankind, and that Shams was a sun ("Shams" means "sun" in Arabic), shining the Light of God on Rumi.

Information collected from: www.wikipedia.org

*5

Khwāja Šhamsaud-Din Muhammad **Hāfez-e Šhirāzi**, or simply **Hafez**, was a Persian mystic and poet. He was born sometime between the years 1310 and 1337 in Shiraz, Medieval Persia. John Payne, who translated the Diwan Hafez, regards Hafez as the greatest poet of the world.

His lyrical poems, known as *ghazals*, are noted for their beauty and bring to fruition the love, mysticism and early Sufi themes that had long pervaded Persian poetry. Moreover, his poetry possessed elements of modern Surrealism. Very little credible information is known about Hafez's life, particularly his early years, there is a great deal of more or less mythical anecdote. Judging from his poetry, he had a good education or found the means by which to educate himself.

In his early thirties Mubariz Muzaffar captured Shiraz and appears to have ousted Hafez from his position. Hafez apparently regained his position for a brief span of time after Shah Shuja took his father, Mubariz Muzaffar, prisoner. But shortly afterward, Hafez was forced into self-imposed exile when rivals and religious characters he had criticized slandered him. Another possible cause of his disgrace can be seen in a love affair he had with a beautiful woman, Shakh-e Nabat. Hafez fled from Shiraz to Isfahan and Yazd for his own safety.

In his old age, Hafez met Tamerlane to defend his poetry against charges of blasphemy. It is generally believed that Hafez died at the age of 69. His tomb is located in the Musalla Gardens of Shiraz (referred to as Hafezieh).

Information collected from: www.wikipedia.org

*6

Sheikh **Saadi** (full name in English: Muslih-ud-Din Mushrif ibn Abdullah) (1184 – 1283/1291) is one of the major Persian poets of the medieval period. He is recognized not only for the quality of his writing, but also for the depth of his social thought.

The unsettled conditions following the Mongol invasion of Persia led him to wander abroad through Anatolia, Syria, Egypt and Iraq. He also refers in his work to travels in India and Central Asia. Saadi is very much like Marco Polo, who traveled in the region from 1271 to 1294. There is a difference, however, between the two. While Marco Polo gravitated to the potentates and the good life, Saadi mingled with the ordinary survivors of the Mongol holocaust. He sat in remote tea houses late into the night and exchanged views with merchants, farmers, preachers, wayfarers, thieves and Sufi mendicants. For 20 years or more, he continued the same schedule of preaching, advising, learning, honing his sermons, and polishing them into gems illuminating the wisdom and foibles of his people. When he reappeared in his native Shiraz he was an elderly man. Shiraz, under Atabak Abubakr Sa'd ibn Zangy (1231-1260) enjoyed an era of relative tranquility. Saadi was not only welcomed to the city but respected highly by the ruler and enumerated among the greats of the province. In response, Saadi took his nom de plume from the name of the local prince, Sa'di bn Zangi, and composed some of his most delightful panegyrics as an initial gesture of gratitude in praise of the ruling house and placed them at the beginning of his *Bustan*. It is believed that he spent the rest of his life in Shiraz.

Information collected from: www.wikipedia.org

*7

Omar Khayyam (born 1048 AD, Neyshapur, Iran—1123 AD, Neyshapur, Iran), was a Persian polymath, mathematician, philosopher, astronomer and poet.

He has also become established as one of the major mathematicians and astronomers of the medieval period. Recognized as the author of the most important treatise on algebra before modern times as reflected in his *Treatise on Demonstration of Problems of Algebra* giving a geometric method for solving cubic equations by intersecting a hyperbola with a circle. He also contributed to calendar reform and may have proposed a heliocentric theory well before Copernicus.

His significance as a philosopher and teacher, and his few remaining philosophical works, have not received the same attention as his scientific and poetic writings. Zamakhshari referred to him as "the philosopher of the world". Many sources have also testified that he taught for decades the philosophy of Ibn Sina in Nishapur where Khayyam lived most of his life, breathed his last, and was buried and where his mausoleum remains today a masterpiece of Iranian architecture visited by many people every year.

Outside Iran and Persian speaking countries, Khayyam has had impact on literature and societies through translation and works of scholars. The greatest such impact was in English-speaking countries; the English scholar Thomas Hyde (1636–1703) was the first non-Persian to study him. However the most influential of all was Edward FitzGerald (1809–83) who made Khayyam the most famous poet of the East in the West through his celebrated translation and adaptations of Khayyam's rather small number of quatrains (*rubaiyaa*s) in *Rubaiyat of Omar Khayyam*

Information collected from: www.wikipedia.org

*8

The **Buddha** was born Siddhartha Gautama, a prince of the Sakya tribe of Nepal, in approximately 566 BC. When he was 29 years old, he left the comforts of his home to seek the meaning of the suffering he saw around him. After six years of arduous yogic training, he abandoned the way of self-mortification and instead sat in mindful meditation beneath a Bodhi tree. On the full moon of May, with the rising of the morning star, Siddhartha Gautama became the Buddha, the enlightened one.

The Buddha wandered the plains of northeastern India for 45 years more, teaching the path or Dharma he had realized in that moment. Around him developed a community or Sangha of monks and, later, nuns drawn from every tribe and caste, devoted to practicing this path. In approximately 486 BC, at the age of 80, the Buddha died.

Buddhism is a religion and philosophy with between 230 and 500 million adherents worldwide, the vast majority living in Asia. The religion consists of two major schools: Mahayana and Theravada. The Mahayana school is in turn divided into East Asian (including Pure Land, Chan/Seon/Thien/Zen, Nichiren, Shingon and others) and Tibetan (sometimes grouped with Shingon under the term Vajrayana). However there are many other sects besides these. These divisions reflect a combination of doctrinal differences and regional syncretism.

Scholars usually categorize Buddhist schools by the ancient languages of surviving Buddhist religious scripture. These are the Pāli, Tibetan, Mongolian and Chinese collections, along with some texts that still exist in Sanskrit and Buddhist Hybrid Sanskrit. While practical, this method does not always correspond to doctrinal divisions. Despite these differences, there are several concepts common to both major Buddhist branches:

- Both accept the Buddha as their teacher.
- Both accept the middle way, dependent origination, the four noble truths and the noble eightfold path, in theory, though in practice these have little or no importance in some traditions.
- Both accept that members of the laity and the Sangha can pursue the path toward enlightenment (Bodhi).
- Both consider Buddhahood to be the highest attainment; however Theravadins consider the nirvana (Nibbana to the Theravadins) attained by Arahants as identical to that attained by the Buddha himself, as there is only one type of nirvana.

According to Theravadins, a Buddha is someone who has discovered the path independently and has taught it to others.

Information collected from:
Dr. C. George Boeree - Shippensburg University
www.wikipedia.org

*9

Aristotle (384 BC - 322 BC) was a Greek philosopher, a student of Plato and teacher of Alexander the Great. He wrote on many subjects, including physics, metaphysics, poetry, theater, music, logic, rhetoric, politics, government, ethics, biology and zoology.

Together with Plato and Socrates (Plato's teacher), Aristotle is one of the most important founding figures in western philosophy. He was the first to create a comprehensive system of western philosophy, encompassing morality and aesthetics, logic and science, politics and metaphysics. Aristotle's views on the physical sciences profoundly shaped medieval scholarship and their influence extended well into the Renaissance, although they were ultimately replaced by modern physics. In the biological sciences, some of his observations were only confirmed to be accurate in the nineteenth century.

His works contain the earliest known formal study of logic, which were incorporated in the late 19th century into modern formal logic. In metaphysics, Aristotelianism had a profound influence on philosophical and theological thinking in the Islamic and Jewish traditions in the Middle Ages, and it continues to influence Christian theology, especially Eastern Orthodox theology, and the scholastic tradition of the Roman Catholic Church. All aspects of Aristotle's philosophy continue to be the object of active academic study today.

Though Aristotle wrote many elegant treatises and dialogues (Cicero described his literary style as "a river of gold"), it is thought that the majority of his writings are now lost and only about one third of the original works survive.

Information collected from: www.wikipedia.org

*10

Socrates (Greek470 BC - 399 BC), was a classical Greek philosopher. Considered one of the founders of western philosophy, he strongly influenced Plato, who was his student, and Aristotle, whom Plato taught. Indeed much contemporary understanding of Socrates' life and work stems from Plato's dialogues.

Principally renowned for his contribution to the field of ethics, Socrates also lends his name to the concepts of Socratic irony and the Socratic Method, or elenchus. The latter remains a commonly used tool in a wide range of discussions, and is a type of pedagogy in which a series of questions are asked not only to draw individual answers but to encourage fundamental insight into the issue at hand.

Socrates also made important and lasting contributions to the fields of epistemology and logic, and the influence of his ideas and approach remains strong in providing a foundation for much western philosophy which followed.

Information collected from: www.wikipedia.org

*11

Plato (428/427 BC - 348/347 BC), was a classical Greek philosopher who, together with his mentor, Socrates, and his student, Aristotle, helped to lay the foundations of western philosophy. Plato was also a mathematician, writer of philosophical dialogues and founder of the Academy in Athens, the first institution of higher learning in the western world. Plato was originally a student of Socrates and was as much influenced by his thinking as by what he saw as his teacher's unjust death.

Plato's sophistication as a writer can be witnessed in his Socratic dialogues. Some of the dialogues, letters and other works that are ascribed to him are considered spurious. Interestingly, although there is little question that Plato lectured at the academy he founded, the pedagogical function of his dialogues, if any, is not known with certainty. The dialogues have since Plato's time been used to teach a range of subjects, including philosophy, logic, rhetoric, mathematics and other subjects about which he wrote.

Information collected from: www.wikipedia.org

*12

Friedrich Wilhelm Nietzsche (October 15, 1844 - August 25, 1900) was a 19th-century German philosopher and classical philologist. He wrote critical texts on religion, morality, contemporary culture, philosophy and science, using a distinctive German language style and displaying a fondness for aphorism. Nietzsche's influence remains substantial within and beyond philosophy, notably in existentialism and post-modernism. His style and radical questioning of the value and objectivity of truth raise considerable problems of interpretation, generating an extensive secondary literature in both continental and analytic philosophy. Some of his major ideas include interpreting tragedy as an affirmation of life, an eternal recurrence (which numerous commentators have re-interpreted), a rejection of Platonism and a repudiation of (especially 19th-century) Christianity.

Nietzsche began his career as a classical philologist before turning to philosophy. At the age of 24 he became the Chair of Classical Philology at the University of Basel (the youngest-ever holder of this position), but resigned in 1879 due to health problems, which would plague him for most of his life. In 1889, he exhibited symptoms of serious mental illness, living out his remaining years in the care of his mother and sister until his death in 1900.

Information collected from: www.wikipedia.org

*13

Johann Wolfgang von Goethe (28 August 1749 - 22 March 1832) was a German writer. George Eliot called him "Germany's greatest man of letters… and the last true polymath to walk the earth." Goethe's works span the fields of poetry, drama, literature, theology, humanism and science. Goethe's *magnum opus*, lauded as one of the peaks of world literature, is the two-part drama *Faust*. Goethe's other well-known literary works include his numerous poems, the Bildungsroman *Wilhelm Meister's Apprenticeship* and the epistolary novel *The Sorrows of Young Werther*.

Goethe was one of the key figures of German literature and the movement of Weimar Classicism in the late 18th and early 19th centuries; this movement coincides with Enlightenment, Sentimentality (*Empfindsamkeit*), *Sturm und Drang* and Romanticism. The author of the scientific text *Theory of Colours*, he influenced Darwin with his focus on plant morphology.

Goethe is the originator of the concept of *Weltliteratur* ("world literature"), having taken great interest in the literatures of England, France, Italy, classical Greece, Persia, Arabic literature, among others. His influence on German philosophy is virtually immeasurable, having major impact especially on the generation of Hegel and Schelling, although Goethe himself expressly and decidedly refrained from practicing philosophy in the rarefied sense.

Goethe's influence spread across Europe, and for the next century his works were a major source of inspiration in music, drama, poetry and philosophy. Goethe is considered by many to be the most important writer in the German language and one of the most important thinkers in western culture. Early in his career, however, he wondered whether painting might not be his true vocation; late in his life, he expressed the expectation that he would ultimately be remembered above all for his work in colour.

Information collected from: www.wikipedia.org

*14

Sigmund Freud, born Shlomo Sigismund Freud (May 6, 1856 - September 23, 1939), was an Austrian physician who founded the psychoanalytic school of psychology. Freud is best known for his theories of the unconscious mind and the defense mechanism of repression, as well as for creating the clinical practice of psychoanalysis for curing psychopathology through dialogue between a patient and a psychoanalyst. Freud is also renowned for his redefinition of sexual desire as the primary motivational energy of human life, as well as his therapeutic techniques, including the use of free association, his theory of transference in the therapeutic relationship, and the interpretation of dreams as sources of insight into unconscious desires.

Information collected from: www.wikipedia.org

*15

Ontology in philosophy is the study of the nature of being, existence or reality in general, as well as of the basic categories of being and their relations.

Traditionally listed as a part of the major branch of philosophy known as metaphysics, ontology deals with questions concerning what entities exist or can be said to exist, and how such entities can be grouped, related within a hierarchy, and subdivided according to similarities and differences.

Students of Aristotle first used the word "metaphysica" (literally "after the physical") to refer to what their teacher described as "the science of being *qua* being," later known as ontology. *"Qua"* means "in the capacity of." Hence, ontology is inquiry into "being" in *so much as* it is being or into being, *in general*, beyond any particular thing which is or exists; and the study of "beings" insofar as they exist, and not insofar as, for instance, particular facts obtain about them or particular properties to them. Take anything you can find in the world, and look at it, not as a puppy or a slice of pizza or a folding chair or a president, but just as something that *is*. More specifically, ontology concerns determining what *"categories of being"* are fundamental and asks whether, and in what sense, the items in those categories can be said to "be."

Ontological approaches

Social scientists adopt one of four main ontological approaches:

1. Realism (the idea that facts are out there just waiting to be discovered)

2. Empiricism (the idea that we can observe the world and evaluate those observations in relation to facts)

3. Positivism (which focuses on the observations themselves, attentive more to claims about facts than to facts themselves)

4. Post-modernism (which holds that facts are fluid and elusive, so we should focus *only* on our observational claims)

Aristotle, Plato, Martine Heidegger, Friedrich Hegel and Jean-Paul Sartre are some of prominent Ontologists.

Information collected from: www.wikipedia.org

411

*16

The full name of **Ibn-i-Yamin**, the Persian Puritan, was "Amir Fakhru'd-Din Mohamud bin Amiru'd-Din Tughral knows as "Feryumadi".

The poet derived his name Ibn-i-Yamin (son of Yamin) from his father's name Yaminu'd-Din, who was a minister in the court of Khudabanda, in Khorasan in the fourteenth century. Ibn-i-Yamin carried on a literary correspondence with his father, who was also a poet, when one of them was in Asia Minor and the other in Khorasan. The letters contained in this correspondence are still prized as example of styles and are much read in Persia (Iran).

According to Dawlatshah, Amir Yaminu'd Din was of Turkish origin who had settled at Faryumad as a landowner, where his son was born (1322 A.D.) in the reign of Mongol Sultan Khudabana; and enjoyed the favor and patronage of Khwajah Ala u'd-Din Muhammad who was in the fiscal service od Sultan Abu Sa'id and who was killed near Astrabad by the Sarbadars in 1336-1337 A.D.

Amir Yaminu'd-Din was also a man of substance who taught his son his craft and when he died in 1322 A.D. he left his son Ibn-i-Yamin not only affluent but also established as a court poet, esteemed by the prince of Khorasan.

Philosophically he may be considered an absolute opposite of Omar Khayyam, in that, he is an unequivocal puritan. Most of his work is a representative of moral aphorism. Apparently he composed them to counteract the sacrilegious quatrains of Khayyam.

Information collected from:
www.books.google.com
"Ethics in Persian Poetry" by Ghulam Abbas Dalal
Mr. Koorosh Angali